Jai Maha Leela

(Victory to The Great Eternal Play,
The Dance of Beauty & Joy, Beauty of Enjoying Beauty)

Jai Maha Leela

(Victory to The Great Eternal Play,
The Dance of Beauty & Joy, Beauty of Enjoying Beauty)

Pramod Sonar

ZORBA BOOKS

ZORBA BOOKS

Published by Zorba Books, November 2021

Website: www.zorbabooks.com
Email: info@zorbabooks.com
Contact: 0124-4259579/8800509579

Title :- Jai Maha Leela

ISBN Print Book - 978-93-90640-23-2
ISBN eBook - 978-93-90640-31-7

Zorba Books Pvt. Ltd. (opc)
Sushant Arcade,
Next to Courtyard Marriot,
Sushant Lok 1, Gurgaon - 122009, India

Highlights of this Book

'A book of Beauty is Joy for All'. You are what you Practice! The great practice of spirituality and meditation will help the reader, the spiritual aspirant, the seeker to develop good health, wealth, improve personality, spiritual upliftment, fulfill needs, desires, and to achieve esteemed goals of life.

This book inspires, motivates, and helps you to make your personality better by using the spiritual knowledge, practice, and meditation techniques in your day-to-day life. You learn the art of exploring, knowing, transforming, experiencing, and enjoying your real being your true-Self. Today, the world needs personalities striving for constant newness, earning good merits, abundance of health, wealth, wellness, and spiritual wellbeing of self and of others who are friendly with humanity and Nature. Transformation of individuals and collective to become integral global personalities is the solution for all worldly problems and for spiritual evolution of mankind. By practice of cessation, concentration, contemplation, meditation, transformation, cultivation, and creation, you can transform and change your shadow illusory personality to real glorious personality of your true-Self. Awakening your hidden inner innate energies and potential and integrating your body, mind, spirit, and Soul. With spiritual wisdom and practice you can transform your stress, anxiety, depression, insecurities, and fear into positive energies for your overall growth. The technique is transforming information to knowledge to practice to wisdom to goodness to joy and beauty.

This book is inspiration to enrich our Soul and for balancing our whole being to pave our path through the turbulence of our inner and outer world. It motivates and nourishes our body, mind, spirit, and Soul. It helps you feel more connected to your real-Self and surroundings to experience peace, bliss, love, happiness, joy, and beauty amidst the chaos. Practicing and developing good habits that can help you to be more creative, loving, kind, compassionate, towards yourself and others and to gain ability to take good decisions to deal with tough situations and times. By developing balance, right mindset, strengths, and confidence you can tackle life's obstacles and challenges. Heal your spirit-Soul and healing of mind and body will follow naturally. Learning self-expression, healing, kindness, emotional intelligence, social and spiritual quotient, and other important life skills to unlock your greatest potential to fulfill your needs, desires, and goals. You are guided towards becoming superhuman.

This book is superbly gleaned, wonderful, and rich with practical worldly scientific and spiritual knowledge and wisdom required for your personal development, spiritual upliftment, and to be in harmony with others and Nature. By practice you get centered, calm, peaceful, loving, compassionate, and joy giving personality. You start trusting your own intuitions, energies, and innate potential and use them for empowering your life. You start rejoicing your work, health, wealth, relationships, friendships, social life, and surrounding nature.

The readers will enjoy reading this book of beauty and joy and will learn to enjoy life with love, peace, joy, and beauty. You will feel your presence in the present and you will be more focused in your creativity, work, artistic activity, physical, mental, and spiritual development. You will explore yourself and understand yourself more deeply embracing the beatitudes. You will learn how to integrate your physical, mental, intellectual, financial, social, emotional, conscious, and spiritual creative energies, powers, qualities, and artistic skills for your progress. By devoted spiritual practice, meditation, and unlocking your intuitive superpowers, and innate potential of your real-Self you can fulfill your intuition and deep desire for your spiritual ascent, self-realization, and Enlightenment. You can have more healthier and stronger body, mind, and spirit by reprogramming through meditation with intense intent and desire for transformation by focusing on positive thoughts and emotions that are spontaneously and continuously reassembling, reorganizing, and recreating our body and mind.

As everyone is aware of the current world scenario, which is full of chaos, confusions, disasters, pollution, the deadly coronavirus pandemic, and ever-increasing stress, worries, tensions, insecurities, disbalances of various kinds. Although the situation world over is very tough, if we see the gleam side of our world, we have enough potential for change and transformation to pave our way victoriously through all these adversities and uncertainties. With great hope, faith, devotion, dedication, and by putting our best efforts with enthusiasm we can transform and make great change to make this world magnanimously beautiful to live healthy, wealthy, happy, and joyful living for all of us and create heaven on earth.

Everyone must awaken to one's life purpose and work to fulfill that purpose for meaningful life and love and enjoy life in harmony with humanity and Nature. One of the great new meditation methods for effective transformation and change in life is the 'Naad-Brahman Synchronous Resonance Transcendence Art', The Great 'Zero-point' Power Transformation. Incredible Turning Point. It is detailed in this book.

Contents

'Jai Maha Leela'

Author's Note

Dear Reader,

My name is Pramod Vasantrao Sonar, aged 61 years, living in Dhule city, Maharashtra, India. I have done Bachelor of Engineering in Electronics and Telecommunications and Master of Science in Electronic Engineering. I have been a businessman since 1987, Managing Director of our own Television factory, a Pvt. Ltd. firm for 7 years, a Partner in a Hotel for 15 years, a Partner in a retail store for 8 years and a Trustee in an educational trust for 20 years. My hobbies are, visiting tourist places, sightseeing nature for its beauty and wonders, reading books on spirituality, personal development, astronomy, motivational leadership. This book is my first experience in writing. I have a great desire to spread the message of universal oneness, unity, love, compassion, peace, bliss, happiness, joy, and beauty through this book. The faith that All is One and One is All is the undertone. The variety in Nature is its beauty.

I am most fortunate to be a disciple of H.H. Shri Mataji Nirmala Devi who is the founder of Sahajayoga meditation. She is my spiritual Guru (Master). By her holy grace, I got my Self- Realization. I have been actively following and practicing Sahajayoga meditation techniques since 1994. I am a spiritual aspirant, seeker, and practitioner. I am enthusiastic and interested in exploring, experiencing, and enjoying the magnificent beauty of Nature and its reality. I have a deep desire to share my spiritual experiences with spiritual aspirants, seekers, and practitioners and make it available for the benefit of the masses. With this vision and deep desire, I had started writing this book 'Jai Maha Leela' on spirituality, spiritual metascience, spiritual practice, meditation techniques, and personal development.

'Jai Maha Leela ' (Victory to The Great Eternal Play, The Dance of Beauty and Joy, The Beauty of Enjoying Beauty) is a book on modern age scientific spiritual practice and meditation techniques for glorious integral personality development, spiritual upliftment, exploring and enjoying our inner innate beauty, wellness, and well-being, achieving success, abundance of health, wealth, and spiritual well-being.

Today, constant newness, earning merits, abundance of health, wealth, wellness, spiritual well-being, friendliness with humanity and nature is the only solution for all worldly problems and for spiritual evolution of mankind. Proven modern age spiritual practice and meditation techniques will help the spiritual practitioner to achieve the esteemed goals of life.

One of the modern age spiritual meditation techniques involves Incredible Zero Point Power Transformation technique, The Great Turning Point. It is a point of infinite possibilities. By using this technique, one can experience divine awareness of our Soul and feel Brahma Chaitanya, Param Chaitanya which is all pervading pure divine cosmic vibrations, the living vital life force and blissful sentient supreme spiritual energy. One can make transformation of body, mind, and spirit gradually as per will and can control hormones, maintain hormonal balance, and reprogram DNA and make changes. Zero point is beyond causation. Zero point and Infinity coexist. Everything is transcended at this point. You experience eternal silence, peace, bliss, joy and beauty. Zero point is the point of spiritual awakening, enlightenment, and self-realization. At this Zero point, your whole body, mind and spirit are synchronized and are in complete harmony with nature.

Zero point is experienced by deep spiritual meditation practice under the guidance of an enlightened self-realized spiritual master, through practice of Asana (an effortless meditation posture), Pranayama (Breathing techniques), Chanting of mantras, and process of Cessation, Concentration, Contemplation, Cultivation, Meditation and Samadhi (Union of body, mind, and spirit with the Soul).

The spiritual awakening, enlightenment and self-realization are experienced by awakening the dormant cosmic divine power within us known as Kundalini Shakti, the feminine cosmic energy which is at the base of the spine coiled on the first Chakra called Muladhara. It is awakened and activated by the grace of Spiritual Guru (Master) through spiritual initiation.

Practitioner experiences distinct feeling of subtle energy flow along the spine rising and flowing through all Chakras, energy centers and central nervous system. Sushumna Naadi emerging out from the top of the head through Brahmarandhra at the crown of the skull, a small opening on the top of the head, the aperture at the crown of the head where you experience Zero Point, Shoonya Shikhar, Summit of aloneness, nothingness, creation, point of victory, to be one with eternal beauty of our Soul, one with the entire cosmos, achieving 'Yoga' Union with All That Is; The Supreme Brahman, The Ultimate Reality.

At this point, the transformation takes place spontaneously and naturally without any effort. Our Intense Intent Manifests. We become ready for the fulfillment of our deep pure desires. We experience physical bliss, mental peace, happiness and joy in our heart. A calm, serene and sublime state witnessing the witnesser, observing the observer, knowing the knower, thoughtless, doubtless, egoless, undifferentiated steady state of pristine effulgent conscious awareness.

To achieve this state, you must surrender and let go of all the impediments to the awakening rather than trying to actively awaken the dormant sleeping Kundalini power. Kundalini is the vital life force or prana which is spread over the macrocosm, the entire cosmos and the microcosm, the human body. In the human body, Prana creates a fine bio-chemical substance which works in the whole organism and is the main agent of activity in the nervous system and in the brain. The brain is alive only because of Prana. As the Kundalini power rises from the lowest to the highest lotus center, and waking the subtle centers, with each waking the psychology and personality of the practitioner will be altogether and fundamentally transformed.

In yogic metascience, it is the Kundalini's coiled body itself that is the Turning Point between emanation and participation, the emission and resorption. It is the source of all energy, which gives pleasure and takes pleasure. Kundalini awakening results in deep meditation, bliss, samadhi, enlightenment, and self-realization. The Self- Realization is liberating knowledge of the true Self. The Self- Realization means removing away the fabricated layers of one's own personality to understand the true Self and hence the true nature of reality. It is considered as the ultimate spiritual attainment. The- Self Realization is the Soul's destiny, awakening to the reality of the undivided whole, realization of this whole. The Self- Realization leads to God- realization. All the mysteries of this universe are unraveled to a man of Self- Realization, and he attains Salvation, Freedom, Moksha, Liberation and Enlightenment. The divine knowledge of the true Self is the real knowledge, for every other kind of knowledge is superficial. Self-Realization illuminates the divine effulgence of the Soul in the heart of a being.

You are what you Practice. One must practice Spirituality with determination, devotion, and dedication. This book emphasizes the most practical benefits of modern age spiritual practice and meditation techniques. It also imparts true knowledge of Spiritual Metascience.

Some of the benefits of modern age spiritual practice and meditation techniques that a good Spiritual aspirant and practitioner experiences are:

- Purification and balancing of gross and subtle energies of all the chakras, naadis, and our whole body, mind, and spirit. Promotes sense of Calm.

- Experiencing Constant newness, practical wisdom, gaining merits, wellness, well-being and spiritual upliftment.
- Improves blood circulation, Boosts cardiovascular and respiratory functions.
- Connects us with Universal Consciousness and enhances our Spiritual experiences.
- Improves intelligence and memory, promotes psychic abilities, and increases sense of perception.
- Development of physical, mental, intellectual, emotional, and spiritual abilities.
- Experiencing calm serene sublime state of peace, bliss, love, happiness, joy, and beauty.
- Developing Concentration, Visualization, and Creativity. Growing in understanding and conscious awareness.
- Promotes achieving esteemed aims and goals of life. Experiencing fulfillment of your needs, desires, and vision.
- Transforming your stress, anxiety, depression, insecurities, and fear into positive energies to boost your physical, mental, financial, intellectual, emotional, and spiritual growth.
- Natural spiritual healing, rejuvenation and transformation of our body, mind, and spirit. Achieving abundance of health, wealth, and success.
- Learning spiritual metascience, gaining pure spiritual knowledge of true divine Self, and Transforming shadow illusory personality into Glorious Integral Personality.

The personality of a person is the inner innate potential of his/her spirit, the fragrance of which spreads like a bloomed flower. The lion stands as a king of the jungle naturally and spontaneously, governed by nature without any elections or support. So, you must sit on a throne, the seat of your Soul in your heart governed by nature and rule your kingdom as a King. The drive for spirituality is inherent in our nature, but the way spiritual path unfolds is unique to each one of us. Spiritual practice is a discipline undertaken in the pursuit of higher esteemed goals. Spirituality is the Beauty of exploring and enjoying our inner innate Beauty which rules eternity. 'Jai Maha Leela' is a book on personality development, wellness, wellbeing, and "Maha Prabhu Yoga" The modern age spiritual practice.

'Jai Maha Leela' book will be very useful and helpful for our personal development, and to spiritual aspirants, seekers, and practitioners in these modern times. With best wishes, I appeal everyone to read this book 'Jai Maha Leela '. Thanking You,

Yours faithfully,
Pramod Sonar

'MahaPrabhu' Saguna Personal Brahman

'MahaPrabhuYoga' Modern Age Spiritual Practice & Meditation Techniques, Introduction:

'Maha' means The Greatest One, a mighty personage, 'Prabhu' means the supreme, the most powerful having control over everything...'The Great Lord' having mastery over everything. 'Yoga' or Yog means Yuj which means union. Oneness with Brahman, union of body, mind, spirit, and Soul with the supreme Soul, Parabrahma, Parmeshwara, Parmatma. 'Mahaprabhuyoga' means union, oneness with "The Great Almighty Lord" Paramatma, Parmeshwara, Parabrahma.

The greatest & highest purpose of human life is to achieve Yoga, Oneness, union with the Supreme Divine Parabrahma and remain in Yoga henceforth. When you are in yoga, you imbibe Divine attributes and Divine Nature and serve "The MahaPrabhu". Your whole Instrument i.e., Body, Mind, and Spirit becomes Peaceful,

Blissful, Joyful & Beautiful. You are in perfect Harmony with Divine Nature. You experience Rutumbhara Prajna, a fully alive Rhythmic Nature with the highest form of Wisdom, Intelligence & Understanding. You become 'synchronous with all creation. In complete coherence with "The Mahaprabhu", The Paramchaitanya (divine sentient cosmic spiritual energy vibrations) of Mahaprabhu flows freely through you. You enjoy Divine Beauty within you. You enjoy the 'Mahaleela', The great eternal cosmic play which is the real beauty of enjoying eternal beauty.

Practice of "Mahaprabhuyoga" is for everyone. All creation is a celebration. Human life is for highest spiritual Satsang celebration which includes all nature, the infinity of Cosmos. Spiritual Satsang is the only reality which gives expression as a whole realizing interconnectedness, interdependence, and respecting each-others independence, with its unbound beauty and joy. 'The Mahaprabhu is our eternal friend. We are all Prabhusakhas with hearts of one accord (Atmaj), Divine Soul Friends.

In "Mahaprabhuyoga" Satsang, you develop profound Integral Personality i.e., your Physical,

Mental, Intellectual, Emotional and Spiritual Abilities. You enjoy Divine Friendship & establish harmonious, peaceful, loving relationship with all human beings and the surrounding Nature. You start enjoying the beauty of nature and the whole creation. You explore & develop your Inner Innate Potential Qualities, Essence, & Energies to achieve your esteemed goals of your life. You promote Peace, Equanimity, Harmony, Love, Compassion & Sharing joy so that everyone should live a healthy life without fear, tensions, stress etc. You spread happiness and divine Joy wherever you go. Every human being must rule his Empire sitting as a king in his heart on the beautiful throne "The Mahaprabhu" has made for oneself and enjoy life. Your Atma "The Soul" is in your heart and "The Supreme Soul" is in the Heart of Hearts.

The growth of "Mahaprabhuyoga" Satsang is our collective growth. Everyone shall grow by sharing and caring with love and compassion for each other. All must contribute Physically, Mentally, Monetarily & Spiritually for the growth of "Mahaprabhuyoga" Satsang. Spirit of "Mahaprabhuyoga" is our real potential & strength. Practice makes one perfect & great. Spiritual Practice of "Mahaprabhuyoga" with faith, devotion, dedication, hard work & patience shall make you a glorious personality.

"Mahaprabhu" The Great Lord is our eternal friend. Be friendly with yourself, with all people & nature. Only Divine Friendship can lead us to peace, harmony, knowledge, prosperity, love, and joy. "Thou shall love thy neighbor as thyself" – (Leviticus). "Fellowship is heaven & lack of fellowship is hell; fellowship is life, and the lack of fellowship is death; and the deeds that ye do upon the Earth, it is for fellowship's sake that ye do them". - (William Morris). If a man does not make new acquaintance as he advances through life, he will soon find himself alone. A man should keep his friendship in constant repair. - (Dr. Samuel Johnson).

Cultivate Divine friends, behold the men who can cure the evils that have already befallen thee and who can guard thee from future ones; cultivate thou their friendship with ardor. It will be the rarest of rare, good fortunes if thou canst secure to thyself the devotion of men of worth. - (Thiruvalluvar)

The friend who always seeks his benefit, the friend whose words are other than his deeds, the friend who flatters just to make you pleased, the friend who keeps you company in wrong, these four, the wise regard as enemies. Shun them from afar as paths of danger.

The friend in happiness and sorrow both, the friend who gives advice that's always good, the friend who is a helper all the time, these four, the wise see as good-hearted friends and with devotion cherish such as these as does a mother cherishes her own child. - (Digha Nikaya)

We secure friends not by accepting favors but by doing them with pure heart. A friend in need is a friend indeed. Giving as a joyful experience is an art. Yet, many feel it is a burden, but all wise men claim that true happiness lies in giving rather than taking. Ofcourse, in real friendship, there is pure heartily give and take relationship. You accept love and gift or needed help from a friend. Why then is the joy of giving experienced by some and not by others? Giving is to be understood in the light of the attitudes that we hold.

One must learn from nature and cultivate the Art of Giving. It is a very easy to receive from a Saint or a real friend because their giving is pure and genuine. It is peaceful to be in Nature because nature is a silent giver & expects nothing in return. The purer the giving, the greater is the happiness it gives. It is not so important what or how much one can give, what really counts is the attitude with which one gives that determines the Joy one experiences.

The Art of Nature's Beauty experiencing is of loving nature and exploring its beauty which is Joy giving. The beauty of nature is fathomless & limitless and it's up to the seeker how much he can explore and enjoy. Nature has abundance to give. When you are completely surrendered to the Divine Nature and establish divine friendship with nature, you start receiving in abundance. Nature is friendly to everyone which is why we have evolved as human beings with great capacities and capabilities. See the pebbles in the river and the secret of their existence. They have been naturally molded round by river waters from their original rough sharp edged rock stone. How smooth and rounded they become after striking with each other so that they can roll easily. Similarly living in spiritual collective, we get transformed.

All our roughness, harshness, selfishness, greed, envy, and all other negativities are completely washed off and we become humble, polite, loving, & compassionate with great divine qualities sharing divine Joy with each other.

We must all meet together, speak together, let our minds be of one accord, may our counsel be common, our assembly common, let our mind, thoughts and purpose be common. Our aim be common and our hearts of one accord so that we all may live well together and enjoy life together. Hear the laughter of the leaves, listen to the whisper of flowers, see the cheerful faces around you & let your spirit soar high in collective joy.

"Vasudhaiva Kutumbakam" means "The world is one family" "Vasudha" means the Earth, eva means indeed and "Kutumbakam" means family. "Vasudhaiva Kutumbakam" is a Sanskrit phrase found in "Maha Upanishad" and in "Rig Veda". It is considered the most important moral value in the Indian society. This verse of "Maha Upanishad" is engraved in the entrance hall of the parliament of India. The world is a family. One is a relative, the other a stranger, say the small minded. The entire world is a family, live the magnanimous.

Be detached, be magnanimous, lift your mind, enjoy the fruit of Brahmanic freedom - Maha Upanishad 6.71-75 subsequent shlokas go on to say that those who have no attachments go on to find the Brahman (the one supreme, universal spirit that is the origin and support of the phenomenal universe). The context of this verse is to describe as one of the attributes of an individual who has attained the highest level of spiritual progress, and one who can perform his worldly duties without attachment to material possessions.

Diversity of culture and tradition is necessary. A garden with diverse flowers with diverse fragrances, colors and adoration looks beautiful and gives divinity to the garden. Oneness in diversity is exhibited in nature with the appearance of a rainbow, which is an aggregation of diverse synchronous colors in the ethereal sky. When colors are separate they disperse and are not visible. By the magical prismatic effect of the Sun and rain clouds, the concerted reflection forms sublime rainbow signifying harmony and equanimity.

In the same way, our culture is a beautiful amalgamation of diverse languages, diverse traditions, and diverse existence. Respecting and celebrating cultures is the beauty of diversity. This is what is respecting the humanity and being human. Universal love and brotherhood make us understand the pains and pleasures of others and to be aware of it and to share the concerns. Let us open our hearts, open our arms to embrace and heal. Inculcate universal love and peace for universal family. All pervading consciousness in the whole humanity is the universal consciousness present in each one of us. We all emanate from one supreme source to merge back to the same source.

"Mahaprabhuyoga" Spiritual Satsang Divine collectivity has great potential, energy, and capabilities to transform everyone as well as the whole collective for the welfare of the world. "The Mahaprabhu" is more gracious on those who pray to him with United hearts. By being voluntarily contributive, physically, mentally, and monetarily to "Mahaprabhuyoga", each one is blessed, benefited to explore, and enjoy his inner innate potential, qualities, essence, powers, & energies. You experience your inner beauty. Only by heartily contributing, you are going to grow. You become a great glorious personality.

"Mahaprabhuyoga" spiritual Satsang program has the collective activities of creativity, art, music, singing, dancing, spiritual development, concentration, & meditation. Scientific spiritual practice is essential for great glorious personality development & spiritual upliftment. Truth and Unity with faith, wisdom, love, compassion, and joy from within our hearts are our foundation.

The Art of experiencing Nature's Beauty is the most creative activity. One must seek and Explore Nature. Beauty is an expression of God's love and has a purpose. It gives immense peace & joy.

This nature's beauty everywhere is to be explored, praised, loved, appreciated, sensed, experienced, and its expression is to be enjoyed.

Many great thinkers, explorers, poets, artists, musicians, scientists, philosophers, spiritualists etc. have tried to describe nature's beauty through their writings, poetry, paintings, dance, drama, and in many great ways for centuries. But still the beauty of this nature keeps its secrets and is multidimensional, limitless, fathomless, and immeasurably Joy giving. Beauty of nature is its variegatedness, vastness, magnificence of its different creations, and the transformatory & evolutionary process of continuous change. The most wonderful and beautiful creation of the earth in the evolutionary process of nature is human beings. Once you are very friendly with nature, its beauty starts unfolding giving you true love, bliss & joy. Scientists have done much research and discovery on material physical science, but now it's a need for scientists to do research on metaphysical and spiritual aspects of nature. No material wealth can buy peace, bliss, and eternal Joy. Spiritual knowledge of divine "MahaPrabhu" (Parabrahma) is the most supreme knowledge the noble human being can imbibe. One should therefore not be attached to material possessions and wealth which lead to insecurity, fear, stress, tensions, worries, hollowness, dryness etc. One must wisely use some part of his wealth for his spiritual upliftment and developing great glorious personality by sharing and contributing to the great spiritual cause of spreading peace, bliss, love, and joy through "Mahaprabhuyoga" .

"The Mahaprabhu" is the supreme creator, sustainer, protector, transformer, and enjoyer of all his creation, variegatedness, magnificence, and beauty. He is the supreme witness to everything. His divine play "Leela" is eternally flowing from eternity to eternity. He is eternally enjoying. There is a very subtle relationship between the enjoyer and the enjoyed; just like a honeybee extracts honey from the flowers and enjoys it without disturbing the beauty and the fragrance of the flower thus fulfilling the basic needs and the purpose for which the flower is created. Both serve the purpose and meaning. Each one of us is enjoyer and enjoyed, experiencing, and enjoying the beauty of "The Self".

Rabindranath Tagore said, truth is inseparable from beauty. Truth is everywhere therefore everything is the object of our knowledge. Beauty is omnipresent; therefore, everything can give us Joy. Through our sense of truth, we realize law in creation and through our sense of beauty we realize harmony in the universe. Tagore celebrated life, I feel the embrace of freedom in thousand bonds of delight. He said, so for the man of detachment his home is his heritage. For him to be one with God is to be one with the universe because our master himself has joyfully taken upon himself the bonds of creation, so he is bound with us all forever. God to him was Sakha, the friend. He sought to find divinity in all existence.

The spiritual knowledge of the divine nature must be imbibed and practiced. Practice in daily life is most important, for an ounce of practice is worth a ton of theory. Knowledge of the Self is to be practiced with full devotion, dedication, and faith on your Self and on God for experiencing divine love, compassion, bliss, peace, joy, and beauty.

Pearls of Wisdom, Power, Peace, Love, Joy, and Beauty:

Good, sublime, and beautiful words are pearls of wisdom and have power. Gentle words bring life and health. Words of true wisdom are refreshing and have the power of healing. The inspirational, spiritual beauty quotes are treasures of heart. Kind words are like honey, sweet to the Soul and are healthy for the body and the mind. It is a good habit to read a few inspirational, motivational, and spiritual quotes daily. Quotes are guiding, comforting, refreshing, knowledge giving, and full of inspiration and wisdom. They energize, encourage, and improve our mood and state of our mind. They help us to see the bright side of life and prompt us to take positive action. The words sink into your mind and give insight and wisdom. Quotes are beacon of light, and they drive away darkness. They have power to brighten your day and awaken happiness. You get good advice from them and can implement them in your life. They open our eyes and the mind to perceive and understand reality; and widen our perspective and uplift our spirit. Positive quotes inspire us to adopt positive thinking and take positive action. Reading good quotes is a fun and is joy giving and does not require much time and effort. It is suggested to read a few quotes in the morning before going to work and in the evening before going to sleep or can be read any time as suitable. Reading quotes reduces stress and makes us more balanced. Quotes are useful to everyone; many successful personalities have been seen reading and chanting words and phrases which empower them to success.

Time is most precious. So, inspirational quotes bridge the gap between availability of time and the need for swift words to motivate success. Quotes capture and appeal to your subconscious mind, which indeed is the major portion of your entire mind. Creativity is found subtly embedded in the subconscious mind. Smiles and words are contagious, and quotes can often bring a huge sparkling smile to your face. Quotes are the new universal language used by successful people and great personalities. In this new modern age of quotes, there is an explosion of inspirational, motivational, and spiritually thoughtful quotes. The humanity is experiencing extraordinary times of global unrest, conflict, and pressures in everyday life. At this juncture, quotes have taken prominence as the people look for simple solutions to complex problems. Quotes strengthen us coping in modern day life. A good selection of a few notable quotes is given below which you will love to read.

Fantabulous Inspirational, Motivational, and Spiritual Beauty Quotes:

- No individual can ultimately fail. The Divinity which descends into humanity is bound to regain its original state. - N. Sri Ram
- There are only two ways to live your life. One is as though nothing is a miracle. The other is as though everything is. - Albert Einstein
- When a man is willing and eager, the gods join in. - Aeschylus
- Friendship has always belonged to the core of my spiritual journey. - Henri Nouwen
- Take care of your inner spiritual Beauty. That will reflect in your face. - Dolores del Rio
- Music is the mediator between the spiritual and the sensual life. - Ludwig van Beethoven

- When you realize there is no lacking, the whole world belongs to you. – Lau Tzu
- If your INTENTION is powerful, your action will be powerful. If your action is powerful, your results will be powerful. - #Fearless Soul
- No dream is too big when you understand ABUNDANCE is your birthright. - # Fearless Soul
- "Rutumbhara Prajna" (Mind full of Rhythm – It represents a state of mind where the thought waves are synchronous with the order of the Universe, microcosm and macrocosm are in coherence with each other.) – Vedas
- "Vasudhaiva Kutumbakam" (The world is one family). – Maha Upanishad
- "Thou shalt love thy neighbor as thyself. "The way is not in the sky; the way is in the heart." – Leviticus.
- Love is the only reality, and it is not a mere sentiment. It is the ultimate truth that lies at the heart of creation. – Rabindranath Tagore.
- "Let what comes come. Let what goes go. Find out what remains". – Ramana Maharshi
- "The privilege of the lifetime is to become who you really are". – Carl Jung
- We are not human beings trying to be spiritual. We are spiritual beings trying to be human. – Jacquelyn Small
- Looking deeply at life as it is in this very moment the meditator dwells in stability and freedom. – Buddha
- "Just as a candle cannot burn without fire, man cannot live without a spiritual life". – Buddha
- Soul is the central point of spiritual discipline. – Mahavira
- Realize deeply that the present moment is all you have. Make the NOW the primary focus of your life. – Eckhart Tolle

- The spiritual life does not remove us from the world but leads us deeper into it - Henri J.M. Nouwen
- Beauty is the illumination of your soul. - John O'Donohue
- Beauty surrounds us, but usually we need to be walking in a garden to know it. - Rumi
- There is nothing that makes its way directly to the soul than beauty. - Joseph Addison
- Real Beauty is to be true to oneself. That's what makes me feel good. - Laetitia Casta
- Anyone who keeps the ability to see Beauty never grows old. - Franz Kafka
- At any moment, you have a choice, that either leads you closer to your spirit or further away from it. - Thich Nhat Hanh
- I have so much to do that I shall spend the first three hours in prayer. - Martin Luther
- You must find the place inside yourself where nothing is impossible. - Deepak Chopra
- The way is not in the sky, the way is in the heart. - Buddha
- God is peace, bliss, beauty, and truth. Focus your energy on that, life will be like that. - Amit Ray.
- There is a light within our soul that burns brighter than the sun. And we ignore it. - Basith
- A thing of beauty is a joy forever: its loveliness increases; it will never pass into nothingness. - John Keats
- The most beautiful things we can experience is the mysterious, it is the source of all true art and science. - Albert Einstein
- Truth is everywhere, therefore everything is the object of our knowledge. Beauty is omnipresent, therefore everything is capable of giving us joy.- Rabindranath Tagore
- Beauty is Truth, Truth Beauty. - John Keats

- Love is the Beauty of the Soul. – Saint Augustine
- Everything has Beauty, but not everyone sees it. – Confucius
- To love beauty is to see light. – Victor Hugo
- Beauty awakens the Soul to Act. – Dante Alighieri
- Yoga is enjoying the beauty of constant-newness (Nitya-Nutana) of your Spirit –Soul.
- GOD is beauty, peace, bliss, love, joy, truth, grace, and goodness.
- Life is to enjoy beautiful eternal cosmic play of pure love and joy of divine Energy and Spirit.
- It is in the compelling zest of high adventure and of victory, and in creative action, that man finds his supreme joys. – Antoine de Saint-Exupery

Introduction

It is truly Joy giving to present this book 'Jai Maha Leela' (Victory to The Great Eternal Play, The Dance of Beauty and Joy, Beauty of Enjoying Beauty) and to establish "Mahaprabhuyoga" Modern Age Spiritual Practice and Meditation Techniques, for glorious integral personality development and spiritual ascent of all individual personalities to have happiness, harmony, love, friendliness, compassion, peace, bliss, and joy among all of us. We must harmoniously live with united hearts as a friendly universal collective to enjoy divine beauty within each one of us and our surrounding nature. 'Divine Mother Nature' is 'MahaGuru' (Great Master) of us all. Guru Principle is the highest principle in the entire Cosmos without which no life and no living is possible.

My first Guru in this life is my mother Mirabai in whose womb I was nourished and developed physically, mentally, and spiritually. Indeed, I am the most fortunate to have a saintly mother. She was also called by the name "Mothi Aai" means big hearted mother. She was very generous and kind to all. My second Guru is my father Shri Vasantrao who took utmost care of our joint family and relatives. He was ex-president of Dhule Municipal Corporation. He had devoted his whole life for social and religious development, respecting people from all walks of life and of all caste, creed, and religions. He has constructed Sri Nagai Mata temple, near Sakri town, Dhule. I have learned the great lessons of my life 'to be very kind, compassionate, and helpful to all' from my mother & father. . They loved us all very much. In my childhood, I was taught the mantra "Matru Devo Bhava Pitru Devo Bhava" which means revere your mother and father as God. I feel everyone of you must revere your mother & father, who have brought you up with love, care, and sacrifice.

My real Gurus are my teachers, relatives, friends, and my surroundings from whom I learnt most valuable lessons of life. It's nature's arrangement to create the best environment for your overall growth, physical, mental, and spiritual. Learning is an ongoing process of life.

Having a spiritual Guru (master) in one's life is very important. One cannot tread on the path of spirituality without the grace of a spiritual Guru. I am the most fortunate to be a Sadhaka, Shishya (Disciple) of H. H. Shri Mataji Nirmala Devi who is my spiritual MahaGuru. The experiences I had through my MahaGuru are beyond words & writing. I joined Sahajayoga in October 1994. I got my initiation at Nashik and self-realization at the Lotus feet of 'H. H. Shri Mataji Nirmala Devi' at Nargol, Gujarat, India on 29th Oct 1995, the occasion of celebration of silver jubilee of 'Sahajayoga', Diwali Puja. This day I became Dwija i.e. I was twice born. I experienced great transformation. It was the turning point of my life. I became a true spiritual seeker of truth. For a spiritual seeker it is foremost essential to completely surrender oneself at the Lotus feet of a spiritual Guru (master), to experience egoless divine oneness, peace, bliss, love, and joy. When the new life begins, the new process of learning, practicing, and experiencing higher dimensions of life exploring the magnificent beauty of divine nature starts.

In my childhood life, the impact of a movie namely 'Sant Dnyaneshwar' was very great on my mind & heart. I liked the song "Jyot Se Jyot Jagate Chalo, Prem Ki Ganga Bahate Chalo", meaning as you light your lamp; embrace the nature of its divine soothing fire that does not diminish when shared with others; and let the great river of divine love flow freely with all together. The character personality of The Great Saint 'Sant Dnyaneshwar' spontaneously touched my heart. In my heart I wanted to be like Sant Dnyaneshwar. He is indeed my first ideal and Sadguru in my life.

'Sant Dnyaneshwar' was a great Saint, poet, philosopher, and MahaYogi in 13th century A.D. When he was only sixteen years of the age, he had written a great commentary on the 'Bhagavad Gita' about the "Great Lord Shri Krishna" known as "Dnyaneswari" and "Amrutanubhav" in Marathi language, reflecting non-dualistic Advaita Vedanta and emphasis on Yoga (oneness with the all- pervading divinity). When I was in third std. in Marathi school, I had fallen from a ladder while playing. I had fracture in my left hand and blood clotted. All my nerves were blocked. My father took me to Mumbai for treatment. But even Mumbai doctors could not make it right after three four months of treatment. My hand and fingers were not moving. My father didn't give up hope. He heard about a specialist Doctor in Ahmednagar. So, he took me there. The treatment was going on for three four months. Almost now nine months had passed and there was very little improvement. One day while on our journey from Dhule to Ahmednagar, my father, grandmother, and myself stopped for Holy Darshan of 'Shri Saibaba of Shirdi'. My father and my grandmother asked me to pray for curing my hand. So, I prayed with my full heart to 'Shri Saibaba' for curing my hand. As we left from Shirdi by bus to Ahmednagar, just after ten fifteen minutes, the bus jumped on a very rough road. Many people in the bus got hurt including my father and grandmother. At that instance my left hand was struck hard with a Rod in the bus and for our surprise by the grace & blessings of Shri Saibaba my left hand became straight & my hand and fingers were now moving normally. I told my father & grandmother. They were astonished with joy and said it's a miracle by 'Shri Saibaba'.

From that instance, I became a staunch devotee of 'Shri Saibaba' who is my Sadguru and Ideal.

At the age of twenty-four, in the year 1984, I was following 'Bhaktivedanta Swami Prabhupada, a spiritual teacher and founder-preceptor of ISKON "Hare Krishna Movement". I started reading Srimad Bhagavatam & Srimad Gita. The most practical and profound spiritual experiences I had were from the year 1994, when I joined 'Sahajayoga' founded by my spiritual MahaGuru 'H. H. Shri Mataji Nirmala Devi'.

Children are a Great Source of Inspiration, Learning, Innocence, Love, Peace, Bliss and Joy. They are all our Gurus. One must learn living life from them. My children Chaitanya, Kashmira, my daughter in law Chetna and my wife Vaishali are my inspiration and my Gurus. I learn a lot from them. To know a person with love is a great experience.

My pure desire with enthusiasm and interest is to explore the beauty of life and nature, process of transformation, evolution of humanity and surrounding nature in Cosmos, to share and spread the divine message of creativity, love, compassion, peace, bliss, joy, and divine beauty. The whole humanity should unite-together in harmonious friendly loving relationship from their hearts to fulfill the purpose of "The Lord's Beautiful Creation" of this Cosmos. Today's greatest need is the collective efforts for global integration of all scientific, philosophical, religious, and spiritual aspects of humanity and nature to contribute towards creation of beautiful heavenly kingdom on earth to explore and enjoy divine beauty.

Since my childhood I always have been inspired and experimenting on the subject matter of knowing one's Spirit-Self-Soul and about creation of entire Cosmos. My hobby was astronomy and was interested in mathematics, physics, biology, and electronics subjects. In September 1994, I received my initiation, awakening and self-realization by the grace and blessings of H. H. Shri Mataji Nirmala Devi through Sahajayoga meditation practice.

Since the creation of mankind, human beings have always tried and struggled to find out solutions, ways and means to experience real pleasures, happiness, peace, bliss, joy, and beauty, and are seeking the real knowledge of divine nature of Cosmos.

Many great divine messengers, incarnations, saints, philosophers, and highly evolved spiritual gurus (masters) have shown us the path towards absolute divine truth. They themselves have explored and experienced enigmatic divine mysteries, beauty of divine nature; and have given us divine knowledge, wisdom, their blessings and wishes for us to explore, experience, and enjoy the divine beauty within us and in surrounding nature. Their preaching, writings and spiritual scriptures are readily available. Marvelous scientific developments have helped humanity to explore the inner realms of nature and its secrets to a greater extent. But despite such vast and in- depth advancement of scientific, philosophical, and spiritual knowledge, today's mankind is in distress, chaos, confusions, disturbances, disasters, etc. and is leading an artificial, illusionary and superficial life with discontentment.

With the very basic purpose of exploring, experiencing, and enjoying real pleasures, happiness, peace, bliss, love, joy, and beauty of life and fulfilling its purpose, I have with my enlightened vision founded and established "MahaPrabhuYoga" the modern age spiritual practice and meditation techniques for glorious integral personality development.

Friendliness with one's own real-Self (Soul), friendliness with humanity, with our surroundings, and friendliness with divine nature, truly lead us to wisdom, peace, harmony, real knowledge, prosperity, love, compassion, real pleasures of life, happiness, contentment, divine truth, joy, and beauty. Friendliness fulfills everything. "MahaPrabhu" (The Almighty Lord) is our eternal friend. I humbly and heartily appeal everyone to join "MahaPrabhuYoga" and spread friendliness all over the world. "May God bless us".

Pramod Sonar

MahaPrabhuYoga, Modern age Spiritual Practice & Meditation Techniques.

Beauty, Love, & Joy of Divine Friendliness - (21st June 2020 Global Message by Pramod Sonar)

'Jai Om Jai', Namaste! Hello, 'All dear friends',

Today is Sunday, 21st June 2020, a very great 'Spiritual Day', Wish you all 'Happy World Music Day', 'Happy Father's Day' and 'Happy International Yoga Day'. The significance of international yoga day is to promote global health, harmony, and peace. 'Yoga' means union or to join. The primary aim of yoga is to integrate our body, mind, spirit and Soul in harmony, oneness, and unity. 'Yoga' also means connection, union of our individual Soul with the Supreme Soul. International yoga day is celebrated Worldwide.

Today is summer solstice. The sun in the sky is farthest North in the Northern hemisphere. It is the longest day of the year in Northern hemisphere. Today is also a day of Annular Solar Eclipse.

It is our great 'Yoga', a divinely blessed coincidence that we all are united together on this auspicious day. Although we are apart, we are close in our Heart. Today the sky is filled with serene gigantic clouds of 'Paramchaitanya' ('The Supreme Divine Cosmic Energy').

I am very glad to introduce on this auspicious day "MahaPrabhuYoga" It is the spiritual practice of exploring, experiencing, and enjoying nature's beauty. Through this, one can experience the joy of divine friendliness and the beauty of enjoyment of beauty. It is the inner innate beauty of our soul which glorifies our personality.

As you all know "A journey of thousand miles begins with a step". Today is the new beginning of "MahaPrabhuYoga" spiritual practice, a journey of spiritual transformation of Humanity. I am very sure that we all with our united hearts, collectively and magnanimously make miraculous transformation of our individual self and world around us into the great heavenly planet in the near future.

The meaning of "MahaPrabhu" in Sanskrit is: 'Maha' means The Greatest One, A Mighty Person- age; "Prabhu" means supremely powerful Personality having control over everything. "Ma- haPrabhu" means "The Great Lord" and "Yoga" means to join or unite; it is union and oneness with Brahman (The all-pervading supreme divine power of "The Great Lord"). So "MahaPrabhuYoga" means union, oneness, and harmony with "The Great Almighty Lord".

The greatest and the highest purpose of human life is to achieve and attain 'Yoga', oneness, union, and harmony with the all-pervading supreme divine energy, nature, & power of "The Great Lord" "MahaPrabhu".

"MahaPrabhuYoga" is a spiritual practice to serve the purpose of attaining our self-realization and enlightenment. It is a new generation modern age spiritual Joy program for all. With this vision in our hearts and with dedicated practice, we all would be able to develop our Glorious Integral Personality.

"MahaPrabhuYoga" is a spiritual practice for gaining real knowledge of divine nature and learning the spiritual techniques of meditation. Using this real knowledge with practical wisdom, we can transform our body, mind, and Spirit-Self to be Glorious Integral Personality. It is an incredible turning point in our life. Our lives are transformed & are filled with love, compassion, peace, bliss, harmony, and joy. We experience abundance of health, wealth, wellness, and wellbeing.

"MahaPrabhuYoga" is an art of experiencing nature's beauty. It is the Beauty of Enjoyment of Beauty. You experience love, peace, bliss, harmony, and joy in your daily life irrespective of the situations and surroundings you are in. There are many great advantages of this practice such as: your personality gets transformed from shadow illusionary personality to great glorious real personality. You explore your inner innate hidden subtle energies, powers, and potential and use them for your speedy transformation. You achieve and fulfill your needs, desires, wishes and esteemed aims and goals of your life.

You learn the art of concentration-contemplation and meditation. With intense practice, you will soon start realizing your real self and reach the state of enlightenment, self-realization, and ultimately liberation (Moksha), where you will experience and enjoy your complete freedom.

All your abilities and competencies at the level of your physical, mental, intellectual, emotional, social, and spiritual will be dramatically improved and enhanced. You experience constant newness in your daily life. You become a glorious spiritual leadership personality.

"Mahaprabhuyoga Mahasatsang", the beautiful divine collective of spiritual seekers and practitioners is for sharing and celebrating divine love, peace, bliss, and joy in harmony and friendliness with each other. You share your creativity, spiritual knowledge, and experiences. You celebrate art, music, singing and dancing. We all individually and collectively practice spiritual healing, wellness and wellbeing methods for our overall development and spiritual upliftment. The "Mahaprabhuyoga Mahasatsang" is the Royal ideal path for your Glorious Integral Personality Development and your Spiritual Upliftment. Experiencing beautiful divine harmony with people from all walks of life and with your surrounding nature, you develop your physical, mental, intellectual, emotional, social, and spiritual essence, qualities, energies, and abilities. The personality of a person is the inner, innate potential of his spirit, the fragrance of which spreads all over like a bloomed lotus flower. You master and become competent in using your physical, mental, intellectual, emotional, and spiritual resources for achievement and fulfillment of your needs, desires, wishes, and esteemed aims and goals of life and your spiritual upliftment.

You all are born great to become great and glorious. It's a practice of strengthening your personality. We all know that greatest power is lodged in the fine, the subtle and not in coarse or gross. It is the fine, the subtle that is really the seat of power, the source of power. So, through practice of concentration, contemplation, and meditation we explore our inner innate subtle realms and awaken our subtle energies, powers, essence, qualities, and potential and use them for our greater development.

The greatest need of the time now is the development of individual to become great glorious personality. Such personalities can collectively transform the whole world miraculously into the great heavenly planet. This is the dream of all great Rishis, Munis, Saints, Gurus, Incarnations, Philosophers, Spiritual Masters, Leaders, Scientists, and the Great Personalities of the world till today. This is our dream too. Now we are all realized souls and I am sure this beautiful and wonderful dream of creating heaven on Earth is now becoming truth very shortly. We all collectively and unitedly will make it happen. Transforming ourselves individually and collectively by continuously investing in our self-development and collective development.

As you are all well aware, the current world scenario is full of chaos, confusions, disturbances, disasters, natural calamities, pollution, etc. and now this novel covid-19 pandemic, and ever-increasing stress, insecurities, worries, tensions, and disbalances of various kinds.

In all these adversities & uncertainties, we all are now paving our way, our path with faith, great hope, devotion, dedication, confidence, enthusiasm for making each one of us healthy, wealthy, prosperous, loving, peaceful, blissful, happy, joyous, and glorious. With our individual and collective efforts, we will create a glorious heavenly life on Earth. Now is the time for making our lives more beautiful and enjoy our journey on this planet.

There are many very important questions, which make us think in depth as regards to our life, such as, why do I live life? What is the meaning and purpose of my life? Who Am I? In our enquiry about Self, we should think and contemplate about, what can I do to my life? What can I do for my self- development? What can I do for fulfilling my needs, desires, wishes, aim and goals of my life? and in a broader vision, what can I do for others to make them happy and joyous? What contributions can I do to make this world more beautiful and a heavenly place for everyone to live happily and joyously.

Upon such great inquiry and deep contemplation, you gain intense momentum for manifesting your elevated desires, and you become a great and glorious personality.

Every great personality had intense desire to become great and they became great & glorious. So, each of us can!

Each one of us individually and collectively must take full interest with zeal and enthusiasm to contribute and serve the Humanity to make this world heavenly and beautiful.

I am very glad and delighted to introduce myself to you. My name is Pramod Vasantrao Sonar. The meaning of my first name "Pramod" is - 'Pra' means big, great, beginning, prior principle, and 'Mod' means joy, pleasure, fragrance, vital. So Pramod means a great lively, joyous, and friendly personality.

My first Gurus in my life are, my mother Mirabai and my father Vasantrao from whom I have learned the great lessons of life; most importantly of unconditional love, compassion and caring for others. They both loved me very much and took utmost care for my upbringing. At every difficult time in my life, they have lovingly and kindly supported me, without which I would not have done progress in my life and reached this stage of life. Their blessings are always with me.

I am a disciple and follower of H. H. Shri Mataji Nirmala Devi. She is the founder of Sahajayoga and its trusts. She is my Mahaguru, The Great Spiritual Master. By her Grace, blessings, and practice of Sahajayoga, I have received my self-realization and enlightenment. She is my Councellor, Comforter, Redeemer, and Spiritual inspiration and motivation in my life. She is everything for me.

I am from Dhule city, which is in the state of Maharashtra, India. I call this Dhule city as "The City of Golden Dust" as there is lot of Golden Dust in this city area; and people are also Golden. I am a post graduate in Electronics Engineering. My occupation is Agriculture and Business. I am a spiritual seeker and practitioner. I am the founder & chief coordinator of "MahaPrabhuYoga" spiritual practice, 'Real Life Cosmos Collective'. This spiritual practice is a new beginning for individual and collective transformation of humanity towards divinity. It's a journey to exploring, experiencing, and enjoying the beautiful divine nature on Earth and of Cosmos. It will help us to promote & share love, compassion, harmony, friendliness, peace, bliss, happiness & joy all over the world.

As you all know "An ounce of practice is worth a ton of theory". Practical seeking, gaining spiritual knowledge, and daily spiritual practice and meditation are very important for our spiritual growth.

Dear friends, this is our new beginning. Every week we will have new learning session of "MahaPrabhuYoga MahaSatsang". With our united hearts, filled with love, compassion, peace, bliss, happiness, and joy, we all will collectively experience and enjoy divine nature and its beauty. I request you all to please practice meditation daily for your spiritual ascent.

Those who are curious, enthusiastic, and interested in spiritual practice, in gaining divine spiritual knowledge and learning new meditation techniques for the development of your Glorious Integral Personality and Spiritual Upliftment can join us for free as a member of "Mahaprabhuyoga Mahasatsang", Real Life Cosmos Collective.

I humbly request you all, to kindly share and spread this message of promoting global love, compassion, harmony, health, prosperity, happiness, wellness, well-being, peace, joy, and beauty, to many around the globe. "May God bless us".

Pramod Sonar

MahaGuru Anubhava

The Great Master's Divine Experience

MahaGuru Mantra

Gurur Brahma Gurur Vishnuh Gurur Devo Maheshwarah |
Guru Sakshat ParaBrahman Tasmai Shri Gurave Namah | |

Realize that The Guru is Brahman Himself. He is Vishnu and He is also Shiva (Maheshwara). The Guru is Para Brahman (Supreme God or The Absolute Truth). With this knowledge, I (Salute) offer my obeisance to The Guru. Our creation is that Guru (Brahma-the force of creation), the duration of our lives is that Guru (Vishnu-the force of preservation, sustenance); our trials, tribulations, illness, calamities, and the death of the body is that Guru (Devo Maheshwara-the force of destruction or transformation). There is a Guru nearby (Guru Sakshat) and a Guru that is beyond the beyond (Param Brahman). I make my offering (Tasmai) to the Beautiful (Shri) remover of my darkness, my ignorance, (Guru) it is to you I bow and lay down my life (Namah).

Guru is the remover of darkness: 'Gu' means darkness, and 'Ru' means remover. Darkness refers to what obscures the light of awareness. Guru is the enlightenment principle that aids one in the realization of the true self, the whole self, the holy self. The Guru removes avidya or ignorance, which is a case of mistaken identity. It is when you think you are your personality, mistaking your body / mind container for who you are and ignore who you really are. It is when you feel separate from the whole.

By reciting this Mantra with a sincere heart, you will see that the power that enlightens is always all around you. The mantra asks for the ability to see the Guru in all names and forms, and even to acknowledge, love and serve the Guru who you cannot see, who is beyond all visible forms. The Guru is your own self. The real self, the inner guiding light.

Your own birth, the creation principle, holds within it the potential for enlightenment. This would include your parents, your day, and the place of your birth and all the circumstances surrounding your birth. Many people find it difficult to recognize the Guru in their parents. Many of us spend a lot of time complaining about the bodies we have been given by our parents and blame our parents for the difficulties in our lives.

The situation we are living in right now is where Guru Vishnu manifests. If we could see our present circumstances - who we work with, who we live with, who our friends are - as embodying the Guru principle, we might stop perceiving them as in the way of our happiness and begin to realize that they might be providing us with the way for our enlightenment to unfold.

The most difficult circumstances to accept in a positive way are the calamities, the injuries and illness that befall us physically or mentally. Guru Devo Maheshwara manifests as the big challenges in our lives, which provide us with the greatest opportunities for clearing away avidya and embracing all that happens to us as a gift from God. Destruction always opens the door for transformation.

To see the Guru in the teacher or master who is right in front of you, giving you the teachings of enlightenment, may be very difficult for us due to preconceived idealistic notions about what a Guru is supposed to look like. This is prejudice may disable us from seeing past the outer form or personality of the teacher. To acknowledge that the Guru is beyond name and form, beyond what we could imagine with the limited vision of the thinking mind, is to begin to open to the mystery of cosmic awareness. The most potent power is the last line of the Mantra in which we ask to have the good sense to be humble enough not to miss our chance to recognize the Guru when they do appear. Only when we can let go our self-cherishing, our pride, our need to be recognized and our yearning to be given credit for the things we do, can we ever hope to encounter the Guru, that which brings enlightenment to our Soul.

Guru dakshina: (Honorarium Offerings, Divine Heartily Giving to the Spiritual Master):

It is the tradition of repaying one's Guru for his Spiritual Guidance on the path of seeking truth, by surrendering, contributing, giving heartily service physically, mentally, and monetarily (Tan, Mann, Dhan) acknowledging with respect and thanks. It includes volunteer service, honorarium donation, Samarpan Rashi (Devotional and dedicated surrendering's, offerings), gift money, divinely giving with reverence, obeisance, and salutations to our beloved Guru. Guru dakshina offerings are to be given to Guru for educating, training & guidance for your spiritual upliftment. Guru dakshina is the offering of gratitude by the Sadhaka Shishya the Spiritual Seeker to his Guru (Master).

It is practically impossible to repay the Guru Runas, Guru Kripa and Guru Blessings. The Guru transforms his disciple with his inner powers by Guru Kripa, blessings, spiritual discourse, love, and compassion knowing a surrendered disciple as his own part; Aatmaja as Soul friend, Sakha. He is always one with his disciple. Gurukripa is the ultimate key towards self- realization of a disciple on his Spiritual Path. Yoga Vasistha considered it to be the only way to transcend the bondage of lifetimes of Karma. Divine Grace enacts through Gurukripa to go beyond the effects of Prarabdha Karma or Sanchita Karma which is the collection of all the past karmas chosen and done by a disciple or a person.

That this Divine Grace is not a Gift from God, but rather must be earned by a person or disciple by dedication and devotional service to the God and Sadguru. Surrendering with devotion and love to ones Guru, one gets liberated from past sins and past Karmas.

The Skanda Purana mentions the grace of a Guru in the Uttarakhand, section Guru Stotram known as 'Guru Gita', in the form of a dialogue between Shiva and Uma (Shakti):

"Gurur Brahma Gurur Vishnu Gurur Devo Maheshwara
Guru Sakshat Param Brahman Tasmei Shri Gurave Namah"

"Dhyana Moolam Guru Murti Puja Moolam Gurur Padam Mantra
Moolam Gurur Vakyam Moksha Moolam Guru Kripa"

"Om Gurukripa Hi Kevalam" is a Divine Mantra which means "The Guru's Grace is Absolute and the only Reality". Every Divine Seeker of Truth needs a Guru (Master, Teacher, Guide, Redeemer, Comforter, Counsellor). Without path you cannot succeed in spirituality, without Guru you cannot know the path of spirituality. Every succeeded Great Spiritual Person has a Guru. In his spiritual life & in the wild abyss of life, to what shall he look? When ships approach a harbor they are guided by a lighthouse. Just as the light house is very important for a sea navigator, Guru is most important for guiding the disciple through the wilderness of life.

If you contemplate carefully, you will realize that you do not really know who you are and where you are. In truth, we do not know anything about ourselves, and if we try to dive deep to acquire self-knowledge, we confront frightening experiences. Therefore, in the darkness of life, there must be one lonely light in the hands of a traveler. That is why they say "Gurukripa Hi Kevalam". The Guru's teachings must be learnt and practiced. The Guru must always be in your heart, and you must always be in rapport with him. That kind of unity must be established with the Guru, then the grace flows automatically. So, the expression is 'Gurukripa' - Grace, blessings, 'Hi' - Indeed, 'Kevalam' - Absolute. We believe in God as many or most of us do, but what is there to think about Him, and how to think about Him? What is He and what is He not? God is not a man; he is not just a little idol; he is the totality. How can I think of totality with this little mind? The mind is finite, and God is infinite. Can you believe that a finite mind can ever visualize the infinite? To experience, know and behold the infinite, you must be infinity first. Therefore, you have to surrender completely and unite with your Guru and become one with him just as salt dissolves in water, sugar dissolves in milk and fragrance dissolves in the air. They unite & become one.

Guru Bhakti & Guru Seva are important factors in spiritual life. Guru bhakti is the devotion to the Guru. It helps to free the disciple from earthly attachments to other worldly things and beings. Guru Seva or service when properly done is effective in removing selfishness, laziness & craving for comfort. True Guru Bhakti is in obeying & following the Upadesha & instructions of your Guru. Real Guru Seva is to live your daily life and conduct yourself in such a manner that your life and personal Vyavahara bring a good name to the Guru. Your living should be in accordance with the Guru's teachings. A flower is known through its fragrance. A country is known by its citizens. A father is known by the nature & behavior of his son. Hence devotees & disciples must try their utmost best to make themselves the embodiment of the Guru's teachings and reflect Guru Upadesha in their daily life.

The True Guru teaches you to achieve Dharma by daily practice of all austerities, service, devotion, and dedication. In Hinduism, Dharma signifies behaviors that are in accord with Rita, the order that makes life and universe possible and includes duties, rights, laws, conduct, virtues and "right way of living". In Buddhism, Dharma means "cosmic law & order and is also applied to the teachings of Buddha. In Jainism, Dharma refers to the teachings of Tirthankara (Jina), Bhagwan Mahavira and the body of doctrine pertaining to the purification and moral transformation of human beings. For Sikhs, Dharma means the path of righteousness and proper religious practice.

In Vedic Sanskrit, 'Dharman'; with a literal meaning of "Bearer, Supporter", in religious sense conceived as an aspect of Rita. Something established or firm, sustainer, supporter of Deities. Dharma also refers to steadfastness and stable powerful, harmonious, law & order, duty, quality. The root of the word Dharman is "Dhri" which means to support, to hold, or bear. It is the thing that regulates the course of change by not participating in change, but that principle which remains constant. Dharman means "right way of living" and "path of righteousness".

Dharman & Self-Realization are free but will cost you. Gurus and Monks sacrifice their life so that they can help you through weal & woe, pain & suffering for your wellness, wellbeing, happiness, joy & spiritual progress. Gurus have their needs & wants for their livelihood and the progress of their disciples, society, and worldly welfare to create heaven on Earth. What do you contribute to them for their teachings, blessings, love, compassion, that help you grow faster on your spiritual journey and invaluable support they extend?

Therefore, you must practice in this regard. What did you do for the Dharma to merit it? What have you done to deserve Gurus Teachings? You must serve with complete surrendering and devotion a Great Master for years to prove yourself for Gurukripa to get Dharma.

"If you protect Dharma, Dharma will protect you". Many people think that spiritual teachings should be free. They are the most important thing in the universe so of course "they should be free" .... but who will support the Guru to do that? No one wants to volunteer on that side equation, which shows how much people really value spiritual teaching, Teachers & Masters.

Once a blind Buddhist Monk called out asking if someone around him wanted to accumulate merit by threading a needle for him so he could repair his garment. Buddha answered and said he would do it. The blind man was shocked. Thinking the Buddha didn't need the merit. Shakyamuni explained that all Buddha's need to make merit, and the merit you make is never enough. In fact, I would venture to say there are only three things that matter in this universe, and thus for your life: 1) Cultivation 2) Accumulating merit 3) Perfecting your conduct, behavior, skills.

You can never ever buy Dharma. But to get it, you must surrender everything to Dharma. Serve the Guru in as many ways as you can to please him.

Spiritual Teachings are free, but they will cost you. The Dharma is free. But if you travel without guidance, it will take very long, or you may just keep wandering. To have a Guru skillful enough to get you a far distance down that road is rarer than a wish fulfilling gem.

What have you done to make the existence of those gems possible in the world, so that the Dharma thrives, is protected, transmitted & maintained, and so that others might succeed & thereby teach you as Karmic reward? Nothing. I bet you just want everything for free.

You must support, protect, propagate, transmit and maintain Dharma. To maintain Dharma, you must heartily contribute with 'Tann' -by physical service, 'Mann'-by devoting mind and 'Dhann' -by contributing money as much as possible with utmost honor.

Enlightened Gurus are themselves embodiment of Dharma. Merit and wisdom are the two wings that can get you everywhere.

Dharma are spiritual teachings which cultivate you & lead you to enlightenment. Ask yourself what you are contributing to propagate Dharma, so that everyone can get it.

Kindly consider the true cost of Dharma. In ancient India, Gurus, Saints and Monks would give up money, marriage & family to learn & pursue 'Dharma', 'The Truth'. You can't say there was no cost to the Dharma if they had to give up a normal life to learn it for the Benefit of the entire Humanity & the world.

A qualified seeker enjoys the "Free Dharma". Once enlightened. he gets it for free, perfectly free; but there is a cost to learning the path, the Tao. 'There is a great cost to pursuing the Dharma' is a definite fact. The point is that nothing is free. Tell me where the free is? Where you get something free, someone has already paid for it, put vast efforts for it. How will you pay those people back if you use what they offer?

You must support your Guru in every way you can. The cost you must pay to learn the Dharma, spiritual practice is tremendous, yet it is nothing, when you get it. That is what it is worth. In fact, it is impossible to buy the Dharma, for you must deserve it by merit. It will descend upon you spontaneously by its own.

The Universe works on Cause & Effect and in Cause & Effect, nothing is free. You get only what you deserve. There is a causal cost to everything even if you didn't see it. You must earn it to receive it. You must support it for it to come back to you. So, what are you willing to do for the Dharma's Sake?

Look at the World! 99.999% is in ignorance of the 'Dharma'. You must merit the 'Dharma' to receive it and do so by practicing it, support it by maintaining it, by respecting it, and experiencing it.

The level of Merit & Understanding of Teachings you get is the level you deserve. If you want more, you must earn it at any cost.

The first Samadhi moment you experience is so powerful, calm & ordinary. You must be in the calm state forgetting your body, mind, intellect, emotions, etc. all the time moment to moment, equanimous, empty and ordinary.

With proper guidance from the enlightened divine masters, you must liberate yourself by your own cultivation efforts, correct daily practice, consistency, intensity & twenty-four hours efforts.

Only readings, rituals, and ceremonies won't do any good. Your Karma is yours. So, it's up to you to practice Dharma to Change, to Transform, to Achieve, to Evolve, to Gain .... To liberate yourself, you need two things - Practice & Merit. Study the principles of cultivation & practice.

To learn anything, you need Good Practice. Learn to let go to experience the Pure Bright Original Nature that runs through everything. You must put in the time & energy to earn. What are the principles of practice? Emptiness all the Way. Mindfulness of Emptiness and Emptiness of Mindfulness. Just let go, with attachments or clinging to States, thoughts, consciousness that arise. Employ the principles of cessation - watching in real practice. Think it through. If you want to succeed in cultivation, you have to think positively and righteously with practical wisdom.

What exactly is Spiritual Enlightenment, Liberation, Nirvana, Self-Realization, Experiencing the clear Light, Attaining the state of no-ego, Union with God or clearly seeing The Path (The Tao)? When Buddha awakened to enlightenment, he awakened to the emptiness of the ego & phenomenon, the emptiness of interdependent origination, & saw through to the root source of the material & spiritual spheres. The Vedas & the Zen school developed the techniques so that the seeds of enlightenment can be transmitted on to the later generations. You must completely transform your body, mind, senses & consciousness, all layers upon your real Self and seeing the Path of truth (The Tao) to reach perfect Enlightenment, which entails transforming your body, mind, intellect, emotions, consciousness, chitta-chit, Atman-tattva, Prakriti... & cultivate all levels of Samadhi.

What is the meaning of life? What is the Purpose? Why are we here on Earth?

The search for life's meaning has produced much philosophical, scientific, metaphysical, and spiritual speculation. The meaning of life as we perceive it is derived from philosophical, religious contemplation, scientific and spiritual inquiries about existence, social ties, consciousness, spirits, energies, love, peace, bliss, happiness, joy and beauty. Many other issues are also involved, such as symbolic meaning, value, purpose, ethics, free will, existence of different realms, afterlife, belief system & faith in God, Soul and Supreme Soul. Nature of meaning in life has basically four component solutions i.e., Purpose, Understanding, Responsibility and Enjoyment (PURE). You need to choose a worthy purpose or a significant Life goal. You need to have sufficient understanding of who you are, what life demands of you, and how you can play a significant role in life. You and you alone are responsible for deciding what kind of life you want to live, and what constitutes a significant and worthwhile Life goal or Goals. You will enjoy a deep sense of significance only when you exercise your responsibility for self-determination and actively pursue a worthy Life goal. Thus, a sense of significance permeates every dimension of meaning, rather than stands as a separate factor. Meaning of life is in attaining the highest form of knowledge, from which all good and just things derive utility and value. Everything in life is done with a goal, and that goal is "Highest Good". Higher goals are for happiness, well-being, flourishing, achieving excellence, good merits, peace, bliss, joy, and beauty, and for freedom from all sufferings. (Lower Goals are conventional desires for wealth, power, pleasures, possessions, fame, etc .)

Living a virtuous life with wisdom and self-control in harmony with universal divine order of nature is essential for goodness of all. Live with dedication, devotion, and subservience to God, and with love, compassion, harmony, non-violence, generosity, selfless service to all, respecting everyone's freedom . The good acts and deeds are those which bring the greatest happiness and joy to the masses. Man must orient himself to give highest meaning to his own life. One must adopt with current environment and be in harmony with divine nature in an ongoing process. The practical understanding of life is more important. The meaning of life is discoverable only via experience. God created the universe, and that God had a purpose in doing so. Humans find their meaning and purpose of life in God's purpose in creating. God has given Purpose, Value, and Ultimate meaning for life. Each person creates the essence and meaning of their life. Each one has freedom of choice, decision, and action. Life is worth living only if there are goals inspiring one to live a good life. To be a Glorious Divine Personality is the purpose of human life, to do greater good for humanity and all living on the Earth. Enlightened self-interest is essential for common good.

Every living being has the right to determine his / her personal and social "meaning of life". Life's purpose is to seek divine salvation through the grace of God. To attain union with God, live a fulfilled life. "Your Purpose in Life is to find your Purpose and give your whole Heart and Soul to it", said Buddha.

In MahaPrabhu Yoga divine cosmos collective, every disciple, Seeker of Truth, Sadhaka, Shishya must surrender completely from within his heart with respect, reverence, and honor to his Guru and to all the Past Gurus, Sadgurus, Mahagurus, Saints, Rishis, Munis, Deities, Devi, Devtas, all true divine Personalities, Mother Nature and "MahaPrabhu" The Great Lord of Cosmos". Sadhaka must pay utmost respect from his heart and always be engaged in devotional Service with love. Wish all spiritual seekers and aspirants a happy and joyous new beginning. "May God bless us".

'MahaPurushartha'

The Great Spiritual Personality

Ideal Model for Glorious Integral Personality Development:

This ideal model is 'Pyramid of Needs and Path of our Ascent' (Refer Image). It has nine Steps as per rising sequence from gross to subtle, from coarse to fine, from basic physical needs to Divine Eternal Needs. This is portrayed in the shape of a pyramid with the largest and the most fundamental needs at the bottom and at top the need for transcending all worldly desires to experience Self Realization and connect with "The Supreme Lord" "The Mahaprabhu" for Divine Eternal Needs. Let us study these nine steps from the bottom of the Pyramid to the highest top in the ascending order.

1. 1st step, level 1: Basic Physical Needs:

This is the largest and the most fundamental need of all human beings and is very common and essential. Our most basic need is for physical survival. As per the ancient spiritual science of India, the great sage Patanjali in his yoga sutras has classified Human Being as Spirit-Soul having seven Koshas which are Annamaya Kosha, Pranmaya Kosha, Manomaya Kosha, Vigyanmaya Kosha, Anandmaya / Bhavanmaya Kosha, Chittamaya Kosha and Aatmamaya Kosha from gross to subtle. So, the basic physical needs come under Annamaya Kosha. Our basic survival needs are Air, Water, Food, Procreation, Clothing, Sleep, Shelter etc. We are motivated by these needs, and we strive to fulfill them by doing work. These needs are all related to our physical gross body. Our physical health is the most important aspect at this level which comes from our Physical Awareness. There is a natural void existing for every level. We naturally get contented when we fill this void. One gets satisfied and fulfilled, experiences the joy of the senses and a sense of achievement after hard work. Unlike animals who have physical and physiological needs such as air, water, food, shelter & procreation; the human beings have much greater needs such as

Mental, Intellectual, Emotional, Conscious, and Spiritual Needs. That is why the human being is the supreme creation of nature on earth. Human beings are created in the image of God. We have macrocosm within our Self (Spirit-Soul).

Although each of the Human Being has great capacity to fulfil most of the higher needs, wants & desires, only very few seem to achieve & fulfil higher intellectual, emotional, conscious, and spiritual needs, desires, & goals. The people who achieve higher steadfast state of conscious spiritual awareness are great glorious personalities. As we are not satisfied with level-1 of our basic physical needs of Annamaya Kosha, we transcend this basic level and rise to the next higher level from a common human being.

2. 2nd Step, level 2: Physiological Needs:

This is about Pranamaya Kosha. The void in this Kosha is created to maintain our physical balance, good health, livelihood, physiological and anatomical body needs, vitality, life force, proper breathing, proper diet, exercise, sports, skill, developing good habits, manners, behavior, wellness, and wellbeing etc. We strive to fulfill our physiological needs and desires. Knowledge and practice about our physiological anatomical body is necessary to develop our strong health. Good food, exercises and pranayam are necessary for our development. At this level, we identify ourselves to be a healthy personality with our physiological awareness. We are aware of our flow of five vital breaths called as Panch Pranavayu; this is the vital life force known as Prana Shaki (chi) which flows throughout our body. We also achieve self-security, security of our family, safety, and hygiene.

We experience Joy of Good Health, security and fulfilling of needs, wants and desires at this level. We must work hard to fulfill this void and transcend it to rise higher to the next level. This physiological anatomical body of Panch Prana is most important and is, to be maintained very healthy because this Pranamaya kosha links our physical gross body to our subtle body energy system, to link with our mind, intellect, thoughts, feelings, and emotions and to our causal & super causal nature. Pranayama (Proper controlled breathing practice) is very important to transcend this level. One who has control over his breath has control over his mind. We fulfill our sustenance needs and develop good habits, manners, and behavior at this level.

IDEAL MODEL FOR INTEGRAL PERSONALITY DEVELOPMENT
Pyramid of Needs and Path of Ascent
Transcending steps and rising sequence

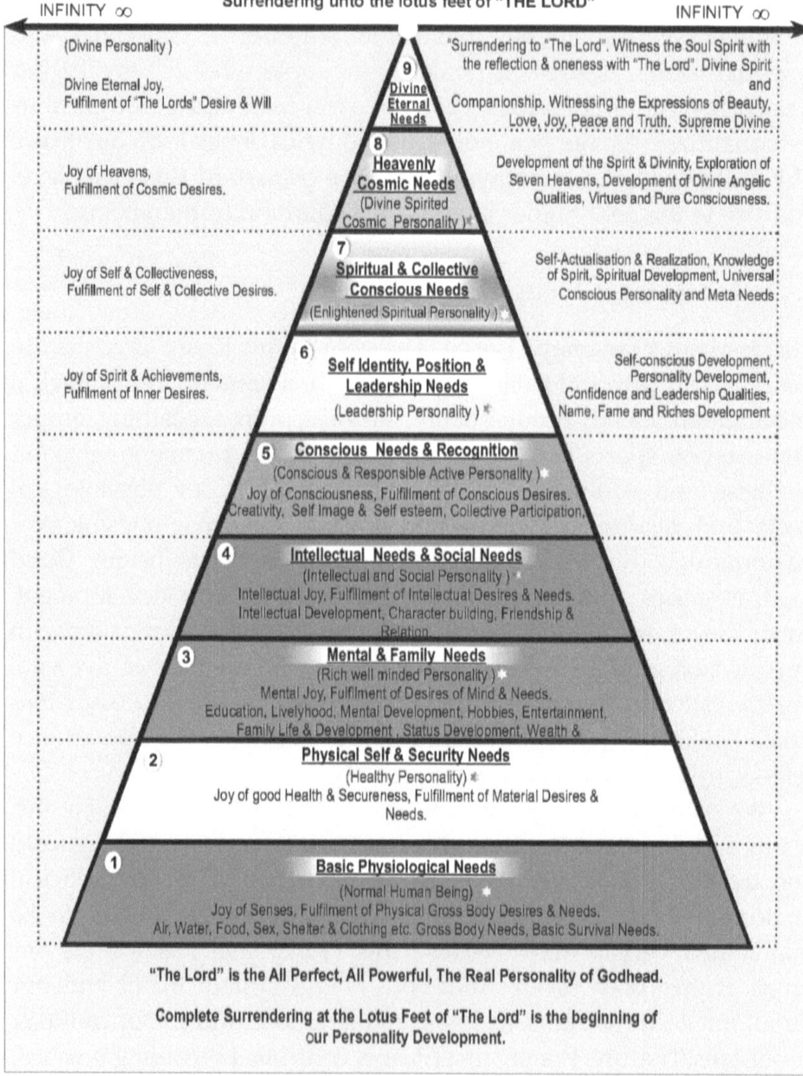

SHADOW SELF

Knowing and understanding our Ego Self, Illusions, Ignorance, cause of sufferings, and inner and outer illusory world. Practice acceptance and surrendering to reality. With determination, devotion, & dedication, practice transformation techniques for living in reality. Practice Spiritual concentration, meditation for our integral, physical, mental, & spiritual growth.

TRANSFORMATION

Change habits, practice self-introspection, imagination, visualization & transformation for what you need, want, and desire to achieve to fulfill your esteem goals of life. Practice with intense intent cessation, concentration, contemplation, cultivation, and creation.

Meditate for attaining yoga samadhi experiencing union with ultimate reality.

REAL SELF

Experiencing transformation of your shadow self with spiritual knowledge of your real Self. Achieving esteemed goals, abundance, wellness, & wellbeing. Enjoying spiritual upliftment, peace, bliss, love, happiness, joy, & beauty. Attaining Self-Realization, Enlightenment, Liberation, Freedom. Oneness with Reality.

3. 3rd step, level 3: Psychological & Family Needs:

This is about Manomaya Kosha which is our subtle body system. This Manomaya Kosha subtle body has void which has been created by nature for human being to strive for higher needs, wants & desires such as education, mental development, livelihood, hobbies, entertainment career development, family relationship, wealth, richness & status development, and all progress related to our mental world. We strive to fulfill our family needs, happiness, security, wellness, wellbeing, social relationship, and our own psychological needs. Here we get Joy of happy family and well minded personality. We become a responsible family member. Manomaya Kosha (subtle mental body) links our physical body to our subtle & causal bodies, Mind controls the brain & physical gross body. It is very difficult to conquer one's own mind, one who has control over one's mind has control over everything. Thoughts can be controlled at the root level by practice of concentration, introspection, contemplation, and meditation. Through mind we achieve our evolution & involution. We must achieve satisfaction, contentment and control over our mental activity and transcend this subtle mental level to higher level of our Identity & Awareness.

4. 4th step, level 4: Intellectual & Social Needs:

This subtle body is called Vigyanmaya or Buddhimaya Kosha. In this subtle body, the void is created for us to strive for using our intellect for learning, knowledge building, IQ development, character building, power of discretion, choice of righteousness, developing friendships, social relationship, good career to do good deeds, Karma, art, creativity, and wisdom etc. We identify ourselves at intellectual level with our intellectual awareness. Here we get joy of intellectual, social, and cultural development and our sphere of vision enlarges. We do intellectual progress. Our personality is recognized as intelligent social personality. Subtle aspects of our intellect develop only when we interact socially with people, friends, communities, and nature. Our discretion power and freedom of choice have great effect on control of our thoughts, minds, and actions. After developing our intellectual and social awareness, needs, wants and desires up to a certain level of satisfaction, we must transcend this level to experience higher level of awareness and identity. Our inner innate existing void at each level enables us to move upwards to rise higher and evolve.

5. 5th Step, level 5: Emotional & Community Needs:

This subtle body is called Anandmaya Kosha / Bhavanamaya Kosha. The subtle body of emotions and joy. The void is created to fulfill our emotional and joy giving individual and social community needs, wants, and desires. Our emotions are responsible for our expressions.

Thought + Feeling + Action = Manifestation

We develop our creativity, art, skills, languages, behavior, feelings, sentiments, empathy, compassion, emotional quotient, countenance, love, care, expressiveness, pleasure, exploring inner beauty of our mind and heart, and spreading peace and joy. Progress of our emotional intelligence; we identify ourselves at emotional level with our emotional awareness as a responsible joyous personality. We get joy of fulfilment of our emotional and community needs, wants and desires. We spread communal love, peace, brotherhood, and joy by understanding and caring for each other's emotions and feelings. We widen our circle of recognition.

Emotions affect our intelligence. Therefore, we must have excellent EQ and IQ (emotional intelligence quotient). Here, our personality is recognized as responsible joyous personality. We must gain full control on this subtle joy giving body of emotions and transcend it to achieve next higher level of identity and awareness.

6. 6th step, level -6: Conscious Needs & Recognition:

The subtle body for this is called Chittamaya Kosha. This is about the subtle body of consciousness and conscience. The void is created to fulfill our conscious needs and desires. Our conscious needs are recognition, self-image, self-esteem, self-respect, name, fame, riches, leadership development, collective participation, work for development of community, enterprise, social circles, national and global development, our evolution, and involution. It pertains to the progress of our communication skills, leadership qualities, and character building; with our conscious awareness for our higher development. We identify ourselves at conscious level with our conscious awareness. We get joy of fulfilment of our conscious needs, wants, and desires. You are recognized as conscious leadership personality at this level of achievement. Very few people reach this stage of great leadership personality; and very few of these personalities transcend this stage and can rise higher to super causal level of awareness to fulfill the Meta needs beyond these materialistic worlds and experiencing higher realm of the spiritual world.

7. 7th Step, Level – 7: Spiritual Collective Conscious Needs:

The subtle body for this purpose is called Aatmamaya Kosha (The subtlest body of spirit, Antakaran, essence of Soul). Our inner innate nature is associated with our spirit, which also includes our ego. This is a causal body. Our life's real purpose lies in this. This realm, we can explore only after our self-realization and enlightenment by enlightened spiritual Guru (spiritual master). The great void is created to fulfill our spiritual quest, spiritual collective conscious needs & desires. Here we gain knowledge of inner innate nature, spirit, universal consciousness, and our real spirit Soul. We get divine joy of collective experiences by our spirit soul. Our ego completely dissolves, and we realize our true self. Our real identity is that we are not this physical gross body, mind, intellect, emotions, and consciousness, but we are the masters of all these. We are pure divine spirited Soul. We are made in the image of "Almighty God" "Mahaprabhu". We develop unconditional love, compassion, caring and divine virtues. We enjoy peace, bliss, inner beauty, & joy. We know self by the Self. We realize our real identity as divine spirit Soul. We get self-realization and enlightenment from an enlightened Guru for our spiritual ascent and increasing our divine awareness. We are recognized as enlightened spiritual personality ready to help fulfill spiritual collective needs, wants, and desires of the people of the entire world and nature.

8. 8th step, level- 8: Heavenly Cosmic Needs:

This subtle realm of divinity is called Virata Shakti Kosha (Virata -The cosmic being of infinite spirit and energy). This is completely out of body experience, where our spirit-soul with divine energy unites with a divine universal consciousness and divine sentient energy. Here, our spirit soul can have communication with higher divine heavenly entities, and deities to have very exceptional divine experience. The evolved spiritual enlightened being contribute to the cosmic inter-activities for universal evolution and transformation. One experiences his spiritual eternal nature in rhythmic harmony with the entire Cosmos, subtle spiritual realms, heavenly realms, with cosmic awareness and heavenly divine joy. A highly realized, enlightened, spiritual being strives to fulfill the heavenly cosmic needs, desires and help other human beings on Earth to evolve to be divine spiritual beings; spreading divinity to establish heavenly Kingdom on earth as it is in heaven. Divine cosmic personality develops divine qualities, virtues, divine essence and is fully devoted to the "Almighty Lord" "Mahaprabhu".

9. 9th step, level - 9: Divine Eternal Needs:

This subtle realm of divinity is called Purushtatwa, Divine Spirit Kosha, Paramdham, Vaikuntha, 'The Kingdom of The Lord'. In the scheme of 'Almighty Lord', the human beings are the ultimate form in creation, who are created in the image of God. The event of union of our spirit- soul with the supreme spirit- soul is also the highest moment for the devotee. Reaching the lotus feet of "The Lord" is our ultimate destiny. This is the ultimate stage of a devotee in the path of spiritual ascent. This is our highest purpose to unite with our source. There is a unique individual experience of each seeker of truth. One must fulfill divine eternal needs, spreading the joy of eternal divine virtues, knowledge, bliss, love, beauty, divinity and share the experiences. One experiences the supreme eternal play of divine sentient cosmic energy and divine spirit. One gains supreme divine conscious awareness. The realized enlightened free spirit soul strives to fulfill the desires and the will of "The Almighty Lord" "Mahaprabhu". The highly realized great spirit soul is recognised as divine godly personality. He transcends space, time, all qualities of nature and experiences the supreme divine love, compassion, peace, bliss, joy, and beauty of the "Kingdom of the Lord" the seeker devotee becomes "Mahapurush" (Glorious spiritual divine personality) who performs higher duties "Mahapurushartha".

The sequence of superiority and supremacy from gross to subtle in Human Beings: Physical Gross body - Physiological Anatomical body - Mental body Mind - Intellectual Knowledge body - Emotional Joy Giving body - Conscience, Consciousness body - Inner Innate Nature with Ego I'ness - Individual Spirit, Life Soul - Divine Nature & Sentient energy - Supreme Divine Spirit, Supreme Eternal Soul.

Energy is the source and cover of all living and non-living entities in the universe. Energy is capacity and strength or power to do work.

Through meditation practice, we must increase our level of conscious awareness in its different capacities, forms, and attributes in connection with the universal consciousness and transcend each level of pyramid of needs and path of ascent. Transcending all gross and subtle levels to ultimately have union and oneness with the divine supreme eternal Soul. This is the ultimate purpose of human life.

'MahaUtthan'

The Great Spiritual Upliftment

The Ideal Path of Divine Spiritual Ascent:

This ideal model is pyramid of spiritual ascent (see image), exploring nine heavenly subtle kingdoms:

Beauty, bliss, love, & joy of Nature and Spirit of the entire Cosmos is magnificent, wonderful, unbounded, limitless, and Divine. It is only to the limitations of the explorer how much one can truly explore and experience Nature's Glorious Divine Beauty. It is the matter of sincere quest, curiosity, zeal, enthusiasm, capability, capacity, dedication, devotion, and faith to explore and experience the sublime magnificent Beauty of Nature and its Secret. It is really a great art of loving Nature's Beauty.

There are seven subtle planes in human subtle body. There are totally forty-nine planes in seven Strata of the entire creation in the Cosmos. Higher planes are Heavens and lowest seven planes are Hell. Human beings are created in the image of "The Lord" by the Grace of "The Lord". We can achieve our complete Spiritual Ascent by transcending the seven subtle planes within us and connect directly to the all-pervading 'Divine sentient cosmic spiritual energy' called as "Paramchaitanya" "Paramtatttva", and thus experience peace, bliss, love, beauty, and joy of divine nature. Let us study these nine steps, levels from the bottom of the Pyramid of the ideal path of divine spiritual ascent to the highest top in the ascending order.

1. First Heavenly Kingdom

This subtle Heavenly Kingdom is located at the Pelvic Plexus at the bottom end of our spinal cord. It is called Mooladhara Chakra the (root chakra) in Sanskrit as per the Vedas. The first subtle energy center is the root center. It has four sub plexuses. Its color is red. The seed Mantra for Mooladhar Chakra is "Om Lam". Its element is

Earth. Physical Responsibility is to control activities and metabolism of Prostate Glands, Procreation, Potency, Excretion, Cohesiveness, and Inertia. At subtle level, it has many Divine Qualities, Essence, Energies and Powers of various sorts such as Auspiciousness, Wisdom, Purity, Chastity, Innocence, Power of Discretion, Mightiness, Prosperity, Opulence, and Holiness required for our wellness and wellbeing and for our Spiritual Ascent.

The Divine Sentient Cosmic Energy known in Vedas as "Kundalini Shakti" rests as three and half coiled energy on this Mooladhara Chakra. This divine kundalini actualizes itself when a true seeker of truth has pure desire for his Spiritual Upliftment and with the guidance and blessings of Sadguru. The seeker is one who is fully surrendered to his "Sadguru" (The enlightened Master) and who has been blessed with "Sadgurukrupa". This actualized coiled kundalini energy then rises to next higher center.

2. The Second Heavenly Kingdom

This is located at our vest vertebrae in the spinal cord between the leg joints with the trunk, the abdomen at the Aortic plexus. It is called Swadhisthana Chakra (The Sacral Chakra) in Vedas. The second subtle energy center. It has six sub plexuses. Its colour is orange. Its seed Mantra is "Om Vam". Its element is Water. Its physical responsibilities are to control the activities of Urinary Bladder, Liver, Spleen, Pancreas. It provides power to the brain cells by converting fat cells into brain cells.

At the subtle level, its qualities are Creativity, All Arts, Interest in Beautiful Creative Works, Intuition, Inner Inspiration, Genius, Intellectual Understanding, Abstract Thought, Aesthetics, Pure Desire, Pure Knowledge, Learning etc. This center is actualized for higher divine experiences by the Divine Sentient Energy "Kundalini Shakti". When this energy freely flows through this center and then it rises to higher center.

The divine path of ascent
Pyramid of spiritual ascent
The nine heavenly kingdoms

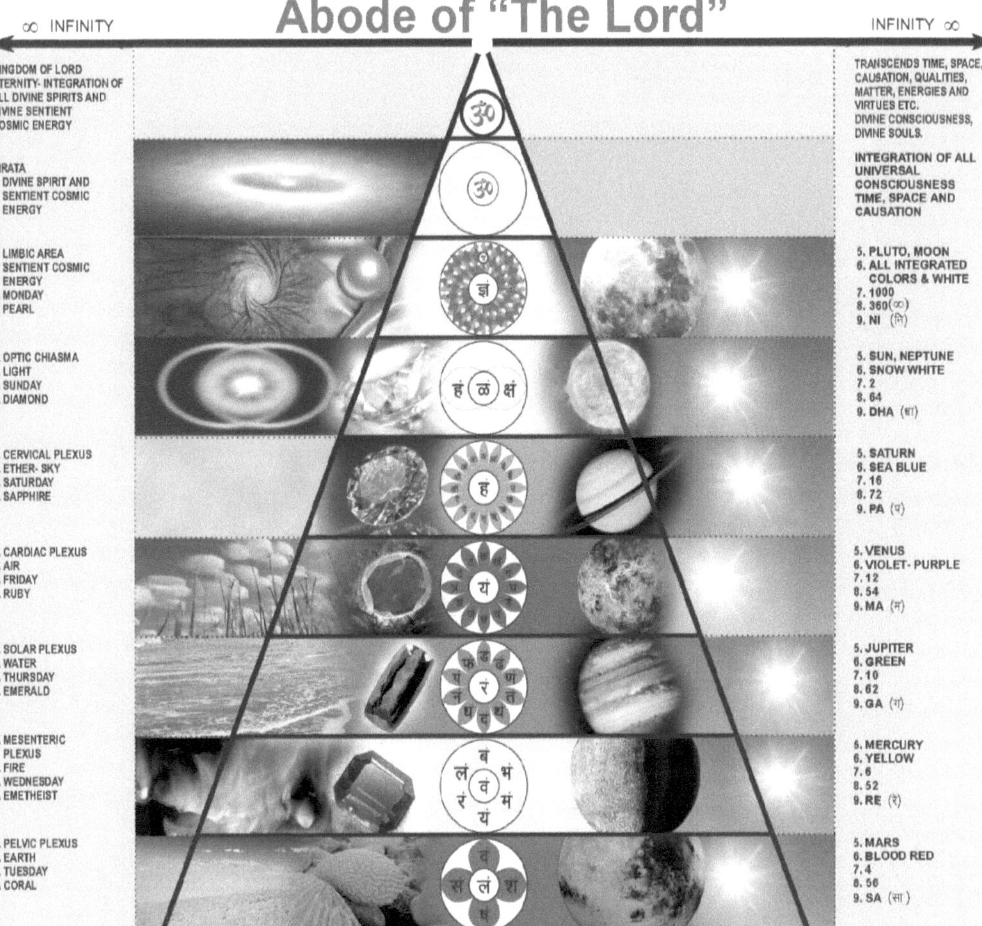

1. NAME OF CHAKRA 2. ELEMENT 3. DAY 4. STONE 5. PLANET 6. COLOUR 7. PETALS 8. RAYS 9. SEVEN NOTES

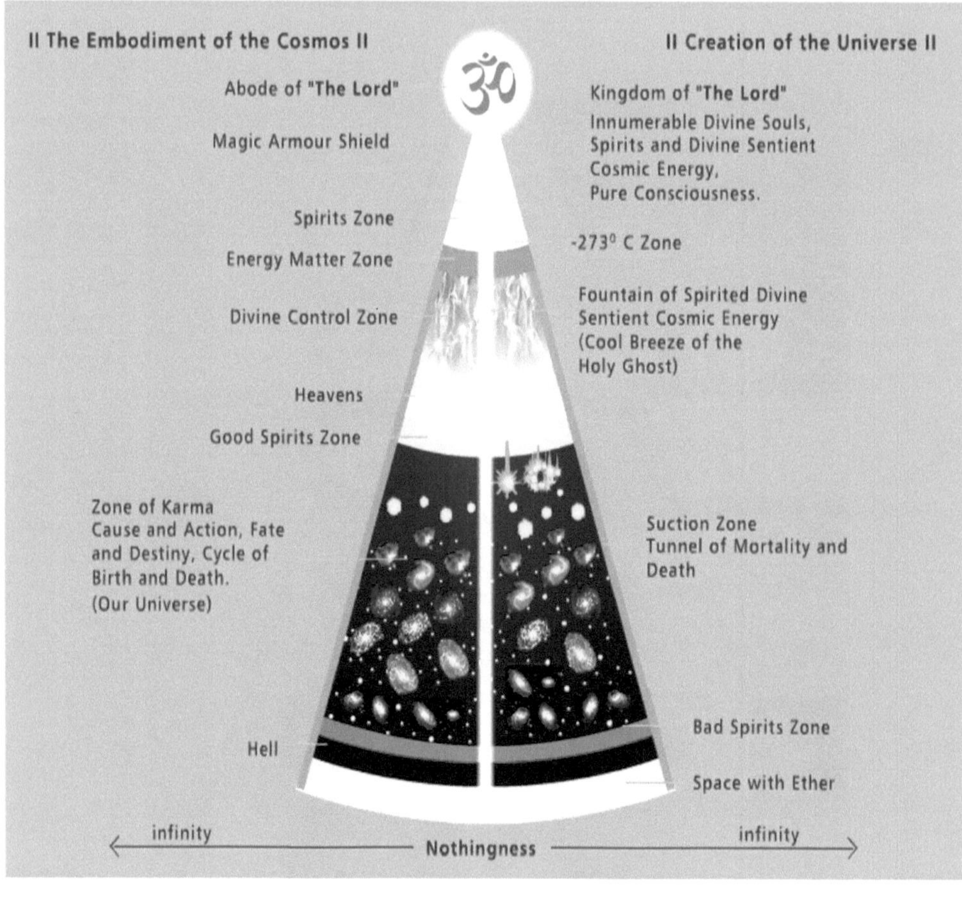
II The Embodiment of the Cosmos II
II Creation of the Universe II
Abode of "The Lord"
Magic Armour Shield
Kingdom of "The Lord"
Innumerable Divine Souls,
Spirits and Divine Sentient
Cosmic Energy,
Pure Consciousness.
Spirits Zone
-273⁰ C Zone
Energy Matter Zone
Divine Control Zone
Fountain of Spirited Divine
Sentient Cosmic Energy
(Cool Breeze of the
Holy Ghost)
Heavens
Good Spirits Zone
Zone of Karma
Cause and Action, Fate
and Destiny, Cycle of
Birth and Death.
(Our Universe)
Suction Zone
Tunnel of Mortality and
Death
Bad Spirits Zone
Hell
Space with Ether
infinity
Nothingness
infinity

3. The Third Heavenly Kingdom

This is located at the spinal cord behind our Navel at Solar Plexus (Coeliac Plexus). It is called Manipur Chakra or Nabhi Chakra (The Solar Plexus Chakra) in the Vedas. It is the third subtle energy center. It has ten sub plexuses. It is surrounded by a great void (Bhavsagar). Its color is Yellow surrounded by Oceanic Blue. Its seed Mantra is "Om Ram". Its element is Fire. Its physical responsibilities are to control the activities of Stomach, Intestine, Adrenal Gland, Parts of Uterus.

At subtle level, its qualities are Happiness, Satisfaction, Peace, our Spiritual Ascent, Dharma (Divine Virtues, Principles, Qualities & Essence), Generosity, Rising in Awareness, Righteousness, Health, Wealth, Welfare, Wellbeing, Evolution, Contentment, Self-guidance, Guru Tattva, Seeking, Path of Self Realization, Enlightenment and Glory.

The subtle energy has an upward consuming movement like fire flames. This subtle Divine Kundalini Shakti is Soothing, Nurturing, Caring, Loving, Benevolent and Blissful. It Controls, Guides, burns and removes all negativities and Doshas of the True Spiritual Seeker of Truth. This subtle Nabhi Chakra is actualized and enlightened by Divine Cosmic Sentient Energy when this powerful energy flows freely through it and rises upward to the next higher center.

4. The Fourth Heavenly Kingdom

This is located at the spinal cord behind the center of our chest at the cardiac plexus. It is called Anahata Chakra or Heart Chakra. It is the fourth subtle energy center, the powerhouse of the body. It has twelve sub plexuses. Its color is green. Its seed Mantra is "Om Yam". Its element is Air, Pranavayu (Vital life force).

Its physical responsibilities are to control the activities of Heart, Lungs, Creation of Antibodies, Developing Immune System. At subtle level, its qualities are Fearlessness, Self- Confidence, Self-Image, Immunity, Fatherhood or Motherhood, Pure Love, Life's Vitality, Compassion, Responsibilities, Existence, Serene Joy, Security, Possibilities, Cosmic Vibration Resonance, Emotional balance. This subtle center helps the union and balance of our Spirit Self with our inner innate Divine Cosmic Sentient Energy. It is actualized and enlightened by the Divine Cosmic Sentient Energy when this energy flows freely through this center and rises upwards to the next higher center.

5. The Fifth Heavenly Kingdom

This is located at the neck vertebrae behind the throat at the Cervical Plexus. It is called Vishuddhi Chakra (The Throat Chakra). It is the fifth subtle energy center. It has sixteen sub plexuses. Its color is sky blue. Its Mantra is "Om ham". Its element is Ether, Sky. It is like a vessel where all elements mingle with each other. Its physical responsibilities are to control Thyroid Glands, Eyes, Tongue, Ears, Nose, Hands, Neck, Teeth, Face Muscles, Parathyroid Glands, Mouth Palate, Eyebrows etc.

At subtle level, its qualities are Collectiveness, Steadfastness, Divine Diplomacy, Sweetness, Gentleness, Humorous, Sportive, Playful, Joyous, Cleverness, Charismatic, Excellent Communication, Emotional Intelligence. It also connects with universal cosmic energies. This subtle energy center is actualized and enlightened by the spirit of divine sentient energy when this divine energy flows freely through this center and rises upwards to the next higher level.

6. Sixth Heavenly Kingdom

This is located at the brain, behind the forehead at the optic chiasma. Two optic nerves cross each other in the brain. It is called Agnya Chakra in Vedas. It is also called the third Eye Chakra. It is believed to reveal insights about the future. It is the sixth subtle energy center. It has two sub plexuses. Its color is Indigo and White (after enlightenment). Its seed Mantra is "Om", "Om Dnyam". Its element is Light.

Its physical responsibilities are to control the activities of Vision, Optic Nerves, Pituitary and Pineal Glands, Part of the body which manifests the Ego and Superego within us, Retina, Optic Lobes, Optic Chiasma.

Its subtle qualities are Thinking, Thought Processing, Politeness, Evolution, Merciful, Pure Vision, Imagination, Forgiveness, Surrendering, Egoless, Faith, Sacrifice, Modesty, Humility, Devotion, Dedication, Determination, Resurrection, Name, Fame, Glory, Balance, Single Pointedness. This subtle energy center is actualized and enlightened by Divine Sentient Energy when this divine energy flows freely through this center and rises upwards to the next higher level.

7. The Seventh Heavenly Kingdom

This is located at the top of the head in the limbic area. It is called Sahasrara Chakra (The Crown Chakra) in Vedas. It is the seventh subtle energy center. It has thousand sub plexuses. Its color is Violet, White, and Colorless. The Sub plexus exhibit star dance of multi colors randomly changing. Its seed Mantra is "Om", "Om Shram", "Om Ahaaa....".

Its physical responsibilities are to control the activities of the Brain, Memory, All Nervous System, Integration of all body parts and subtle energy centers, and Hypothalamus. There are thousand sub plexuses of fine nerves, Lotus like structure of The Brain.

Its subtle qualities are Consciousness, Awareness, Attention, Integration of All Gross, Subtle and Causal Energies and Spirit. Illumination of Mind, Radiance, Beauty, Faith, Doubtlessness, Thoughtlessness, Integration of All Energy Centers, Chakras and Nadis (Nervous System), Desirelessness, Knowledge about Self and Divinity, Renunciation, Witness state, Self-realization, and Enlightenment.

Here, the divine spirit and divine sentient energy sport with each other in a divine play. This center is enlightened by divine sentient energy and divine spirit. The seeker by his Dedication, Devotion, Steadfast Practice and by Grace and Kripa of Sadguru can Transcend this stage and rise higher to experience the next level which is totally out of body experience of our spiritual subtle body.

8. The Eighth Heavenly Kingdom

This does not have any physical location inside our physical body. But it is realized by an individual seeker just around two to four inches above the top of the Head. It is called the Virata Chakra which connects an individual spirit self to the Universal Cosmic Energies and spirits. It is the eighth energy center of complete universal consciousness. Here our spirit soul and divine sentiment cosmic energy and our original nature become one with the universal consciousness of Virata (Universal Cosmic Being). This Chakra color is pure white and colorless. It is a Whirlpool of spirited conscious Divine Sentient Energy. Its seed Mantra is "Om", "Om Jai", "Om Shri". "Om" which means Unity, Oneness, Harmony, Wholeness. It transcends all physical gross body experiences. This realization is totally outside our body above our Sahasrara Chakra at the top of our head. We can clearly experience our physical body completely detached from our subtlest body of divine sentient energy-Spirit-Soul.

Its subtle qualities are Immense gravity, electromagnetic field, potencies, powers of various sorts, divine energies and spirit, pure divine knowledge of Cosmos, communication with other cosmic beings possible. It is the integration of all divine energy and spirits. It is the fulfilment of the void of the earlier seven stages, cosmic Synchronicity and Rhythm; Connection with the Cosmic Intelligence, Experiencing higher Divine Nature. This stage is achieved by a sincere spiritual practitioner who is a completely surrendered and devoted seeker under the guidance of Sadguru (Spiritual Master) by the Grace, Blessings, and Kripa of Sadguru.

9. The Ninth Heavenly Kingdom

This is the kingdom of "The Lord" "Mahaprabhu" in which "The Lord" lives eternally at his Abode. This Kingdom of "Mahaprabhu" is separated from all the other six strata of creation. Each stratum is having seven worlds as per superiority. The kingdom of Mahaprabhu also has seven worlds known as 'Lokas' in the Vedas.

The kingdom of "The Lord" is separated from the rest of the World, Universes by his Yogmaya, divine maya. 'Maya' means Illusion or that which is not. It is an illusionary separation between the materialistic world and divine spiritual world by a divine magic shield.

'The Lord's Kingdom' cannot be described by words. The experience is beyond all intellect overshadowed by divine play of maya.

The ninth heavenly kingdom is the destination home of a great devotee of "Mahaprabhu", who has completely transcended the eight heavenly kingdoms. This Kingdom of "The Lord" is beyond all physical & metaphysical existences. It is divine spiritual heavenly realm, which creates, sustains, and transforms all other creations, existences, universes of the entire Cosmos. It has infinite potencies and is Eternal.

The heavenly Kingdom of "Mahaprabhu" has infinite potencies, sentient energies, powers, divine supreme consciousness, divine spirits with divine nature, and all supreme qualities of divinity which transcend all creation.

There are innumerable divine spirited souls eternally existing with "The Mahaprabhu" who are always in divine servitude following the will of "The Mahaprabhu". It is impossible to express and comprehend about the greatest Kingdom of "The Mahaprabhu".

The Three Subtle Channels and the Void

The seven Chakras are connected by the three gross and subtle channels of our body. These are the Left Sympathetic Nervous System, Right Sympathetic Nervous System and The Central Parasympathetic Nervous System. These are the main three gross and subtle channels through which the blood, subtle life force, vital pranavayu and divine sentient energy circulate and flow within our entire body and mainly to the seven chakras.

The Left Channel

It is called the Moon channel, known as Ida Nadi in Vedas. It is the Left Sympathetic Nervous System. At subtle level, the left channel governs desire, emotions, conditioning related to our past. It is responsible for keeping us away from danger. More left sided activity is responsible for disbalance of gunas, increasing tamoguna, ignorance, inertia, lethargy, laziness, repentance, over thinking of past and dormant consciousness. Our subconscious activities take place through this channel. Through left channel, we can get connected to the universal subconscious wherein we can know the abstract past.

Its positive good qualities are pure desire & emotions, willpower, learning from Past experiences, devotion, determination, dedication, development of our attitudes, use of Anger for Righteousness and depletion of our superego of the past. It helps in gaining pure knowledge and developing skills, etc.

The Right Channel

It is called the sun channel or pingala nadi in the Vedas. It is The Right Sympathetic Nervous System. At subtle level, the right channel governs thoughts, actions, planning and our future. It is responsible for helping us fight for our survival. More right sided activity is responsible for disbalance of the three gunas, increases rajoguna, disturbs attention, more futuristic, supra conscious, shadowy creativity, obsession for power, passionate, workaholic, physical & mental activities. Through right channel, we get connected to the universal supra consciousness, wherein we can know the abstract future.

Its positive good qualities are positive good karmic action, future visualization, positive planning, helping others with Justice, and depletion of our ego on the left side of our brain, etc.

The Central Channel

It is called the Cosmic Energy Channel, Sushumna Nadi in the Vedas. It is central parasympathetic nervous system, autonomic nervous System. The central channel governs our automated 'pre- programmed' functions, such as heartbeats, breathing, and other metabolic activities in our body. This channel is the spiritual channel as well. It maintains the balance between two channels, left and right channels. It is responsible for soothing us, lowering blood pressure, relaxing us, healing us to make progress. After our self-realization from our spiritual master, this channel is awakened and provides a path of ascent for the divine sentient cosmic energy called "Kundalini Shakti" to rise through to provide divine sentient energy to all the chakras, our heart, brain, and to the whole of our body at gross and subtle levels. It helps us to balance the functioning of the left and the right channels and avoid the extremes and excesses such as too much lethargy on the left side or over activity on the right side. It keeps us maintained, balanced, and centered.

Its positive good subtle qualities and essence are sattwaguna, goodness, path of truth, wisdom, righteousness, to be present in a moment, path of our ascent, perfect balance, divine knowledge of truth, bliss, peace, beauty, and Joy. Helps to practice moderation in life. Through this Central path we know the present, we get connected to the universal pure consciousness.

The Great Void

At all levels of our evolution and ascent, there is a void which propels us to evolve and rise higher. It is this void which makes us to do work, practice and develop various skills, to gain physical materialistic knowledge and spiritual knowledge at various levels. There is an ocean of void for worldly materialistic life and higher spiritual life called bhavasagara of samsara and anandasagara of spiritual world, devout sea of earthly concern and of Paramartha (Spiritual Path of seeking Truth) the divine concern. Without this great void, we wouldn't have had this beautiful, wonderful, and magnificent creation and evolution in this entire Cosmos. This creation itself is to fill this great void.

All nine heavenly kingdoms in the path of our evolution and spiritual ascent of human beings have a great ocean of void. Each one of us is striving, making effort, earning merits to fill and cross these voids at different levels to rise higher. This creation itself is to fill the infinite void as per one's own needs, wants, desire in limitations with one's satisfaction and contentment to rise higher. One may be satisfied and contented with very little, and one may not be even with abundance. The most essential void for every living being is the basic need for air, water, food, shelter, and procreation, the basic needs for survival. This void is in the Annamaya Kosha. We get satisfaction and joy when we strive and work to fulfil this basic needs for moderate living.

There is a great void called bhavasagara which is surrounding our solar plexus (Coeliac Plexus) called nabhi chakra in Vedas.

At each level, physical, subtle, and causal, there is void, which create and propel us to fulfil our needs, wants, wishes and desire at each level for which we put our efforts and work hard to fulfil them hence performing our karmas, actions. The fruits of karma depend upon how we perform them. We must transcend all physical materialistic and spiritual levels by performing good karmas, righteous actions. Thus, while fulfilling void at every level, we gain life experiences, pleasures, worldly & divine knowledge, satisfaction, contentment, happiness, love, peace, bliss, and joy. We enjoy our inner innate beauty, nature's beauty, and our path (The Tao).

'MahaMantras – MahaYantras – MahaTantras – MahaShlokas'

The Great Spiritual Power Boosters

'MahaMantras'
Great subtle divine formulae of nature

"Om": It signifies the essence of the ultimate reality, consciousness, Atman (Soul, the Self within) and Brahman (ultimate reality, entirety of the universe, truth, divine supreme spirit, cosmic principle). Referred as Pranava.

Origin of light and sound: In the beginning was the word and the word was with God, and the word was God. That word is "Om". "Om" is the word of God.

Nikola Tesla said, "If you want to find the secrets of the universe, think in terms of energy, frequency and vibration". The very foundation of our universe of matter and thought, appear to lie in sound vibration. From a yogic perspective, there is a profound connection between speech (the expression of our thoughts) and prana (the life energy carried on the breath). When we speak, we are naming our reality, while using the power of the breath to form and express our words. Speech is prana in action. Prana naturally creates sound. The potential of sound vibration and intention in creating our reality has been explored in great depth by the ancient Yogis. Patanjali taught this, Chant "Om" and you will attain your goal. If nothing else works; just chant "Om". You experience a non-dual awareness.

"Om" is the original seed Mantra, the first syllable carrying immense pranic life force energy. "Om" is the primal or primordial sound of the entire Cosmos. "Om" connects us to and carries the divine in vibrational form, It makes our prayers and mantras more effective with its increased pranic energy. The sound "Om" is a vibration from which all the manifest universe emanates. Form and creation are from vibrations. "Om" is the most elemental of vibrations. It is the sound of the great Void. It is the sound of the creator, preserver and destroyer or transformer of the universe. Is also the inner Guru and prime teacher. It attunes us with our true nature. It reflects both the manifest & unmanifest Brahman, sustaining the vibration of being, life, and consciousness in all worlds and all creatures. "Om" in prolonged pronounciation as "AUM" correspond to different aspects of divine. The first sound 'A' invokes "Brahma", the creative aspect. The "U" sound invokes "Vishnu", the preserver and the "M" sound invokes "Shiva" who represents the destructive or transformative aspect of God, without which nothing exists and everything is sustained and dissolved back into the Void. In the yogic tradition, Mantra is a powerful tool to focus and quite the mind. With proper breathing and holding your attention and awareness at the crown of your head, chant the mantra "Om" 108 times, this keeps the mind focused and infuses the body, mind, and heart with the qualities of the mantra. "Om" is all encompassing sound of the entire cosmos, essence of all reality, and unifies everything in the universe.

The letter "A" represents the waking state, "U" represents the dream state and "M" is the unconscious state, or state of deep sleep. In the "Om", "ॐ" symbol the waking state is represented by the bottom curve, the dream state is the middle curve, and the state of deep sleep is represented by the upper curve. The crescent shape of the above the curve denotes Maya, or illusion, which is the obstacle that sits in the way for reaching the highest state of Bliss. The dot at the top of the symbol represents the Absolute state; which is the fourth state of consciousness and is Absolute Peace, Bliss, and Beauty; it is also called "Turiya State" or "Sat Chit Anand" in which a true devotee could get connected with the Divine.

Mahamantras: "Mantra" is the chanting of protected or secret sound. Mantra has supernatural power. These are subtle formulae of nature. Mantras contain praise and invocation for divine power or deity. Mantras are magical and have spiritual efficiency. Mantras are recited, muttered, sung, or meditated upon. Each 'Mantra' has power, shakti (energy), and divine essence.

Mantras are structured formulae of thoughts, prayers, sacred utterance, spell and weapon of supernatural power. Mantra are used for worshipping, developing divine virtues and qualities for spiritual development and ascent. Mantras are used for pleasing and invoking a deity requesting for achieving good intention and goal. Mantras are also used to cope with the uncertainties and dilemmas of daily life. Mantras are to be recited with a transcendental redemptive goal as intention for experiencing a spiritual connection with God. Mantras are a spiritual language and instrument of thought. Mantras may be spoken aloud or recited in the mind. Mantras are silent instruments of meditation. Mantra "Om" is the Pranava Mantra, the source of all mantras. There is only one reality which is Brahman, and first manifestation of Brahman is expressed as "Om". Thus "Om" is prefixed and suffixed to all mantras, prayers, and devotional songs, Bhajans etc. Mantras invoke divine principles, essence & qualities and ultimately focus on the one reality. The universe is sound. "Om" the supreme "Parashabd" "Shabd Brahma" is reverberating in the entire Cosmos and is eternal. Creation consists of vibrations at various frequencies and amplitude giving rise to the phenomena of the world. Bija Mantra are prefixed and appended to other Mantra, thereby creating complex mantras. Mantra japa is the practice of repetitively uttering the same mantra for an auspicious number of times, the most popular being 108 times. Mantra japa purifies the mind, heart and spirit and achieves God consciousness. Mantra is that which saves one by pondering over the light of supreme I-consciousness. The divine supreme I-consciousness is the dynamo of all mantras. Shiva Sutras originated from Shiva's Tandav Nritya (Dance). In Shiva sutras, Deha or body has been compared to wood, "Mantra" has been compared to Arani -a piece of wood used for kindling fire by friction; Prana has been compared to fire. Sikha or flame has been compared to atma (Self); ambara or sky has been compared to Shiva. When prana is kindled by means of mantra used as arani, fire in the form of udana arises out of sushumna, and then just as flame arises out of Kindled fire and gets dissolved in the sky, so also atma (Self) like flame having burnt down the fuel of the body, gets absorbed in Shiva.

The best effect of Mantra is when Mantra is experienced and absorbed as thought sound only, listening to the inner voice. The mantras are used for enhancing intellect, prosperity, health, wealth and developing spiritual qualities. It is also used for experiencing love, peace, bliss, joy & beauty. It is used for praising and invoking deities. Mantras are magic spells for developing enlightened mind. The term Mantra is traditionally said to be derived from two roots, 'man' -to think, and the action-oriented suffix 'tra'. Mantras are also used for protection from negativities, worries, tensions, stress, anxieties, natural calamities, troubles, disasters, diseases, enemies, and other negative evil forces. Mantras are used for concentration of the mind on God. Through proper repetition of the mantra, and listening to one's own voice, thoughts reduce, and the mind rises above materialism to tune into the Voice of God. Mantra eliminates ego.

As per neuroscience pilot study, activity in the default mode network was suppressed in group practicing on Mantra based meditation, but not in the control group practicing tapping fingers on a four-button keypad. The default mode network is a large-scale brain network, active during, passive rest and mind-wandering, and is the neurological basis for the self. Chanting Mantra are proven to be more beneficial. Mantra meditation decreases heart rate and blood pressure, increases our immunity and system functionality and decrease intrusive thoughts. It elevates the mind. Just as water nourishes the plants in a garden, so Mantras nourishe all that are beneficial for our lives. Each time we chant Mantra, we plant seeds for transformation and tend to the garden of our being. Eventually, the garden begins to bear fruits in the form of abundance, health, wealth, prosperity, healing, love, compassion, peace, bliss, joy, and beauty and elevated state of consciousness. The benefits radiate outwards and be a fruitful offering for friends, relatives, family members, neighbors, and for the entire planet. Mantras empower and increase radiance. Mantras enhance positive alpha, gamma, delta, and the brainwaves. The whole brain synchronizes, balances the left and right brain hemispheres leading to super creativity and more.

| | MAHAPRABHU MAHAMANTRA | |

| | Om Jai | |
| | Om Param Sundaram Shri Mahaprabhuyoga Mahashivshakti Mahamantram Namo Namah: | |

OM JAI ~ OM JAI ~ OM JAI |
Om Paramsatyam ~ Om Paramsatyam ~ Om Paramsatyam | |

Om Aham Bramhasmi ~ Om Ayam AtmaBrahma
~ Om Tattvamasi |
Om Prajnyanam Brahma ~ Om Sarvamkhalvidam Brahma
~ Om Soham | |

Om Shivoham ~ Om Shivoham ~ Om Shivoham |
Om ParamShanti ~ Om ParamShanti ~ Om ParamShanti | |

Om SarvaVyaptam ~ Om Sarvadnyam ~ Om Sarvaatmaaka |
Om SarvaShaktiman ~ Om SarvaSiddhi ~ Om Sarveshvara | |

Om Bhavyadivyam ~ Om Prasannachittam
~ Om BrahmaChaitanyam |
Om Mangalyam ~ Om Kalyanam ~ Om Anandam | |

Om ParamSunderam ~ Om ParamSunderam
~ Om ParamSunderam |
Om Tat Sat ~ Om Tat Sat ~ Om Tat Sat | |

Om Jai ~ Om Jai ~ Om Jai |
Om ParamSunderam Shri Bhagavati Narayani MahaShakti
Trigunatmika Kundalini Jagadamba Namo Namah | |

Om Shri Brahma Namo Namah |
Om Shri Vishnu Namo Namah |
Om Shri Mahesh Namo Namah |
Om Shri MahaSaraswati Namo Namah |
Om Shri MahaLakshmi Namo Namah |
Om Shri MahaKali Namo Namah | |

Om Shri MahaVishnu Namo Namah |
Om Shri Ram Namo Namah |
Om Shri Krishna Namo Namah |
Om Shri Bhagavan Mahavira Namo Namah |
Om Shri Gautama Buddha Namo Namah |
Om Shri Kalki Namo Namah ||

Om Shri Parameshwara Namo Namah |
Om Shri ParamDaata Namo Namah |
Om Shri Paramaatma Namo Namah |
Om Gam Ganapataye Namah |
Om Namah Shivaya Namaha |
Om Namo Narayanaya ||

|| Om Shri Sat-Chit_Ananda Mahamana Sadashiva
Parabrahma Divya Omkar Paramchaitanya Swaroopa
Mahaveda ParamPurushaya ParamSunderam
Shri Mahaprabhu Namo Namah ||

Om ParamSunderam Shri MahaPrabhuYoga Namo Namah |
Om Yogakshemam Vahamyaham |
Om Tathastu ||
Om Jai ~ Om Jai ~ Om Jai ||

Om ParamSunderam Om ParamSunderam Om ParamSunderam |
Om Tat Sat ~ Om Tat Sat ~ Om Tat Sat ||
Om Jai ~ Om Jai ~ Om Jai ||

- Pramod Sonar

"MahaPrabhuYoga MahaShivShakti Mahamantram" Meaning:

"Om Jai" - "Om" The word of "The Almighty Lord" "MahaPrabhu", 'Om' is great, glorious, and victorious. "Om" is Omnipresent, Omnipotent, and Omniscient, "The Almighty Lord is Victorious".

"Om ParamSatyam" - "Om" is the Supreme Truth. The ultimate reality.

"Om Aham Brahmasmi" - I am Om the Absolute. I am Brahma, the Infinite reality.

"Om Ayam Atma Brahma" -This Atma is a Brahman

"Om Tattvamasi" - 'I Am That', 'Thou Art That'.

"Om Prajnnanam Brahma" - Intelligence is Brahman. 'Pra' means Supreme, 'Jnana' means knowledge or wisdom, awareness, consciousness, understanding.

"Om Sarvam Khalvidam Brahma" - The Universe is Brahman, 'One in All and All in One', 'All is One and One is All'. All this is Brahman alone. Everything is Brahman.

"Om Soham" - 'Soham' He am I. This shows the Identity of the Self Atman with the Brahman, Parmatma, Divine Lord inherent within the natural movement of our breath. I Am He. I Am that I Am. "So" is the natural sound of inhalation, "ham" of exhalation.

These are statements of the Identity of the individual consciousness with the Absolute Divine reality "Brahman". These are called "MahaVakyas" in Vedas.

They all derive from & merge into "Om" (AUM) the divine word of "I Am All".

Turiya State in which pure awareness does its Dance, Pure Silence after "Om" ॐ "Bindu" (The Dot) consciousness itself permeating & being All; is Atman (Self)- Brahman, Absolute Reality.

"Om Shivoham" - I am Shiva. It is a Mantra which reminds us of our oneness with the absolute, the transcendent, the ultimate reality - The Truth, Eternal Knowing, Peace, Bliss, Love, Beauty, Pure Consciousness, Auspicious, Benevolent.

"Om ParamShanti" - Absolute Peace, The Supreme Peace, calm and quiet in harmony with Nature.

"Om SarvaVyaptam" - All embracing, omnipresent, "Om" the "Supreme Divine" is present everywhere at the same time. Eternally present.

"Om Sarvadnyam" - All knowing, Omniscient, "Om" the "Supreme Divine" is all knowing, sees everything.

"Om Sarvaatmaaka" - All- soul, all containing and contained in everything, all-pervading.

"Om Sarvashaktiman" - All powerful, "Almighty", omnipotent, having unlimited power, poten- cy, everlasting.

"Om SarvaSiddhi" - All perfect, All accomplishing, obtainment of all one's objects, universal success, completion of everything, entire proof.

"Om Sarveshvara" - "Lord of All", Omnipotent, Omnipresent, Omniscient, "The Lord of the Entire Cosmos".

"Om Bhavyadivyam" - 'Bhavya'- All that is Glorious, Magnificent, Grand, and Super. 'Divya'- Al ,l that is Divine, Heavenly, Brilliant, Extraordinary, Beautiful, and Angelic.

"Om Prasannachittam" - Pleased, Delighted, Clear, Soothing, Tranquil, Kind, Glorious, Happy Conscious, Lighthearted, Going Merry, Good Tempered, Glad, Successful, Good Spirits, Divine.

"Om Brahmachaitanyam" - Ultimate, impersonal divine reality of the Cosmos, Supreme eternal spirit, highest Universal principle. All pervading divine power of "The Almighty Lord" "Mahaprabhu", living divine force. 'ParamChaitanya' which works out everything, all pervading divine vibrations, holy spirit, Omnipresent, limitless, infinite and eternal, divine self-awareness, divine creative - sustaining - transformative (destructive de-constructive) power, it knows, understands, organizes, and does all living divine work. It is pure consciousness, cosmic intelligence, cosmic spirit, vital life force, universal love, bliss, and joy giving beauty.

"Om Mangalyam" - Auspicious, sanctity, good fortune, prosperity, well-being, welfare, festivity, beautiful, Holy, pious, pure, sacred, blissful, benevolent, confers happiness and joy.

"Om Kalyanam" - Goodness, auspicious, benevolent, blessed union, good spirit, merry, cheer- fulness, blissful, brings good health and prosperity, always helpful.

"Om Anandam" - Great divine Joy, extreme happiness, elation, delightful, gaiety, enjoyment, jolliness, playfulness, cheerfulness, serene, merriment, enthusiastic.

"Om Paramsunderam" - Supreme Beauty.
Param - supreme absolute, highest, greatest, paramount, sublime, beyond, across, perfect.

"Sunderam" - Beautiful, divine beauty within, ocean of beauty, formless divinity, lovely, excellence, wellness, righteousness, goodness, dispassion to oneself. Dedication to whole creation, loving nature, and devotion to God is the secret of undying beauty within.

"Om Tat Sat" - 'Om' is the Mantra of Brahma (Akshar Brahma), 'Tat' is the secret Mantra of Par- brahma and 'Sat' is the secret Mantra of Parambrahma. Mantra of complete salvation. "Om Tat Sat" is the eternal sound pranava which represents the unmanifest and absolute reality, total existence. "Om Tat Sat" is a threefold name of the supreme Soul – 'Paramatma' with which at the beginning of the universe the Brahman, Vedas & Yajna were made. Om is one (1), Om is Tat (0, zero), Om is Sat (Infinite). "Om" is the primordial sound of God. "Om" is transcendental. "Tat" means "that"; it refers to God only. "Sat" means ultimate 'truth' which is God which is eternal. In the beginning was the "Om", and the "Om" was with God, and the Om was God. "Om Tat Sat" means 'All that is'. "The Supreme Absolute Truth". Om is the sound of Brahman, the cosmic vibration or primordial sound. 'Tat' translates as "that" and symbolizes the universal consciousness. 'Sat' means "Truth" & represent pure existence or the Supreme Soul.

According to the Bhagavad Gita, all auspicious work or sacrifice should begin with the sound of 'Om'. The sound of 'Tat' reminds the faithful to renounce any reward for the work or sacrifice. The sound of 'Sat' declares what is Good & True, as is work that is done well. 'Om Tat Sat' means 'I/We are that Truth'.

"Om Jai" - Meaning (see above)

| | Om Paramsunderam Shri Bhagavati Narayani Mahashakti Trigunatmika Kundalini Jagdamba Namo Namah | |

"Om Paramsunderam" _ Meaning (see above)

"Shri" - Holy, supreme consciousness, "Shri" is used as honorific veneration as prefix, title for deities, God such as Shri Krishna, Shri Rama, Shri Mahalaxhmi, Shri Mahaprabhu. Shri means great respect, prosperity, wellbeing, Grace, Splendor, loveliness, beauty, affluence, Glory, light, Riches, radiance, adorning, beautifying, bestowing success, sacred, holy, Goddess of wealth, benevolence, bliss, beatitude.

"Bhagavati" - Used in addressing Goddesses. 'Bhagavati' meaning - holy, Prakriti (Nature, Divinity), Shakti (Divine energy), Devi (Goddess), Maya (Power of creating illusion), Ishwari.

"Narayani" - Goddess Sri Durga, Goddess Mahalakshmi, expression and exposure of conscious- ness, feminine primordial power of God; personification of salvation, Adya Shakti or Adi Shakti, Power of illusion (Maya). Yogmaya, Lalita, beatitude, bliss, love, compassion.

"MahaShakti Trigunatmika" - Mahashakti means Supreme power, energy, strength, primordial energy. Trigunatmika - possessing three qualities of Nature – Rajas, Tamas, and Sattva; Trigunatmika is the name of AdiShakti, Goddess Durga. She is personification of the three gunas (modes) - Mode of goodness, mode of ignorance, & mode of passion. JnanaShakti which is reflected in Sattvaguna which leads to liberation, limpidity of mind, realization of one's own self, supreme peace, contentment, great joy and being anchored always in the Paramatman which ensures the experience and enjoyment of love, peace, bliss, beauty, and joy without intermission. VikshepShakti pertains to Rajoguna and is of the nature of activity. From it the attachment and pain take place. Desire, anger, avarice, pride, jealousy, egoism, envy etc. are its terrible characteristics that are inducements to actions of men and hence cause bondage.

AvaranaShakti pertains to Tamoguna whose effects are - ignorance, apathy, sloth, sleep, negligence, foolishness etc. It makes for the wrong projection of objects differently from what they are and is the root cause of the functioning of the projecting power and the original cause for the procession of Samsara (Man's transmigration). The person overpowered by Tamoguna & by this Shakti does not see clearly because they envelope the nature of an object and makes it appear otherwise; he considers what is super-imposed by his delusion as true and attaches himself to its qualities. The concealing power of this Shakti makes for untold hardships.

"Kundalini Jagadamba Namo Namah"-

"**Kundalini**" is the latent Divine Feminine Cosmic energy which lies dormant coiled at the base of the spine. It is the innate intelligence of embodied consciousness responsible for experience, enjoyment, bliss, pleasure, love and joy, spiritual liberation (Moksha).

"Jagadamba" - Adishakti, Primordial energy, divine cosmic mother. Mahashakti.

Namo Namah - Many great salutations to the auspicious One. Salute again and again, Adoration, Prostrations, respect, great honour, Bow with respect and humility, all glory to You.

"Om Shri Brahma Namo Namah, Om Shri Vishnu Namo Namah, Om Shri Mahesh Namo Namah"

'Brahma' - The creator, 'Vishnu' - The preserver & sustainer, 'Mahesh' (Shiva) - The destroyer & transformer, known as Trimurti. Represent the three natural attributes, principles, essence, qualities of all spirits and energies of nature and entire Cosmos. They are divine masculine energies, powers, and spirits.

"Om Shri Mahasaraswati Namo Namah, Om Shri Mahalaxmi Namo Namah, Om Shri Mahakali Namo Namah"

Three Goddesses are called Tridevi. They are the feminine consorts of Trimurti (masculine).

"MahaSaraswati" is the Goddess of learning, arts, and cultural fulfillment. She is cosmic intelligence, consciousness and cosmic knowledge.

"MahaLakshmi" is the Goddess of wealth, fertility, and material fulfillment. She bestows Glory, magnificence, exaltation, greatness, and joy.

"MahaKali" is the Goddess of power, beauty, love, and spiritual fulfilment, she also represents the transformational power of divinity.

God is both male and female. But all different forms of energy or powers of God are with the Trimurti in the form of MahaSaraswati, MahaLakshmi, and MahaKali (Tridevi). That is a non-dimensional God who created this world through Srishti-Shakti (MahaSaraswati, sound or knowledge), preserves through Sthiti-Shakti (MahaLakshmi, light or resources), and destroys through Samhara-Shakti (MahaKali, heat or strength). It is also seen that God cannot create, generate, or destroy because God does not possess any attribute. So true energy or Adishakti does everything on God's behalf.

"Om Shri MahaVishnu Namo Namah, Om Shri Ram Namo Namah, Om Shri Krishna Namo Namah, Om Shri Bhagwan Mahaveera Namo Namah, Om Shri Gautam Buddha Namo Namah, Om Shri Kalki Namo Namah"

"MahaVishnu" is the Super Soul of all living beings (Jivaatmas) in all material universes in the entire Cosmos. Brahman, Almighty, absolute, supreme personality of Godhead. This means that the absolute truth is realized first as Brahman (impersonal aspect) then as Paramatma (personal aspect) and finally as Bhagavan (Incarnate perfection). Bhakti (loving devotion) goes to Bhagavan, Rama or Krishna for instance (Avatars or incarnations of Vishnu, Narayana). In this way, Bhakti surpasses even Yoga, which is aimed at the Super Soul, Parmatma. Mahamaya remains ever obedient material energy of the "Supreme Lord MahaVishnu", 'The Absolute' which is beyond human comprehension and is beyond all attributes.

"Shri Rama" - He is the seventh Avatar, incarnation of MahaVishnu. Prabhu Ramchandra is the central figure of "The Great Epic Ramayana". King Rama was married to Devi Sita. In Advaita Vedanta, Rama connotes the metaphysical concepts of Supreme

Brahman who is the eternally blissful spiritual self (Atman, soul) in whom Yogis delight non- dualistically.

The root of the word Rama is 'Ram' - which means "stop, stand still, rest, rejoice, be pleased, support, witness, make evident. Rama is Maryada Purushottama or the best of upholders of Dharma. The views of Rama combine "reason with emotions" to create a "thinking hearts" approach; he emphasizes through what he says and what he does, a union of consciousness and action to create an "ethics of character", Rama's life combines the ethics with the aesthetics of living. Rama killed the demon Ravana.

"Shri Krishna" - The cosmic supreme being. Divine Hero Krishna's life is generally titled as Krishna Leela. He is a central character in the Mahabharata, the Bhagavad Purana, and the Bhagavad Gita. His lover Radha Rani is his Shakti. He gave counsel to Arjuna. Krishna is worshipped as Svayam Bhagawan. He is all attractive. Krishna is the eighth incarnation of "MahaVishnu" in the great Epic Mahabharata that constitutes the Bhagavad Gita which contains the advice of Krishna to Arjuna on the battlefield. Krishna leelas are playing for fun and enjoyment and not for sport or gain. He is the spiritual essence and eternal love in the existence, the Gopis metaphorically represent the Prakriti, matter, and the impermanent body.

Krishna in Mathura overthrows and kills the tyrant king, his uncle Kamsa/Kansa, after quelling several assassination attempts by Kamsa.

Krishna is universal consciousness. Krishna is auspiciousness, extremely pleasing, effulgent, Brahma Jyoti, strongest, ever youthful, wonderful linguist, truthful, super intelligent, extremely clever, expert, grateful, firmly determined, sees and speaks on the authority of Vedas or scriptures, self-controlled, steadfast, forbearing, forgiving, grave, self-satisfied, possessing equilibrium, magnanimous, heroic, gentle, respectful, compassionate, liberal, shy, the protector of surrendered souls, well-wisher of devotees, controlled by love, all auspicious, all worshipable, all honourable, the supreme controller, changeless, ever fresh, all cognizant. Krishna's body is eternal, full of knowledge and bliss, Sat-Chit-Anand, possessing all mystic perfections. He is inconceivable, attractor of liberated souls, by playing his flute, he can attract all living entities all over the universes; he has a wonderful excellence of beauty which cannot be rivaled anywhere in the creation.

"Bhagavan Mahavira" - Mahavira was named 'Vardhamana' meaning "One who grows", because of the increased prosperity in the kingdom at the time of his birth. Born in 599 BCE,at the age thirty, Mahavira abandoned royal life and left his home and family to live an ascetic life in the pursuit of spiritual awakening. He meditated under the Ashoka tree. Mahavira achieved Kevala Jnana (Omniscience or infinite knowledge) after twelve years of rigorous penance. Mahavira is all seeing, all knowing and most auspicious free from all imperfections. He taught Ahimsa (non- violence). Five ethical principles were taught by Mahavira to all his disciples and for the whole humanity.

1)Ahimsa (non-violence or non-injury). 2) Satya (Truthfulness) for oneself and others. 3) Asteya (non-stealing) not taking anything that has been given. 4) Brahmacharya (Chastity) Abstinence from sensual pleasures for monks and faithfulness to one's partners for householders. 5) Aparigraha (non-attachment) for lay people, an attitude of non-attachment to property and worldly positions; for mendicants not owning anything.

The goal of these principles is to achieve spiritual peace, upliftment and finally liberation. Ahimsa is the supreme moral virtue. Mahavira taught that the Soul is dravya (substantial), eternal, and yet temporary. Mahavira taught Anekantvada (many-sided-reality). 'Mahavira' meaning very brave and courageous, greatest enlightened personality to liberate oneself. Mahavira taught the necessity of right faith (Samyak Darshana), right knowledge (Samyak Gyana) and right conduct (Samyak Charitra). Bhagavan is an epithet for a deity or Divine Avatara (incarnation), The blessed one, fortunate (bhaga meaning "fortune", "wealth"), lustrous, divine, holy, glorious, revered, Splendor, might, wisdom, dispassion, Lord, realized impersonal Brahman.

"Gautama Buddha" - Also known as Siddhartha Gautama, Shakyamuni. He was a philosopher, mendicant, meditator, spiritual master and teacher. His teaching is based on his insight into duhkha (suffering) and the end of dukkha, the state called Nibbana or Nirvana. He was born in 563 BCE. The name Buddha means the fully awakened one the fully enlightened. He found the answer to suffering when he became enlightened after long days of meditation under the Bodhi tree. This answer was called the four Noble Truths. He taught about the four noble truths and the noble eightfold path to Nirvana. Gautama Buddha taught that old age, sickness, death, and suffering is a part of everyone's life. He taught that pain is caused by craving. And he showed that there is a way to end craving and end suffering by doing good things and training one's mind. When a person perfects these qualities, they will gain enlightenment. He taught non-harm and balance, not going too far one way or the other. He taught people to meditate. Buddha believed that it is up to each person to become enlightened. Buddha preached Dharma. His path was called the middle way. To be your own light. He taught "Four Noble Truths"- The first is the truth of suffering, which holds that existence in all the realms of rebirth is characterized by suffering. The sufferings particular to humans are birth, aging, sickness, death, losing friends, encountering enemies, not finding what one wants, finding what one does not want.

The second truth identifies the cause of this suffering as non-virtue, negative deeds of body, speech and mind that produce the Karma that fructifies in the future as physical and mental pain. These deeds are motivated by negative mental states, called Klesha (afflictions), which include desire, hatred, and ignorance.

The third truth is the truth of cessation, the postulation of a state beyond suffering, called Nirvana. Cessation entails the realization of both the destruction of the causes of suffering and the impossibility of future suffering.

The fourth truth; "The Path", is that method. "The Path" was delineated in a number of ways, often as the three trainings in ethics, meditation, and wisdom. In his first sermon, The Buddha described the great eightfold path of correct view, correct attitude, correct speech, correct action, correct livelihood, correct effort, correct mindfulness, and correct meditation. The Buddha taught Dharma for the benefit of all humans, each day & night he surveyed the world with his omniscient eye to locate those that he might benefit, often travelling to them by means of his supernormal powers.

In Vaishnava Hinduism, Gautama Buddha is considered as the ninth Avatar (incarnation) of MahaVishnu. Buddha taught compassion and path of Ahimsa (non-violence). In Sanskrit 'Budh' means 'to wake'. He is a man who has woken fully, as if from a deep sleep, to discover that suffering, like a dream, is over. He discovered a way of achieving true wisdom, compassion, and freedom from suffering. Through his own efforts, he was able to find the way out of suffering to liberation, and those that have followed him have kept that way open. He pointed to a great law Dharma running through everything that exists. It is by living in accordance with this law (divine laws of nature) that true wisdom and compassion and hence freedom from suffering may be achieved.

"Kalki" - 'Kalki' is prophesized the tenth Avatar (incarnation) of 'MahaVishnu' who will take birth to end Kaliyuga and start a new cycle with Satyayuga. Presently we are living in Kaliyuga. He is described in the Puranas as the avatar who rejuvenates existence by ending the darkest and destructive period to remove adharma and ushering in the Satyayuga. He will destroy evil forces and transform chaos to order. A new era will begin where people will live long, and happy life, righteousness will reign supreme and golden age will begin.

"Om Shri Parameshwara Namo Namah, Om Shri Param Daata Namo Namah, Om Shri Parmatma Namo Namah"

"Om Gam Ganapataye Namo Namah, Om Namah Shivaya Namah, Om Namo Narayanaya Namah"

"Parmeshwara" - Supreme Being, the creator, omnipresent, Lord (Prabhu), God (Ishwar), Supreme Ruler.

"Paramdaata" - Supreme donor, giver, bestower of boons, blessings, prosperity, generous, liberal, provider, sustainer, supporter, creator.

"Parmaatma" - Lord, Supreme Soul, Prime Soul, God, the Supreme Spirit, Absolute Atman, Supreme Being, Complete, Almighty.

"Om Gam Ganapataye Namah" - This Mantra is of "Lord Ganesha". Lord Ganesha governs our roots chakra (mooladhara) at subtle level. Gam is the Bija Mantra of mooladhara Chakra. Ganesha is deity who removes our obstacles and bestows the devotee with wisdom and intellect. This Mantra is translated as "salutations to the remover of obstacles. Ganesha represents the pure consciousness. Ganesha is also called Ganapati. He is the Lord of good fortune, prosperity, protection, grace, bliss, growth, health He removes fear, gives contentment and shows the right path.

"Om Namah Shivaya Namaha" – 'O' salutations to the auspicious 'Lord Shiva', Adoration to 'Lord Shiva'. This mantra bestows deep spiritual experiences and boons (supernatural gifts) when practiced deeply & correctly. This mantra leads you to the transcendental mode. It heals your accumulated toxic emotions & thoughts. It gives you peace, clarity, develops intellect, prosperity, and purifies your whole being.

"Om Namo Narayana" - Salutations to the "Lord Vishnu". He preserves and maintains balance in the universe. This Mantra bestows balance, peace, equanimity, God's Love, calmness, self-realization, oneness, right direction, and divine shelter.

"Om Shri Sat-Chit-Ananda Mahamana SadaShiva Parabrahma Divya Omkar Paramchaitanya Swaroopa Mahaveda Parampurushaya Paramsunderam Shri MahaPrabhu Namo Namaha"

Sat-Chit-Ananda: Experience of realizing the unity and wholeness of all existence. God or Brahman (absolute reality), source of all consciousness and all perfections. As per the Vedas, 'Yoga' is essential to experience Sat-Chit-Anand state and to achieve the goal of the spiritual journey.

Sat: Truth, absolute being or existence, which is eternal.

Chit: Consciousness, understanding and comprehension.

Ananda: Bliss, a state of pure happiness, joy, and sensual pleasure, delight, eternal joy.

"Sat-Chit-Anand" is translated as "Truth-Consciousness-Bliss". It is the eternal and unified concept of the Soul, which is beyond space, matter, and time.

"Mahamana" – Noble, greathearted, magnanimous, greatness, grandeur.

"SadaShiva" – Ever auspicious, benign, transcendent. Supreme Lord Parashiva. Sada meaning always, Shiva means the auspicious one.

"Parabrahma" - Ultimate Brahma, Supreme Brahma, Nirguna Brahma, Supreme Truth, Absolute Reality, eternal, source of the universe, creator, sustainer and destroyer or transformer of all life. 'Para' meaning supreme, highest, beyond and 'Brahma' means sacred, divine, and absolute.

"Divya Omkar" - 'Divya' means Divine, Heavenly, Brilliant, Extra-Ordinary, Beautiful, Celestial, Angelic, Splendid and Superb. "Omkar" - "Om", Omkar is Pranav meaning both "controller of life force (Prana)" and "life giver (infuser of prana)". Omkara is the primordial sound from which the whole universe was created, also called the Shabd Brahman.

"ParamChaitanya Swaroopa" - 'Paramchaitanya' means living divine force that is working everything, all pervading power of God, divine vibrations, supreme consciousness, supreme intelligence, divine sensation, pure cosmic intelligence, enthusiasm, wisdom, spiritual force, supreme understanding, sentience, vital life force, divine spirit, divine feeling, divine joy and divine essence. 'Swaroopa' means form, character, spectacular beauty, divine qualities, nature, beautiful, great appearance, divine manifestation and true nature.

"MahaVeda Parampurushaya" - 'Mahaveda' - Great supreme spiritual divine scripture. Maha means great, grand, noble, superior, mighty, brilliance. 'Veda' - Vedas are the most ancient spiritual divine scriptures, consisting of the RigVeda, SamaVeda, YajurVeda, and AtharvaVeda. These are classical sacred scriptures. Sanskrit word 'Veda' is derived from the root 'Vid'- "to know", "to see", "experience", "to imbibe", what is heard and remembered, cognitive aspect. The Vedas are hidden mysterious sacred knowledge. It is the knowledge of truth, divinity, and nature of the entire Cosmos and Bhraman. It is Brahma Gyana, the divine wisdom.

"ParamPurushaya" - Supreme Purusha, VedaPurusha, cosmic being, universal consciousness, abstract essence of the self, spirit and the universal principle that is eternal and all pervasive. Purusha is the unchanging principle which connects everything & everyone. As per Mandukya Upanishad - Purusha is splendid and without a bodily form is this Purusha, without and within, unborn, without life breath and without mind, higher than the supreme element. From him are born life breath and mind. He is the Soul of all beings.

Purusha is Spirit-Soul, and Prakriti is Energy-Matter. Purusha is vital sentient truth that sets in action the entire Prapancha (Phenomenal world). Purusha is Virata, the invisible principal pervading entirety.

"Param Sunderam" - (see above)

"Shri" - (see above)

"Mahaprabhu" - 'Maha' means great, mighty, noble, and superior. "Prabhu" means "The Lord", "God", who excels everything, Parameshvar, Paramaatma. "Mahaprabhu" means "The Great Almighty Lord".

"Namo Namah" - (See above)

"Om Paramsunderam Shri Mahaprabhuyoga Namo Namah"

"Mahaprabhuyoga" - Means union and oneness with the "Great Almighty Lord", Paramaatma, Parameshvara, Parabrahman and to be one with divine Paramchaitanya.

"Om Yogakshemam Vahamyaham"

"The Lord" says - those who worship me always, without thinking of anything else and who are constantly engaged in devotion, I take upon myself the responsibility to look after their material & spiritual welfare. With single pointed meditation, those who are constantly engaged in my worship, I carry the burden of acquisition and preservation of their needs. I will take care of my devotees securing and giving protection. When a devotee is in Yoga union and oneness with "The Lord", "The Lord" takes care of his complete welfare, wellbeing, protection, prosperity, spiritual development, peace, bliss, happiness, and joy. The devotee experiences Ritambhara Prajna, the higher intuitive insight, intuitive knowledge, enlightened consciousness, and receives divine love, grace, and blessings.

"Om Tathastu" - 'Tathastu' means 'So be it', your wish is complete, so let be, as you wish, Amen, certainly, verily, truly, your wish be fulfilled, heartily approval. Receiving blessings from "The Lord".

"Om Jai", "Om Paramsunderam", "Om Tat Sat" - (See above)

Shanti Mantras:

-1-

Om Asato Maa Sad - Gamaya |
Tamaso Maa Jyotir - Gamaya |
Mrtyor - Maa Amritam Gamaya |
Om Shaantih Shaantih Shaantih | |

-2-

Om Puurnnam-Adah Puurnnam -
Idam Puurnnat -Puurnnam - Udacyate |
Puurnnasya Puurnam - Aadaaya
Puurnnam - Eva -Avashissyate | |
Om Shaantih Shaantih Shaantih | |

-3-

Om Sarveshaam Svastir - Bhavatu |
Sarveshaam Shaantir - Bhavatu |
Sarveshaam Purnnam - Bhavatu |
Sarveshaam Manggalam - Bhavatu |
Om Shaantih Shaantih Shaantih | |

-4-

Om Sarve Bhavantu Sukhinah
Sarve Santu Nirramayaah |
Sarve Bhadraanni Pashyantu
Maa Kashcid - Duhkha - Bhaag - Bhavet |
Om Shaantih Shaantih Shaantih | |

-5-

Om Dyauh Shantir - Antarikssam Shaantih
Prthivi Shaantir - Aapah Shaantir - Ossadhayah Shaantih |
Vanaspatayah Shaantir - Vishvedevaah Shaantir - Brahma Shaantih
Sarvam Shaantih Shaantir - Eva Shaantih Saa Maa Shaantir - Edhi |
Om Shaantih Shaantih Shaantih | |

'Namaste' - I honour the place in you in which the entire universe dwells. I honour the place in you that is Love, Truth, Light, and Peace. When you are in this place in you, and I am in this place in me, we are one.

Namaste is also said as namaskar, namaskaram, pranam, "I bow to the divine in you". It is an expression of reverence, an "offering of homeage and adoration in Vedas. It is a greeting done by pressing palms of both hands together with a smile. It is also called Anjali mudra. In Sanskrit 'Namah' means 'bow', obeisance, reverential salutation, or adoration and 'te' means 'to you'. It also means "the sacred in me recognizes the sacred in you". In Anjali mudra, the palms pressed together are held at the heart chakra with thumbs resting lightly against the sternum, with a slight bowing of the head.

'Jai Om Jai' - The Victory and Praise to the Glorious 'Om' 'The Great Lord' 'MahaPrabhu'. Heartily greetings and salutations to the divine in your heart. It is a heartily wish and greeting like 'Namaste' said when you meet a person or persons.

'Mantra' of Deities -

Om gam ganapataye namaha |
Om shri ganeshaya namaha |
Om namah shivaya namaha |
Om namah shivaya |
Om narayanaya namaha |
Om namo narayanaya |
Om aim mahasaraswatyai namaha |
Om hreem shreem lakshmibhyo namaha |
Om shri hanumate namaha |
Om shri kuberaya namaha |

Om shri......................Namo Namaha |

The Mantra can be taken by filling the Gap above by the Name of Gods, Deities such as Krishna, Rama, Mahaveer, Gautama Buddha, Ganesha, etc.

Shri Ganesh Mantra:

Vakra–Tundda Maha- Kaaya Suurya-Kotti Samaprabha |
Nirvighnam Kuru Me Deva Sarva-Kaaryessu Sarvadaa | |

Gayatri Mantra:

Om Bhuur-Bhuvah Svah
Tat-Savitur-Varennyam
Bhargo Devasya Dhiimahi
Dhiyo Yo Nah Prachodayaat | |

Maha Mrityunjaya Mantra:

Om Try-Ambakam Yajaamahe
Sugandhim Pusstti-Vardhanam
Urvaarukam-Iva- Bandhanaan
Mrtyor-Mukssiya Maa-Amrtaat | |

Kuber Mantra:

Om Yakshaya Kuberaya Vaishravanaya Dhanadhanyadhipataye
Dhanadhanyasamriddhim Me Dehi Dapaya Svaha | |

Shri Vishnu ShantaKaram Mantra:

Shaanta-Aakaaram Bhujaga-Shayanam
Padma-Naabham Suresham Vishva-Aadhaaram
Gagana-Sadrsham Megha-Varnam Shubha-Anggam |
Lakshami-Kaantam Kamala-Nayanam
Yogibhir-Dhyaana-Gamyam Vande Vishnnum
Bhava-Bhaya-Haram Sarva-Lokaia-Eka-Naatham | |

Guru Mantra:

Gurur Brahma Gurur Vishnu Gurur Devo Maheshwarah Guru
Saakshat Para-Brahma, Tasmai Shri Guruve Namaha | |

Hare Rama Hare Krishna Mantra:

Hare Rama Hare Rama, Rama Rama Hare Hare |
Hare Krishna Hare Krishna, Krishna Krishna Hare Hare | |

Shri Durga Mantra:

Sarva Mangala Mangalye Shive Sarvartha Sadhike
Sharanye Triambake Gauri Narayani Namostute | |

Surya Namaskar Mantra:

Om Mitraaya Namaha, Om Ravaye Namaha,
Om Suryaya Namaha, Om Bhaanave Namaha,
Om Khagaya Namah, Om Pooshne Namah,
Om Hiranya Garbhaya Namaha, Om Mareechaye Namaha,
Om Aadityaaya Namaha, Om Savitre Namaha,
Om Arkaaya Namah, Om Bhaskaraya Namaha | |

Navkar / Namokar Mantra of Bhagavan Mahavira -

Namo Arihantanam, Namo Siddhanam
Namo Ayariyanam, Namo Uvajjhayanam
Namo Loe Savrasahunam, Eso Panch Namokkaro
Sarva Pava Ppansano, Mangalanancha Sarvesim
Padhamam Havei Mangalam | |

"Om Namo Arihantanam" |. "Om Namo Arihantaya Namaha"
"Om Mani Padme Hum" (The Jewel Is in The Lotus)

Buddha Mantra:

Buddham Sharanam Gacchami
Dhammam Sharanam Gacchami
Sangham Sharanam Gacchami | |

Guru Nanak Devji "Mool Mantar" (GurBani):

"Ek Onkar"
"Ek Onkaar Satnaam Kartaa Purakh Nirbhau Nirvair
Akaal Moorat Ajooni Saibhang Gurprasaad." "Wahe Guru"

Sai Baba Mantra:

"Om Sai Ram"
"Om Sacchidanand Sadguru Sainath Maharaj Ki Jai –
Anant Koti Brahmaand Nayak Rajadhiraj Sai Baba Ki Jai"

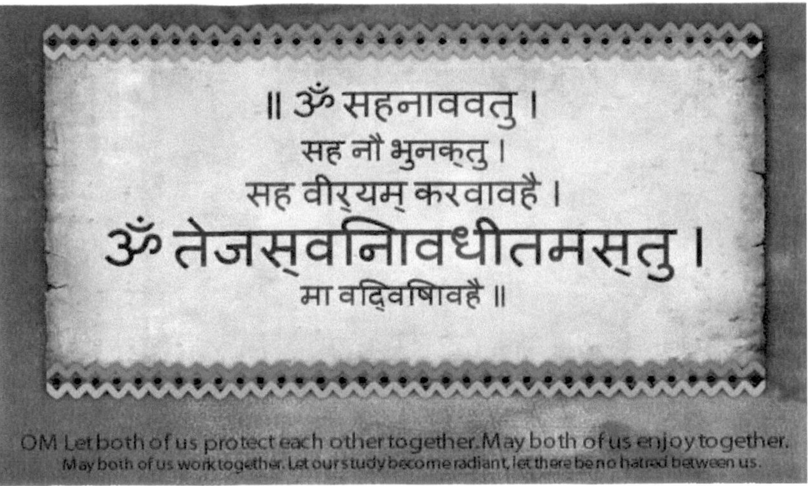

| | VEDIC MANTRA | |

| | SHRI YANTRA | |

| | DHYANA - MEDITATION | |

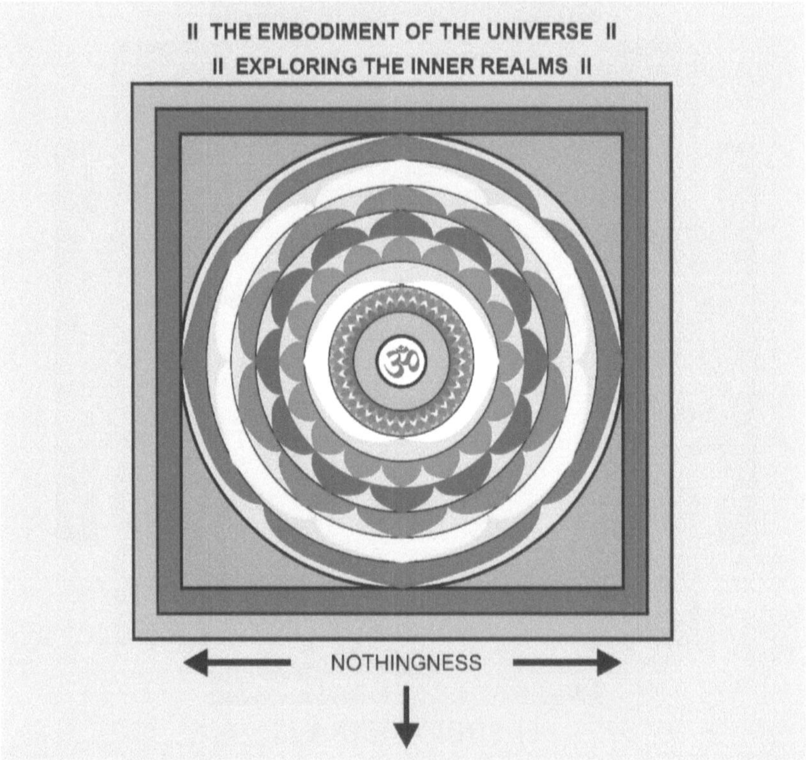

II THE EMBODIMENT OF THE UNIVERSE II

II EXPLORING THE INNER REALMS II

NOTHINGNESS

'MahaYantras'

Yantra literally means loom, instrument, or machine. Yantra is a symbol of the divine, such as the mother goddess Durga. It is made of interlocking geometric figures, circles, triangles, and floral shape that forms a pattern. The yantra is primarily a meditation tool. Yantras function as revelatory symbols of cosmic truth. It is an art of sacred geometry. Yantra is an instrument (tra) for holding (yam) the mind as it enables one to focus one's concentration.

'Shri Yantra'

The shri yantra or shri chakra is shri vidya of Tripura Sundari (The divine Goddess). It is a yantra or mandala formed by nine interlocking triangles surrounding a dot in the center called a bindu (point). Four of these triangles are oriented upright representing Shiva, Shiva Tattwa, Spirit the divine masculine. Five of these triangles are inverted triangles representing Shakti, Divine energy, Nature the divine feminine. Because it is composed of nine triangles, it is also known as the navayoni chakra. Together the nine triangles are interlaced in such a way as to form forty-three smaller triangles in a web symbolic of the entire Cosmos or a womb symbolic of creation. Together they express Advaita non-duality. This is surrounded by a lotus of eight petals, sixteen petals and an earthsquare resembling a temple with four doors.

The Shri chakra is also known as the Nava Chakra because it can also be seen as having nine levels. Each level corresponds to a mudra, a yogini, and a specific form of the deity Lalita Tripura Sundari along with her Mantra. These levels starting from the outside or bottom layer are:

1. Trailokya Mohana, a square of three lines with four Portals.
2. Sarvasa Paripuraka, a sixteen petal Lotus.
3. Sarvasa Sankshobhana, an eight petal Lotus.
4. Sarva Saubhagyadayaka, composed of fourteen small triangles.
5. Sarvarthasadhaka, composed of ten small triangles.
6. Sarva Rakshakara, composed of ten small triangles.
7. SarvaRogahara, composed of eight small triangles.
8. Sarva Siddhi Prada, composed of one small triangle.
9. Sarvaanandamaya, composed of a point or Bindu.

In Sanskrit, the word "Yantra" comes from the root word "Yan" or "Yam" which means "instrument" or "support", and "tra" derived from "trana" meaning release from bondage. A yantra is an instrument or tool for meditation and contemplation to support spiritual liberation.

There are hundreds of yantra designs related to deities, principles, qualities, Spiritual Energies and Planets.

'Mantra' - 'Tantra' - 'Yantra'

Maha Tantras:

Tantra in Sanskrit means "Weave", "Continuity", derived from 2 words - "Tanoti", which means liberation of energy and "Trayati" meaning Expansion of Consciousness. Tantra is a type of ritualistic worship, as mentioned in Shiva Purana. The rite of worship is performed in accomplishment with Mantra, Tantra, Yantra applications. Mantra is a magical spiritual formula. Yantra is a mystical diagram possessed of occult spiritual powers and Tantra is a ritual, the chief peculiarity of which is the worship of Divine Feminine Energy, Shiv Shakti. Tantra is an intuitional science which stands for the progressive realization of the Divine. It liberates one from the Cimmerian darkness and leads unto the divine effulgence. It is a path of salvation. It is a spiritual science of the soul. The authoritative definition of Tantra is that which brings emancipation from the bondage of Maya. Tantra is the method of pleasing the Gods in an easy manner and thereby attaining material and spiritual advantages and finally moksha or salvation by following the Yoga Tantra Shastra. Tantra is a course or way, a line of conduct, a path of procedure.

Mantra - Tantra - Yantra: The whole Brahmanda (Cosmos) contains sounds of Mantra and functions as Tantra and Yantra. These three, combinedly generates enormous power responsible for inner growth of an individual and collective, which benefits All.

Mantras are spiritual universal formulas as are the formulas of modern science. Tantra is a spiritual technique which is similar to the technology to use the formulas for specific purpose. Yantra is the Spiritual Instrument similar to the scientific instrument for machinery which use formulas and technique for getting the desired result. Thus Mantra – Tantra - Yantra are the aspects of spiritual science similar to Formula, Technology and Instrument or Machine of modern physical material science.

Tantra Yoga:

Tantra yoga employs various rituals to study the universe through the human microcosm. From the Sanskrit "Leading Principle" or "Woven Together". Tantra yoga seeks to balance - not renounce, human instincts to reach enlightenment. Tantra yoga rituals encourage its participants to build up Kundalini energy in the top Chakras so it "spills from the top". Some common Tantra yoga rituals include Asanas, Meditation, Breathing Exercise, Mantra, Mudra, Physical Gross & Subtle Cleaning, Purification and Yantras. Tantra yoga originates from the worship of the Deities. Demigods represent the dynamic and static principles of the universe: Shakti (Divine Energy) – Dynamic – Creative, Feminine and Shiva (spirit) - static destructive / trans- formative, masculine. Tantra yoga practitioners seek to comprehend the continual play between these two divine principles. "Atma – Tantra" means doctrine of theory of Atman (Soul, Self).

When an action or thing once complete, becomes beneficial in several matters to one person, or to many people, that is known as Tantra. Because it elaborates (tan) copious and profound matters, especially relating to the principles of reality (Tattwa) and sacred mantra and because it provides liberation (tra), it is called Tantra. Tantras are the techniques, rituals, practices, and experience of meditation.

Yoga and Ideology:-It is a sacred technique of complete purification of body, mind and spirit which brings complete transformation. The exploration of the subtle energies within the body and their connection to the universe provide the opportunity to understand the purpose of life and the principles of union in new dimensions. That Tantra yoga helps us to develop emotional wellbeing, physical health, and spiritual upliftment. It enables us to prosper, to thrive and to merge material world and the spiritual world in one. Tantra yoga integrates, blends, waves all spiritual knowledge, practices, experiences, techniques to finally experience and realize, oneness, unity, union of spirit and energy to be one with the Supreme Divine "The Almighty Lord".

Nirvana Shatkam / Atmashatkam

Mano Budhyahankaar Chittani Naaham,
Na Cha Shrotra Jihve Na Cha Ghraana netre
Na Cha Vyoma Bhumir Na Tejo Na Vayuh,
Chidananda Rupah Shivoham Shivoham | |

Na Cha Praana Sanjno Na Vai Pancha Vaayuhu,
Na Vaa Sapta Dhaatur Na Va Pancha Koshah
Na Vaak Paani Paadau Na Chopasthapaayuh,
Chidaananda Rupah Shivoham Shivoham | |

Na Me Dvesha Raagau Na Me Lobha Mohau,
Mado Naiva Me Naiva Maatsarya Bhaavah
Na Dharmo Na Chaartho Na Kaamo Na Moksha,
Chidaananda Rupah Shivoham Shivoham | |

Na Punyan Na Paapan Na Saukhyan Na Dukham,
Na Mantro Na Tirthan Na Vedaah Na Yajnaah
Aham Bhojanan Naiv Bhojyan Na Bhoktaa,
Chidaananda Rupah Shivoham Shivoham | |

Na Mrityur Na Shanka Na Me Jaati Bhedah,
Pitaa Naiva Me Naiva Maataa Na Janma
Na Bandhur Na Mitram Guru Naiva Shishyah,
Chidaananda Rupah Shivoham Shivoham | |

Aham Nirvikalpo Niraakaara Rupo,
Vibhutvaaccha Sarvatra Sarvendriyaanaam
Na Chaa Sangatan Naiva Muktir Na meyah
Chidananda Rupah Shivoham Shivoham | |

Meaning of Nirvana Shatkam / Atmashatkam

1) I am not mind, nor intellect, nor ego, nor the reflections of inner self. I am not the five senses. I am beyond that. I am not the ether, nor the earth, nor the fire, nor the wind (i.e., the five elements). I am indeed, 'That' eternal knowing and bliss, Shiva, love and pure consciousness.

2) Neither can I be termed as energy (Praana), nor five types of breath (Vaayu), nor the seven material essences (dhaatu), nor the five coverings (pancha-kosha). Neither am I the five instruments of elimination, procreation, motion, grasping, or speaking. I am indeed, 'That' eternal knowing and bliss, Shiva, love and pure consciousness.
3) I have no hatred or dislike, nor affiliation or liking, nor greed, nor delusion, nor pride or haughtiness, nor feelings of envy or jealousy. I have no duty (dharma), nor any money, nor any desire (refer: kama), nor even liberation (refer moksha). I am indeed, 'That' eternal knowing and bliss, Shiva, love, and pure consciousness.
4) I have neither virtue (punya), nor vice (paapa). I do not commit sins or good deeds, nor have happiness or sorrow, pain, or pleasure. I do not need mantras, holy places, scriptures, rituals, or sacrifices (yajna). I am none of the triad of the observer or one who experiences, the process of observing or experiencing, or any object being observed or experienced. I am indeed, 'That' eternal knowing and bliss, Shiva, love and pure consciousness.
5) I do not have fear of death, as I do not have death. I have no separation from my true self, no doubt about my existence, nor have I discrimination based on birth. I have no father or mother, nor did I have a birth. I am not the relative, nor the friend, nor the guru, nor the disciple. I am indeed, 'That' eternal knowing and bliss, Shiva, love, and pure consciousness.
6) I am all pervasive. I am without any attributes, and without any form. I have neither attachment to the world, nor to liberation. I have no wishes for anything because I am everything, everywhere, every time, always in equilibrium. I am indeed, 'That' eternal knowing and bliss, Shiva, love and pure consciousness.

'Shri Ganesha Atharvashirsha'

Om Namste Ganpataye Tvameva Pratyaksham Tatvamasi
Tvamev Kevalam Kartasi Tvamev Kevalam Dhartasi
Tvamev Kevlam Hartasi Tvamev Sarvam Khalvidam Bramhasi
Tvam Sakshadatmasi Nityam | | 1 | |

O Lord Ganesha! I Pay my deep homage to you,
the Lord of the Deva-Gana
You are the first facet of the Bramha-Tatva to arise, You have alone created this Entire universe You alone can maintain this universe,
You are indeed the all-conquering
supreme Lord, Indeed you are the "ATMA" | | 1 | |

Rritam Vachmi Satyam Vachmi | | 2 | |

Speak noble fact, Speak complete Truth | | 2 | |

Ava tvam Mam Ava Vaktaram Ava Shrotaram Ava Dataram
Ava Dhataram Avanuchanamv Shishyam Ava Paschatat
Ava Purastat Avo Uttaratat Ava Dakshinatat Ava Chordhvatat
Ava Dharatat Sarvatomam Pahi Pahi Samantat | | 3 | |

Protect me Protect the one who Describes you
Protect all who hear about your characteristics
Protect me & the disciples who are under Tutelage
Protect me from the obstacles (which arise during Rituals)
From the east (Similarly) Protect me from the West,
From the North From the South Protect me from above & below
Protect me from all directions | | 3 | |

Tvam Vangmayastvam Chinmaya
Tvam Anandmayastvam Bramhamaya
Tvam Sachitananda Dvitiyosi Tvam Pratyaksham Bramhasi
Tvam Jnanmayo Vijnanamayo Asi | | 4 | |

You are the constituent of speech,
You are Joy & Immortal Consciousness,
You are Truth, Mind & Bliss... one without a second,
You are none other than divinity,
You are Knowledge of Gross & Subtle types | | 4 | |

Sarvam Jagadidam Tatvo Jayate
Sarvam Jagadidam Tvat Sti Shastati
Sarvam Jagadidam Tvay Layamesyati
Sarvam Jagadidam Tvayi Pratyeti
Tvam Bhumi Rapo Nalo Nilo Nabha
Tvam Chatvarim Vak Padaini | | 5 | |

All the Universes manifest due to you,
All the Universes are sustained by you,
All the Universes get destroyed in you,
All the Universes finally get merged in you,
You alone are Earth. Water, Fire, Air & Ether,
You are the 4 types of speech & the root source of sound | | 5 | |

Tvam Guna Traya Atitaha Tvam Deha Treya Atitaha
Tvam Kala Treya Atitaha Tvam Avastreya Atitaha
Tvam Muladhar Stiti Yosi Nityam Tvam Shakti Treya Atmakaha
Tvam Yogino Dhayayanti Nityam
Tvam Bramhastvam, Vishnustvam, Rudrastvam, Indrastvam
Agnistvam, Vayustvam, Suryastvam, Chandramastvam,
Bramha Bhur Bhuva Svorom | | 6 | |

You are beyond the 3 'GUNAS',
(Satva; Pure, Rajas: Activating & Tamas: Dull)
You are beyond the 3 Bodies; (Gross, Subtle & Casual)
You are beyond Past, Present & Future (3 State of Time)
You are beyond 3 states of being; (Awake, dream & Deep Sleep)
You always Reside in the "MULADHARA" Chakra
You are the trinity of Power;
(Creative Maintaining & Destructive Powers)
Sages always Meditate on you
You are the Creator. Sustainer, Destroyer,
The Lord of 3 worlds, Fire, Air, Sun, Moon,
You are all inclusive & all Pervading | | 6 | |

Ganadim Purvamuccharaya Varnadim Tada Nantaram
Anusvara Paratarah Ardhendu Lasitam Taren Hridam
Etatva Manu Svarupam Gakarah Purva Rupam
Akaro Madhyam Rupam Anu Svaraschantya Rupam

Bindu Ruta Rupam Nadah Sandhanam
Sagm Hitaa Sandihi Sesha Ganeshvidhya
Ganal Rishi; Nichrud Gayatri chandah Ganpatir devata
Om 'GUNG' Ganpataye Namah | | 7 | |

After Describing the Characteristics & Cosmic Attributes Of Lord Ganesha, Atharvan Rishi Gives us the Sacred "GANESH VIDYA" i.e. the Mantra which Reveals the Sacred Form of Lord Ganesh. The Letter "GA" is to be enunciated, following by "NA" This one-word Mantra is then Potentiated with the "PRANAVA" "OM". This is Sacred Mantra. (In order to make it Simpler, Atharvan Rishi Present the above easier FASHION; Remember that Knowledge was transmitted orally in those days.)

"GA" is the first part, "Na" is the middle & end "UM" formed by the bindu is conjoined with the foregoing & all of them form the Sacred word. This Mantra if pronounced properly, has the power of revealing The Divine Lord Ganesh; The sage who receives the Mantra is Ganaka & the Meter is "NICHRAT GAYATRI" The Deity is Ganapati. Om 'GANG' Ganapati My salutation to you | | 7 | |
Saying Thus, The Devotees should bow to the Lord.

Ek Dantaya Vid Mahe vakra Tundaya Dhimahi
Tanno danti Prachodayat | | 8 | |

Mediate on the single Tusked Lord, with bent Trunk
May He Grant Knowledge & Inspire me | | 8 | |

Ek Dantam Chatur Hastam Pashmam Kusha Dharinam
Radamch Vardam Hastair Bhi Bhranum Mushaka Dhvajam
Raktam Lambodaram Shoorpakarnkam Rakta Vasasamam
Raktam Gandhanu Liptangam Rakta Pushpaihi saupujitam
Bhaktanu Kampinam Devam Jagat Karnam Achutam
Avir Bhutam Cha Shrasta Yadao, Prakruthe Purushat Param
Evam Dhayayati Yo Nityam, Sa Yogi Yoginam Varah | | 9 | |

The "SAGUNA" Form of Lord Ganesha is presented
in the above Shloka I salute the Lord with
1 tusk (Right side) Who has 4 hands;
Upper Right carrying binding rope;
Upper left hoalding goad; lower left carrying Broken tusk
& the lower right blesses us,
the mouse on his banner is also his vehicle.
He is blood red in color; Pot-Bellied;
He has elephant ears & wears red clothes
He is smeared with red sandalwood & decorated with red flowers
He is eternally blessing his devotees & was existing before Cosmos
He is beyond "PRAKRITI" & "PURUSHA" & is ever creating universes
One who meditates on him constantly, is a Supreme Yogi | | 9 | |

(This is the Ganesh "Gayatri", Which is Self Sufficient)

Namo Vrat Pataye, Namo Ganapataye
Namo Pramatha patye, Namste Stu Lambodaraya
Ekdantaya, Vighna Nashine
Shiv Sutaya, Sri Varad Murtiye Namo Namah | | 10 | |

Salutations to you Lord of all Deities, Ganas & all beings (Salutations To) The Post-Bellied one with 1 Tusk who destroys all obstacles, son if Shiva, The Divine Lord who grants, Boons (We bow to you) Taking your name | | 10 | |

'MahaShlokas'

Shanti Shloka:

Om Sarveshaam Swastir Bhavatu
Sarveshaam Shaantir Bhavatu Sarveshaam Poornam Bhavatu
Sarveshaam Mangalam Bhavatu Sarve Bhavantu Sukhinah
Sarve Santu Niraamayaah Sarve Bhadraani Pashyantu
Maakaschit Duhkha Bhaag Bhavet

Bhagavad Gita Shlokas: "Lord Shri Krishna" The Supreme Personality of Godhead said:

Yadaa Yadaa Hi Dharmasya Glaanirbhavati Bhaarata |
Abhyuktaanamadharmasya Tadaatmaanam Srijaamyahamh | |

Paritraanaya Sadhuunaam Vinaashaayacha Dushkritam |
Dharma Samsthaapanaarthaaya Sambhavaami Yuge Yuge | |

Karmanyevaadhikaaraste Maa Phaleshu Kadaachana |
Maa Karmaphalaheturbhuu Maatesangotsva Karmani | |

Janma Karma Cha Me Divyamevam Yo Vetti Tattvatah |
Tyaktvaa Deham Punarjanma Naiti Maameti So Arjuna | |

Patram Pushhpam Phalam Toyam Yo Me Bhaktyaa Prayachchati |
Tadaham Bhaktyupahritamashnaami Prayataatmanah | |

Tasmaadasaktah Satatam Kaaryam Karma Samachara |
Asakto Hyagcharankarma Paramaapnoti Puurushah | |

Brahmanyaadhaaya Karmaani Sangam Tyaktvaaa Karoti Yah |
Lipyate Na Sa Paapena Padmapatramivaambhasaa | |

Manmanaa Bhava Madbhakto Madyaajii Maam Namaskuru |
Maamevaishhyasi Satyam Te Pratijaane Priyo Asi Me | |

Manushhyaanaam Sahasreshhu Kashchidyatati Siddhaye |
Yatataamapi Siddhaanaam Kashchinnaam Vetti Tatvatah | |

Yadyadvibhuutimatsatvam Shriimadurjitameva Vaa |
Tattadevaavagachcha Tvam Mama Tejo Nashasambhavamh | |

Yagyaarthaatkarmano Anyatra Loko Ayam Karmabandhanah |
Tadartham Karma Kaunteya Muktasangah Samaachara | |

Paartha Naiveha Naamutra Vinaashastasya Vidhyate |
Na Hi Kalyaanakritkashchidh Durgatim Taata Gachchati | |

Api Chetsuduraachaaro Bhajate Maamananyabhaakh |
Saadhureva Sa Mantavyah Samyavyavasito Hi Sah | |

Sarvadharmaanparityajya Maamekam Sharanam Vraja |
Aham Tvaa Sarvapaapebhyo Mokshayishhyaami Maa Shuchah | |

Yatra Yogeshvarah Krishno Yatra Paartho Dhanurdharah |
Tatra Shriirvijayo Bhuutirdhruvaa Nitir Matirmama | |

Na Jayate Mriyate Va Kadachin
Nayam Bhutva Bhavita Va Na Bhuyah |
Ajo Nityah Shasvatoyam Purano
Na Hanyate Hanyamane Sharire | |

Nainam Chindanti Shastrani Nainam Dahati Pavakah |
Na Chainam Kledayantyapo Na Sosayati Marutah | |

Yogasthah Kuru Karmani Sangam Tyaktva Dhananjaya |
Siddhyasiddhyoh Samo Bhutva Samatvam Yoga Uchyate | |

Sreyansvadharmo Vigunah Paradharmatsvanusthitat |
Svadharme Nidhanam Shreyah Paradharmo Bhayavahah | |

Asamsayam Mahabaho Mano Durnigraham Chalam |
Abhyasena Tu Kaunteya Vairagyena Cha Gruhyate | |

Yad Yad Acharati Shresthas Tad Tad Evetaro Janah |
Sa Yat Pramaanam Kurute Lokas Tad Anuvartate | |

Sa Evayam Maya Te Dya Yogah Proktah Puratanah |
Bhakto Si Me Sakha Ceti Rahasyam Hy Etad Uttamam | |

Janma Karma Ca Me Divyam Evam Yo Vetti Tattvatah |
Tyaktva Deham Punar Janma Naiti Mam Eti So Arjuna | |

Tad Viddhi Pranipatena Pariprasnena Sevaya |
Upadeksyanti Te Jnanam Jnaninas Tattva Darshinah | |

Ye Hi Samsparsha Ja Bhoga Duhkha Yonaya Eva Te |
Ady Antavantah Kaunteya Na Tesu Ramate Budhah | |

Yuktahara Viharasya Yukta Cestasya Karmasu |
Yukta Svapnavabodhasya Yogo Bhavati Duhkha Ha | |

Yoginam Api Sarvesam Mad Gatenantar Atmana |
Shradhavan Bhajate Yo Mam Sa Me Yuktatamo Matah | |

Raja Vidya Raja Guhyam Pavitram Idam Uttamam |
Pratyaksavagamam Dharmyam Su Sukham Kartum Avyayam | |

Maya Tatam Idam Sarvam Jagad Avyakta Murtina |
Mat Sthani Sarva Bhutani Na Caham Tesv Avasthitah | |

Avajananti Mam Mudha Manusim Tanum Asritam |
Param Bhavam Ajananto Mama Bhuta Mahesvaram | |

Ananyas Chintayanto Mam Ye Janah Paryupasate |
Tesam Nityabhiyuktanam Yoga Kshemam Vahamyaham | |

Yanti Deva Vrata Devan Pitrun Yanti Pitru Vratah |
Bhutani Yanti Bhutejya Yanti Mad Yajino Pi Mam | |

Yat Karosi Yad Asnasi Yaj Juhosi Dadasi Yat |
Yat Tapasyasi Kaunteya Tat Kurusva Mad Arpanam | |

Samo Ham Sarva Bhuteshu Na Me Dvesyo Sti Na Priyah |
Ye Bhajanti Tu Mam Bhaktya Mayi Te Tesu Capy Aham | |

Api Cet Su Duracharo Bhajate Mam Ananya Bhak |
Sadhur Eva Sa Mantavyah Samyag Vyavasito Hi Sah | |

Man Mana Bhava Mad Bhakto Mad Yaji Mam Namaskuru |
Mam Evaisyasi Yuktvainam Atmanam Mat Parayanah | |

Tri Vidham Narakasyedam Dvaram Nasanam Atmanah |
Kama Krodhas Tatha Lobhas Tasmad Etat Trayam Tyajet | |

Dharma- Eva Hato Hanti, Dharmo Rakshati Rakshitah |
Tasma - Dharmo Na Hantbhyo, Ma No Dharmo Hato- Vadhit | |

Manusmruthi -

"Yatra Naryastu Pujyante Ramante Tatra Devata,
Yatraitaastu Na Pujyante Sarvaastatrafalaah Kriyaah."

Sanskrit Shlokas -

"Lokah Samastah Sukhino Bhavantu."

Yatha Chittam Tatha Vacha Yatha Vachastatha Kriya |
Chitte Vachi Kriyayam Cha Sadhunamekarupata | |

Manasvi Mriyate Kamam Kaarpanyam Na Tu Gacchati |
Api Nirvanamayati Naanalo Yati Shitatam | |

Dadati Pratigruhyanati Guhyamakhyati Prucchati |
Bhunkte Bhojayate Chaiva Shadvidham Pritilakshanam | |

Shatahasta Samahara Sahasrahasta Samkira |

Manache Shlok by Shri Swami Ramdas:

Mana Sajjana Bhakti Panthechi Jaave |
Tarii Shree Harii Paavije To Swabhave | |
Janii Nindyate Sarva Soduuni Dyaave |
Janii Vandyate Sarva Bhaave Karave | |

Mana Vaasna Dushta Kama Na Ye Re |
Mana Sarvatha Paap Buddhii Nako Re | |
Mana Sarvatha Niiti Sodu Nako Ho |
Mana Antarii Saar Veechaar Raaho | |

Nako Re Mana Krodh Haa Khedkaarii |
Nako Re Mana Kaam Nana Vikarii | |
Nako Re Mana Lobh Hey Angikaru |
Nako Re Mana Matsaru Dambh Bhaaru | |

Mana Shresth Dharishta Jiivii Dharave |
Mana Bolane Neech Soshiit Jaave | |
Svaye Sarvada Namra Vaache Vadave |
Mana Sarva Lokansi Re Niivavaave | |

Dehe Tyaagitaa Kirti Maage Uravi |
Mana Sajjana Hechi Kriya Dharavi | |
Mana Chandanache Pari Twam Jhijaave |
Pari Antari Sajjana Nivavaave | |

Prabhate Manii Ram Chintiit Java |
Pudhe Vaikhri Ram Aadhii Vadava | |
Sadachaar Haa Thor Saandhu Naye To |
Janii Tochi To Manavii Dhanya Hoto | |

Sada Sarvada Preeti Raamii Dharavii |
Sukhachii Svaye Saandi Jeevii Karavii | |
Dehe Dukh Hey Sukh Maaneet Jaave |
Viveke Sada Svasvaroopii Bharave | |

Sanskrit Shlokas-

Yogaschittavruttinirodhah |

Asvasya Bhushanam Vego Mattam Syad Gajabhushanam |
Chaturyam Bhushanam Narya Udyogo Narabhushanam | |

Nirapeksho Nirvikaro Nirbharah Shitalashayah |
Agadhabuddhirakshubdho Bhava Chinmatravasanah | |

Nischitva Yah Prakramate Nantarvasati Karmanah |
Avandhyakalo Vashyatma Sa Vai Pandita Uchyate | |

Svasmai Svalpam Samajaya Sarvasvam |

Etadapi Gamishyanti | (This Too Shall Pass |)
[Mantra for Perseverance]

Na Kalamativartante Mahantah Sveshu Karmasu |

Vidyam Chavidyam Cha Yastadvedobhya Saha |
Avidyaya Mrityum Tirtvamrutamasnute | |

Prabhat Shlokam-

Karagre Vasate Lakshmih Karamadhye Sarasvati |
Karamule Sthita Gauri Prabhate Karadarshanam | |

Shubham Karoti Kalyaannam - Aarogyam Dhan-Sampadaa |
Shatru - Buddhi - Vinaashaaya Diipa - Jyotir - Namostute | |

Diipa - Jyotih Para - Brahma Diipa - Jyotir - Janaardanah |
Diipo Haratu Me Paapam Diipa - Jyotir - Namostute | |

Yaam Rakshanty - Asvapnaa Vishva - Daaniim Devaa
Bhummim Prithiviim - Apramaadam

Mahakavya - Pasayadaan by Saint Dnyaneshwar - (In Marathi Language)

Aata Vishwatmake Deve | Yene Wagyadnye Toshave |
Toshoni Maj Dnyave | Pasaayadaan He | |

Je Khalanchi Vyankati Sando | Taya Satkarmi Rati Wadho |
Bhuta Paraspare Pado | Maitra Jeevache | |

Duritanche Timir Javo | Vishwa Swadharme Surye Paho |
Jo Je Wanchil To Te Laho | Praanijat | |

Varshat Sakal Mangali | Ishwarnisthanchi Maaadiyalii |
Anavarat Bhumandali | Bhetatu Bhutam | |

Chala Kalpatarunche Aarava | Chetana Chintamaninche Gaava |
Bolate Je Arnav | Piyushache | |

Chandrame Je Alaanchan | Martand Je Taaphina |
Te Sarvaahi Sada Sajjana | Soyare Hotu | |

Kimbahuna Sarva Sukhi | Puurna Houni Ternhi Loki |
Bhajijo Aadipurukhi | Akhandit | |

Aani Gramthopajiviye | Visheshi Loki Iye |
Drushtaadrushta Vijaye | Ho Aave Ji | |

Yeth Mhanne Shri Vishvesharaao | Ha Hoila Daan Pasaavo |
Yene Vare Dnyandeo | Sukhiyaa Jhaalaa | |

-0-

"Dharmo Rakshati Rakshitah."
(It means that dharma protects those who uphold or protect dharma)

"Vasudhaiva Kutumbakam"- ("Vasudha"-Earth, "Iva"-Is,"Kutumbakam"-Family) (The whole world is one family)

Ayam Bandhuryaneti Gannana Laghuchetasaam |
Udaarcharitanaam Tu Vasudhaiva Kutumbakam | |

Ayam Nijah Paro Veti Ganana Laghuchetasam |
Udaracharitanam Tu Vasudhaiva Kutumbakam | |

'Devi Stuti Mantra' - Yaa Devi Sarva Bhuteshu-

Yaa Devi Sarvabhuteshu Vishnumaayeti Shabdita |
Namas-Tasyai Namas-Tasyai Namas-Tasyai Namo Namah | |

Yaa Devi Sarvabhuteshu Chetanety-Abhidhiiyate |
Namas-Tasyai Namas-Tasyai Namas-Tasyai Namo Namah | |

Yaa Devi Sarvabhuteshu Buddhi-Ruupenna Samsthitaa |
Namas-Tasyai Namas-Tasyai Namas-Tasyai Namo Namah | |

Yaa Devi Sarvabhuteshu Nidra-Ruupenna Samsthitaa |
Namas-Tasyai Namas-Tasyai Namas-Tasyai Namo Namah | |

Yaa Devi Sarvabhuteshu Kshudhaa-Ruupenna Samsthitaa |
Namas-Tasyai Namas-Tasyai Namas-Tasyai Namo Namah | |

Yaa Devi Sarvabhuteshu Chaayaa-Ruupenna Samsthitaa |
Namas-Tasyai Namas-Tasyai Namas-Tasyai Namo Namah | |

Yaa Devi Sarvabhuteshu Shakti-Ruupenna Samsthitaa |
Namas-Tasyai Namas-Tasyai Namas-Tasyai Namo Namah | |

Yaa Devi Sarvabhuteshu Trishnnaa-Ruupenna Samsthitaa |
Namas-Tasyai Namas-Tasyai Namas-Tasyai Namo Namah | |

Yaa Devi Sarvabhuteshu Kshaanti-Ruupenna Samsthitaa |
Namas-Tasyai Namas-Tasyai Namas-Tasyai Namo Namah | |

Yaa Devi Sarvabhuteshu Jaati-Ruupenna Samsthitaa |
Namas-Tasyai Namas-Tasyai Namas-Tasyai Namo Namah | |

Yaa Devi Sarvabhuteshu Lajjaa-Ruupenna Samsthitaa |
Namas-Tasyai Namas-Tasyai Namas-Tasyai Namo Namah | |

Yaa Devi Sarvabhuteshu Shaanti-Ruupenna Samsthitaa |
Namas-Tasyai Namas-Tasyai Namas-Tasyai Namo Namah | |

Yaa Devi Sarvabhuteshu Shraddhaa-Ruupenna Samsthitaa |
Namas-Tasyai Namas-Tasyai Namas-Tasyai Namo Namah | |

Yaa Devi Sarvabhuteshu Kaanti-Ruupenna Samsthitaa |
Namas-Tasyai Namas-Tasyai Namas-Tasyai Namo Namah | |

Yaa Devi Sarvabhuteshu Lakshmii-Ruupenna Samsthitaa |
Namas-Tasyai Namas-Tasyai Namas-Tasyai Namo Namah | |

Yaa Devi Sarvabhuteshu Vritti-Ruupenna Samsthitaa |
Namas-Tasyai Namas-Tasyai Namas-Tasyai Namo Namah | |

Yaa Devi Sarvabhuteshu Smriti-Ruupenna Samsthitaa |
Namas-Tasyai Namas-Tasyai Namas-Tasyai Namo Namah | |

Yaa Devi Sarvabhuteshu Dayaa-Ruupenna Samsthitaa |
Namas-Tasyai Namas-Tasyai Namas-Tasyai Namo Namah | |

Yaa Devi Sarvabhuteshu Tushtii-Ruupenna Samsthitaa |
Namas-Tasyai Namas-Tasyai Namas-Tasyai Namo Namah | |

Yaa Devi Sarvabhuteshu Maatru-Ruupenna Samsthitaa |
Namas-Tasyai Namas-Tasyai Namas-Tasyai Namo Namah | |

Yaa Devi Sarvabhuteshu Bhraanti-Ruupenna Samsthitaa |
Namas-Tasyai Namas-Tasyai Namas-Tasyai Namo Namah | |

Indriyaannaam - Adhishtthaatrii Bhutaanaam Cha-Akhileshu |
Yaa Bhuteshu Satatam Tasyai Vyaapti - Devyai Namo Namah | |

Chiti - Ruupenna Yaa Kritsnam - Etad - Vyaapya Sthitaa Jagat |
Namas-Tasyai Namas-Tasyai Namas-Tasyai Namo Namah | |

‘MahaBodhaVakyas’

The Great Life Quotes

In Sanskrit "Maha" means "Great". "Bodha" means awakening, sensibility, perceptiveness, comprehension, cognition, feeling, knowledge, sense, realization, consciousness and reason. "Vakya" means sentence, saying, speech, a rule, a word, what is spoken, a precept, statement, an assertion and declaration, "Maha Bodha Vakyas" means "Great Enlightened Sentences". These Vakyas are inspirational, motivational, and most beneficial for one's physical, mental, and Spiritual development.

'Mahabodhavakyas' The Great Life Quotes:

"Develop the right attitude towards your work and even the most mundane work becomes a source of joy".

- Lord Shri Krishna

"These are three gates to the self-destructive hell: lust, anger, and greed"

-Lord Shri Krishna

"Set your heart upon your work but never its reward".

- Lord Shri Krishna

"It is better to perform one's own duties imperfectly than to master the duties of another".

- Lord Shri Krishna

"Fear not. What is not real, never was and never will be. What is real always was and cannot be destroyed".

- Lord Shri Krishna

"A man is made by his belief. As he believes, so he becomes".

- Lord Shri Krishna

"The key to happiness is the reduction of desires".

- Lord Shri Krishna

"For one who has conquered his mind, the mind is the best friend, but for one who has failed to do so, his mind is the greatest enemy".

- Lord Shri Krishna

"When a person responds to the joys and sorrows of others as if they were his own, he has attained the highest state of spiritual union."

- Lord Shri Krishna

"Calmness, gentleness, silence, self-restraint and purity: these are the disciplines of the mind."

- Lord Shri Krishna

"He who has no attachments can really love others, for his love is pure and divine."

- Lord Shri Krishna

"When a person is devoted to something with complete faith, I unify his faith in that, then when his faith is completely unified, he gains the object of his devotion."

- Lord Shri Krishna

"When meditation is mastered, the mind is unwavering like the flame of a lamp in a windless place."

- Lord Shri Krishna

"The mind is fickle. It won't obey you. Every time the mind misbehaves, use your discretionary intellect to bring it back to the equanimous position."

- Lord Shri Krishna

"Each man is mixture of all the three tendencies: divinely noble, vibrantly restless and indolently dull. The wise man transcends all these three qualities."

- Lord Shri Krishna

"Think about all that I have said and then do as you please."

- Lord Shri Krishna

(In essence "Lord Sri Krishna" is not just preaching but asking Arjuna to make his own choice. Respecting one's complete freedom of choice.)

"Dharma is born from truth".

- Ramayana

"If you want to be happy, be."

- Ramayana

"Conduct is the best proof of character."

- Ramayana

"You can't protect Dharma if you don't know what it is."

- Ramayana

"Only the timid and the weak leave things to destiny. But the strong and self-confident never bank on destiny or luck (Bhagya)."

- Ramayana

"Live and allow others to live; hurt no one; life is dear to all living beings."

- Bhagwan Mahavira

"Don't accumulate if you do not need."

- Bhagwan Mahavira

"All are my friends. I have no enemies."

- Bhagwan Mahavira

"Modes are infinite, and laws are infinite."

- Bhagwan Mahavira

"All souls are equal and alike and have the similar nature & qualities."

- Bhagwan Mahavira

"The nature of things is Dharma."

- Bhagwan Mahavira

"Faith and prayer both are invisible, but they make impossible things possible."

- Bhagwan Mahavira

"Kill not, cause no pain. Ahimsa (non-violence) is the greatest religion."

- Bhagwan Mahavira

"It is better to conquer yourself than to win a thousand battles. Then the victory is yours. It cannot be taken from you."

- Gautam Buddha

"I never see what has been done; I only see what remains to be done."

- Gautam Buddha

"You only lose what you cling to."

- Gautam Buddha

"The past has already gone, and the future is not yet here. There's only one moment for you to live."

- Gautam Buddha

"The trouble is you think you have time."

- Gautam Buddha

"As you walk and eat and travel, be where you are, otherwise you will miss most of your life."

- Gautam Buddha

"No matter how hard the past, you can always begin again."

- Gautam Buddha

"Your work is to discover your work and then with all your heart to give yourself to it."

- Gautam Buddha

"Teach this triple truth to all: A generous heart, kind speech, and a life of service and compassion are the things which renew humanity."

- Gautam Buddha

"Every human being is the Author of his own health or disease."

- Gautam Buddha

"Avoid evil deeds as a man who loves life avoids poison."

- Gautam Buddha

"Holding onto anger is like drinking poison and expecting the other person to die."

- Gautam Buddha

"What you think, you become, what you feel, you attract, what you imagine, you create."

- Gautam Buddha

"Meditation brings wisdom, lack of meditation leaves ignorance. Know well what leads you forward and what holds you back and choose the path that leads to wisdom."

- Gautam Buddha

"No one saves us but ourselves. No one can and no one may. We ourselves must walk the path."

- Gautam Buddha

"Anger will never disappear so long as thoughts of resentment are cherished in the mind. Anger will disappear just as soon as thought of resentment are forgotten."

- Gautam Buddha

"Your body is precious. It is our vehicle for Awakening. Treat it with care."

- Gautam Buddha

"One should strive to understand what underlies suffering & diseases and aim for health & well-being while gaining in the path."

- Gautam Buddha

"If you are quite enough, you will hear the flow of the universe. You will feel its rhythm. Go with this flow. Happiness lies ahead. Meditation is key."

- Gautam Buddha

"Better than a thousand hollow words, is one word that brings peace."

- Gautam Buddha

"Peace comes from within. Do not seek it without."

- Gautam Buddha

"The whole secret of existence is to have no fear. Never fear of what will become of you, depend on no one. Only the moment you reject all help are you freed."

- Gautam Buddha

"You cannot travel the path until you have become the path itself."

- Gautam Buddha

"Purity or impurity depends on oneself. No one can purify another."

- Gautam Buddha

"However many holy words you read, however many you speak, what good will they do you if you do not act on upon them."

- Gautam Buddha

"If you light a lamp for somebody, it will also brighten your path."

- Gautam Buddha

"If we could see the miracle of a single flower clearly, our whole life would change."

- Gautam Buddha

"Those who have failed to work toward the truth have missed the purpose of living."

- Gautam Buddha

In separateness lies the world's greatest misery: in compassion lies the world's true strength."

- Gautam Buddha

"All that we are is the result of what we have thought. The mind is everything. What we think we become."

- Gautam Buddha

"You will not be punished for your anger you will be punished by your anger."

- Gautam Buddha

"To understand everything is to forgive everything."

- Gautam Buddha

"In the end, these things matter most: How well did you love? How fully did you live? How deeply did you let go?"

- Gautam Buddha

"Even as solid rock is unshaken by the wind, so are the wise unshaken by praise or blame."

- Gautam Buddha

"One moment can change a day, one day can change a life, and one life can change the world."

- Gautam Buddha

"There is no path to happiness. Happiness is the path."

- Gautam Buddha

"You yourself, as much as anybody in the entire universe, deserve your love and affection."

- Gautam Buddha

"One should respect his motherland, his culture and his mother tongue because they are givers of happiness."

- Vedas

"Ego is the biggest enemy of humans."

- Vedas

"By enthusiasm one acquires unimaginable strength."

- Vedas

"One should offer oblation to his own body & nurture it well."

- Vedas

"Those who are active shun the company of lethargic."

- Vedas

"It is impossible for the fools to tread the path of learned ones."

- Vedas

"O God! You are the friend of all because of your merits. A good person embellished with good thoughts becomes the friend or benefactor of all. Such a person influences others, because of his positive personality traits and attracts them and as a result, he befriends all."

- Vedas

"Mutual affection only leads to co-operation and peace this propagates happiness and prosperity in the society."

- Vedas

"Develop Ananda: then evil impulses and tendencies will vanish, for they will not get any foothold in the heart."

- Vedas

"Do not talk evil of others; see only good in them."

- Vedas

"Enshrine the feet of the Guru within your heart; your pains, enemies and bad luck shall be destroyed."

- Vedas

"All men are mine so the whole world has to be saved from the consequences of ignorance or limited knowledge."

- Vedas

"He that is without sin among you, let him cast the first stone."

- Jesus Christ

"Love your enemies! Pray for those who persecute you! In that way, you will be acting as true children of your father in heaven. For he gives his sunlight to both the evil and the good. And he sends rain on the just and the unjust alike."

- Jesus Christ

"Everyone who seeks, finds. And everyone who knocks, the door will be opened."

- Luke

"With man this is impossible, but with God all things are possible."

- Mathew

"Except a man be born again, he cannot see the kingdom of God."

- Jesus Christ

"Jesus saith unto him, I am the way, the truth and the life: no man cometh unto the father, but by me."

- Jesus Christ

"But seek ye first the kingdom of God. And his righteousness; and all these things shall be added unto you."

- Jesus Christ

"Do to others whatever you would like them to do to you. This is the essence of all that is taught in the law and the prophets."

- Jesus Christ

"Thou shalt love thy neighbor as thyself."

- Jesus Christ

"Thou shalt not have adulterous eyes."

- Jesus Christ

"If thine eye be single, thy whole body shall be full of light."

- Jesus Christ

(To be "single eyed" means to realize that "God" is omnipresent, omniscient, omnipotent, eternal)

"Do not be proud of wealth, people, relations and friends, or your youth. All these are snatched by time in the blink of an eye. Giving up this illusory world, know and attain the supreme."

- Adi Shankaracharya

"Do not look at anybody in terms of friend or foe, brother or cousin; do not fritter away your mental energies in thoughts of friendship or enmity. Seeking the self everywhere be amiable and equal minded towards all. Treating everyone alike."

- Adi Shankaracharya

"The world, like a dream full of attachment and aversions seems real until the awakening."

- Adi Shankaracharya

"Reality can be experienced only with the eye of understanding not just by a scholar."

- Adi Shankaracharya

"There is a sorrow in finitude. The self is beyond time, space and objects. It is infinite and hence of the nature of absolute happiness."

- Adi Shankaracharya

"What is enquiry into the Truth? It is the firm conviction that the Self is real, and all, other than that is unreal."

- Adi Shankaracharya

"The witness of the three states of consciousness (waking, dream and deep sleep) and of the nature of the Existence, Consciousness-Bliss is the Self. Thus one should know oneself to be of the nature of Existence-Consciousness-Bliss [Sat-Chit-Anand]."

- Adi Shankaracharya

"Reining in your mind, the God has appeared in your heart. Now with his omnipresence there is no emptiness."

- Sant Dnyaneshwar

"Jalashaya Nirmave, Vaanechi laavavi, Nagarechi Rachavi Nanaviddhe."

- Sant Dnyaneshwar

"Wisdom is that, by which all troublesome activities melt away."

- Sant Dnyaneshwar

"When salt is put in the water, it becomes water, so with unity, there remains no animosity."

- Sant Dnyaneshwar

"The true mark, Therefore, of purity of intelligence is, that the mind is directed towards the true form (of Self) and the intelligence has no other purpose except this."

- Sant Dnyaneshwar

"Thou art the doer and thou art the experiencer."

- Sant Dnyaneshwar

"The ideal path to cross over Maya or illusion is of spiritual devotion. Alertness is re- quired to avoid the pitfalls of ego and desire."

- Sant Dnyaneshwar

"The ultimate reality exists in Itself and is beyond the conceptions of existence or non-existence."

- Sant Dnyaneshwar

"Be kind, for whenever kindness becomes part of something, it beautifies it. Whenever it is taken from something, it leaves it tarnished."

- Prophet Muhammad

"A good man treats women with honor."

- Prophet Muhammad

"And be moderate (or show no arrogance) in your walking and lower your voice."

- Prophet Muhammad

"O people, remain straight upon the path and you will have taken a great lead, but if you swerve right or left then you will be led far astray."

- Prophet Muhammad

"The best among you is the one who doesn't harm others with his tongue and hands."

- Prophet Muhammad

"The greatest of richness is the richness of soul."

- Prophet Muhammad

"Strive always to excel in virtue and truth."

- Prophet Muhammad

"The greatest jihad (struggle / striving) is to battle your own soul, to fight the evil within yourself."

- Prophet Muhammad

"The strongest among you is the one who controls his anger."

- Prophet Muhammad

"There is reward for kindness to every living thing."

- Prophet Muhammad

"God does not look at your forms and possessions but he looks at your hearts and your deeds."

- Prophet Muhammad

"Exchange gifts, you will love one another."

- Prophet Muhammad

"Seek knowledge from cradle to the grave."

- Prophet Muhammad

"Speak good or remain silent."

- Prophet Muhammad

"Whatever is prayed for at the time of breaking the fast is granted and never refused."

- Prophet Muhammad

"In Paradise there are things which, no eyes have seen, no ears has heard, and no human mind has thought of."

- Prophet Muhammad

"Beware of jealousy, for it destroys your character just as fire destroys wood."

- Prophet Muhammad

"Speak the truth even if it is bitter."

- Prophet Muhammad

"The cure for ignorance is to question."

- Prophet Muhammad

"The Charity you give while you fear poverty, is the best Charity."

- Prophet Muhammad

"Do not let your difficulties fill you with anxiety, after all it is only in the darkest nights that stars shine more brightly."

- Hazrat Ali

"Nothing hurt's a good soul and a kind heart more than to live amongst people who can- not understand it."

- Hazrat Ali

"The best deed of a great man is to forgive and forget."

- Hazrat Ali

"When the world pushes you to your knees, you're in the perfect position to pray."

- Hazrat Ali

"He who trusts the world, the world betrays him."

- Hazrat Ali

"Patience ensure victory."

- Hazrat Ali

"A brother is like gold and a friend is like diamond. If gold cracks, you can melt it and make it just like it was before. If a diamond crack's, it can never be like it was before."

- Hazrat Ali

"Beware of speaking too much, for it increases mistakes and engenders boredom."

- Hazrat Ali

"Have you forgotten God? Even if you have, he has not forgotten you."

- Moses

"Fear not! stand your ground ... the Lord himself will fight for you; you have only to keep still."

- Moses

"... the dust returns to the ground it came from, and the spirit returns to God who gave it."

- Moses

"You shall not steal, not deal falsely, nor lie to one another."

- Moses

"The only true wisdom is in knowing you know nothing."

- Socrates

"The unexamined life is not worth living."

- Socrates

"I cannot teach anybody anything. I can only make them think."

- Socrates

"There is only one good, knowledge and one evil ignorance."

- Socrates

"Wonder is the beginning of wisdom."

- Socrates

"To find yourself, think for yourself."

- Socrates

"By three methods we may learn wisdom: first, by reflection, which is noblest; second, by imitation, which is easiest; and third by experience, which is the bitterest."

- Confucius

"Everything has beauty, but not everyone sees it."

- Confucius

"Wheresoever you go, go with all your heart."

- Confucius

"It does not matter how slowly you go as long as you do not stop."

- Confucius

"Respect yourself and others will respect you."

- Confucius

"Silence is a true friend who never betrays."

- Confucius

"Being deeply loved by someone gives you strength, while loving someone deeply gives you courage."

- Lao Tzu

"Simplicity, patience, compassion are your greatest treasures."

- Lao Tzu

"The journey of a thousand miles begins with a single step."

- Lao Tzu

"A good traveler has no fixed plans and is not intent on arriving."

- Lao Tzu

"Care about what other people think and you will always be their prisoner."

- Lao Tzu

"Nature does not hurry, yet everything is accomplished."

- Lao Tzu

"Silence is a source of great strength."

- Lao Tzu

"The higher we soar the smaller we appear to those who cannot fly."

- Zarathustra

"You must be ready to burn yourself in your own flame; how could you rise anew if you have not first become ashes.?"

- Zarathustra

"Silence is worse; all truths that are kept silent become poisonous."

- Zarathustra

"Become who you are!"

- Zarathustra

"There is more wisdom in your body than in your deepest philosophy."

- Zarathustra

"And once you are awake, you shall remain awake eternally."

- Zarathustra

"One must be sea, to receive a polluted stream without becoming impure."

- Zarathustra

"I tell you: one must still have chaos within oneself, to give birth to a dancing star."

- Zarathustra

"You great star, what would your happiness be, had you not those for whom you shine?"

- Zarathustra

"Of all that is written, I love only what a man has written with his own blood."

- Zarathustra

"It is true: we love life not because we are used to living, but because we are used to loving."

- Zarathustra

"Do not be content with showing friendship in words alone, let your heart burn with loving kindness for all who may cross your path."

- Zarathustra

"The Earth is but one country and mankind its citizens."

- Baha'u'llah

"Regard man as a mine rich in gems of inestimable value. Education can, alone, cause it to reveal its treasures, and enable mankind to benefit from."

- Baha'u'llah

"Religion without science is superstition. Science without religion is materialism."

- Baha'u'llah

"Let your vision be world embracing rather than confined to your own self."

- Baha'u'llah

"The essence of faith is fewness of words and abundance of deeds."

- Baha'u'llah

"He who has no faith in himself can never have faith in God."

- Guru Nanak

"Even kings and emperors with heaps of wealth and vast dominion cannot compare with an ant filled with the love of God."

- Guru Nanak

"The world is a drama, staged in a dream."

- Guru Nanak

"Speak only that which will bring you honor."

- Guru Nanak

"Those who have loved are those that have found God."

- Guru Nanak

"Nanak, the whole world is in the distress. He, who believes in the name, becomes victori- ous."

- Guru Nanak

"If there is one God, then there is only His way to attain Him, not another. One must follow that way and reject the other."

- Guru Nanak

"Be humbler than a blade of grass, more tolerant than tree, always offering respect onto others and never expecting anything in return."

- Chaitanya Mahaprabhu

"Be like a tree. The tree gives shade even to him who cuts of its boughs."

- Chaitanya Mahaprabhu

"The Vedic literatures composed by the Mahamuni Vyasadeva are evidence of all spiritual existence. Only through these revealed scriptures can all conditioned souls attain knowledge."

- Chaitanya Mahaprabhu

"The essence of all religious principles in the age of Kali is chanting of the holy names of the Lord. One cannot be delivered by following any other religious principles."

- Chaitanya Mahaprabhu

"The word Brahman indicates the complete supreme personality of Godhead,who is Shri Krishna. That is the verdict of all Vedic literatures".

- Chaitanya Mahaprabhu

"In this age of Kali, the holy name of the Lord, the Hare Krishna maha-mantra, is the incarnation of Lord Krishna."

- Chaitanya Mahaprabhu

"No one belongs to me; I belong to no one. There is no "I" or "mine"; all is blissful alone- less."

- Vyasa

"One should never do that to another which one regards as injurious to one's own self."

- Vyasa

"Time is the seed of the Universe."

- Vyasa

"Misfortune the best fortune. Rejection by all is victory."

- Valmiki

"In all this world, I pray thee, who is virtuous, heroic, true.?"

- Valmiki

"Be quiet in your mind, quite in your senses, also quite in your body. Then, when all these are quiet, don't do anything. In that state truth will reveal itself to you."

- Kabir

I laugh when I hear that the fish in the water is thirsty. I laugh when I hear that people go on pilgrimage to find God."

- Kabir

"What is holy person? The one who is aware of other's suffering."

- Kabir

"The beloved is inside you and inside me, you know the tree is hidden inside the seed. Let your arrogance go. None of us has gone far. Inside love there is more power than we realize."

- Kabir

"All know that the drop merges into the ocean, but few know that the ocean merges into the drop."

- Kabir

"The truth of love is the truth of universe: it is the lamp of the soul that reveals the secret of darkness."

- Kabir

"Don't forget love; it will bring you all the madness you need to unfurl yourself across the universe."

- Meera

"Some praise me, some blame me. I go the other way."

- Meera

"I went to the root of things and found nothing but Him alone."

- Meera

"O my companion, worldly comfort is an illusion, as soon you get it, it goes."

- Meera

"Even your pity is like blast of wind and the words you speak would strip a tree of its blossoms."

- Tulsidas

"There are three all-powerful evils: lust, anger and greed."

- Tulsidas

"All the sleepers in a night of delusion beholding so many dreams. In this world of dark- ness, only those who sever themselves from the material world, become absorbed in the contemplation of the Supreme. None can be regarded as really woken up from sleep till they have renounced all sensuous delights."

- Tulsidas

"The life ahead can only be glorious if you learn to live in total harmony with the Lord."

- Sai Baba

"There is only one caste, the caste of humanity. There is only one religion, the religion of love. There is only one language, the language of heart."

- Sai Baba

"Love all. Serve all. Help ever. Hurt never."

- Sai Baba

"You are not one person, but three: The one you think you are; the one others think you are; the one you really are."

- Sai Baba

"Learn to speak what you feel, and act what you speak."

- Sai Baba

"You should not stay for even one second at a place where people are speaking disrespectfully of a Saint."

- Sai Baba

"Do not wail! wait a bit and have patience. Your wish will be fulfilled."

- Sai Baba

"Keep faith and patience and your prayer shall be answered."

- Sai Baba

"Whatever you are, be good one."

- Abraham Lincoln

"Do I not destroy my enemies when I make them my friends?"

- Abraham Lincoln

"Nearly all men can stand adversity, but if you want to test a man's character, give him power."

- Abraham Lincoln

"Those who deny freedom to others, deserve it not for themselves."

- Abraham Lincoln

"I am a slow Walker, but I never walk back."

- Abraham Lincoln

"The best way to predict your future is to create it."

- Abraham Lincoln

"Arise, awake and do not stop until the goal is reached."

- Swami Vivekananda

"You cannot believe in God until you believe in yourself."

- Swami Vivekananda

"All the powers in the universe are already ours. It is we who have put our hands before our eyes and cry that it is dark."

- Swami Vivekananda

"Truth can be stated in the thousand different ways, yet each one can be true."

- Swami Vivekananda

"All differences in this world are of degree, and not of kind, because oneness is the secret of everything."

- Swami Vivekananda

"The world is the great gymnasium where we come to make ourselves strong."

- Swami Vivekananda

"The Vedanta recognizes no sin it only recognizes error. And the greatest error, says the Vedanta is to say that you are weak, that you are a sinner, a miserable creature, and that you have no power, and you cannot do this & that."

- Swami Vivekananda

"Where can we go to find God if we cannot see Him in our own heart and in every living being."

- Swami Vivekananda

"Anyone who is steady in his determination for the advanced stage of spiritual realization and can equally tolerate the onslaughts of distress and happiness is certainly a person eligible for liberation."

- Swami Prabhupada

"Religion means to know God and to love him."

- Swami Prabhupada

"One whose happiness is within, who is active within, who rejoices within and is illumined within, is actually the perfect mystic. He is liberated in the Supreme, and ultimately he attains the Supreme."

- Swami Prabhupada

"Our only business is to love God, not to ask God for our necessities."

- Swami Prabhupada

"For man, mind is the cause of bondage and mind is the cause of liberation. Mind absorbed in sense objects is the cause of bondage, and mind detached from sense objects is the cause of liberation."

- Swami Prabhupada

"A Yogi is greater than the ascetic, greater than the empiricist and greater than the fruitive worker. Therefore, in all circumstances, be a Yogi."

- Swami Prabhupada

"Devotional service is more or less a declaration of war against the illusory energy."

- Swami Prabhupada

"One cannot reach the real point of factual knowledge without being helped by the right Guru who is already established in the knowledge."

- Swami Prabhupada

"The living being is in the state of forgetfulness of his relation with God, due to his being overly attracted to material sense gratification from time immemorial."

- Swami Prabhupada

"We must forget bodily consciousness like a deer which is infatuated by music. We must look up to God, as the young one's of a tortoise look up to their mother. As a fountain rises upwards, even so must one's spirit rise to God. One should entertain no idea whatsoever except that of God."

- Sant Tukaram

"Words are the only jewels I possess, words are only clothes I wear, words are only the food that sustain my life, words are the only wealth I distribute among people."

- Sant Tukaram

"I am looking for a poem that says everything, so I don't have to write anymore."

- Sant Tukaram

"He who utters the name of God while walking gets the merit of a sacrifice at every step. His body becomes a place of pilgrimage. He who repeats God's name while working al- ways finds perfect peace. He who utters the name of God while eating gets the merit of a fast even though he has taken his meals."

- Sant Tukaram

"Even if one were to give in charity the whole Earth encircled by the seas it would not equal the merit of repeating the 'Name'. By the power of the 'Name', one will know what cannot be known. One will see what cannot be seen. One will speak what cannot be spoken. One will meet what cannot be met. Tuka says, incalculable is the gain that comes from repeating the 'Name of God'."

- Sant Tukaram

"Faith is the bird that feels the light when the down is still dark."

- Rabindranath Tagore

"You can't cross the sea merely by standing and staring at the water."

- Rabindranath Tagore

"Everything comes to us that belongs to us if we create the capacity to receive it."

- Rabindranath Tagore

"I slept and dreamt that life was joy. I awoke and saw that life was service. I acted and behold service was joy."

- Rabindranath Tagore

"Love does not claim possession but gives freedom."

- Rabindranath Tagore

"Where the mind is without fear and the head is held high, where knowledge is free, where the world has not been broken up into fragments by narrow domestic walls. Where words come out from the depths of truth, where tireless striving stretches its arms to-

wards perfection, where the clear stream of reason has not lost its way into the dreary desert sands of dead habit. Where the mind is led forward by thee into ever widening thought and action. Into that heaven of freedom, my father let my country Awake.!"

- Rabindranath Tagore

"Love's gift cannot be given it waits to be accepted. The butterfly counts not months but moments and has time enough.

- Rabindranath Tagore

"Problems or successes they all are the results of our own actions, Karma. The philosophy of action is that no one else is the giver of peace and happiness. One's own Karma, one's own actions are responsible to come to bring either happiness or success or whatever."

- Maharshi Mahesh Yogi

"The philosophy of life is this: Life is not a struggle, not a tension ...... Life is bliss. It is eternal wisdom, eternal existence."

- Maharshi Mahesh Yogi

"Problems will disappear as darkness disappears with the onset of Light."

- Maharshi Mahesh Yogi

"Whatever we put our attention on will grow stronger in our life."

- Maharshi Mahesh Yogi

"Life finds its purpose & fulfilment in the expansion of happiness."

- Maharshi Mahesh Yogi

"Your own self-realization is the greatest service you can render the world."

- Ramana Maharshi

"No one succeeds without efforts .... Those who succeed owe their success to perseverance."

- Ramana Maharshi

"Your hands may do the work, but your mind can remain still. You are that which never moves."

- Ramana Maharshi

"Everything is perfect in God's creation. Ignorance and suffering exist only in the minds of people."

- Ramana Maharshi

"The only useful purpose of the present birth is to turn within and realize the Self. There is nothing else to do."

- Ramana Maharshi

"Solitude is an attitude of the mind; a man attached to the things of life cannot get solitude, wherever he may be. A detached man is always in solitude."

- Ramana Maharshi

"As soon as you open your heart you will widen yourself, you will grow."

- Shri Mataji Nirmala Devi

"Nothing is more important for me than to see you all rise to the level where you under- stand your own values."

- Shri Mataji Nirmala Devi

"After all we are all human beings created by one God, on one Earth, in complete unison. We are part and parcel of that one primordial being. We are cells in the body of that great being."

- Shri Mataji Nirmala Devi

"Meditation, where you are connected to the all-pervading divinity, is the starting point in self-realization."

- Shri Mataji Nirmala Devi

"Change Yourself, Change the World."

- Shri Mataji Nirmala Devi

"Not to forgive is difficult, but to forgive is the best. At least when you forgive, there is no headache for you."

- Shri Mataji Nirmala Devi

"The reality is that You are the spirit. The rest is a myth."

- Shri Mataji Nirmala Devi

"Self-realization is the first encounter with reality."

- Shri Mataji Nirmala Devi

"The aim of your life is to seek your Spirit."

- Shri Mataji Nirmala Devi

"The most dynamic power in this world is that of love."

- Shri Mataji Nirmala Devi

"You cannot know the meaning of your life until you are connected to the power that created you."

- Shri Mataji Nirmala Devi

"Be conscious of your spirit. Spirit is the only thing that can Kindle another Spirit."

- Shri Mataji Nirmala Devi

"The best way to practice the witness state is not to criticize anyone."

- Shri Mataji Nirmala Devi

"A realized Soul is always on the Axis of Wheel, which is unmoving, which is silent. So, he has peace within himself."

- Shri Mataji Nirmala Devi

"This all-pervading divine power of love is the ocean of knowledge, is the ocean of bliss and compassion, but above all it is the ocean of forgiveness."

- Shri Mataji Nirmala Devi

"Spirit is the source of peace. It is the source of joy. It is not a duality of happiness and unhappiness, but singular Joy."

- Shri Mataji Nirmala Devi

"Freedom is when you really get your own powers which are within you."

- Shri Mataji Nirmala Devi

"When you get your self-realization or your second birth you become entitled to an awareness by which you can find out the roots of everything."

- Shri Mataji Nirmala Devi

"An innocent person is really like a magnet, and it attracts, he attracts, the people towards himself, just like a flower attracts bee towards itself."

-Shri Mataji Nirmala Devi

"There's only one pure desire and that is to be one with the divine."

- Shri Mataji Nirmala Devi

"This power of Kundalini, which is your individual mother; is waiting in the sacrum bone and knows all about your past and all about your aspirations, your future. So, she knows your problem. She is your individual mother, and she is anxious to give you your second birth. Once it happens automatically you start seeing things very clearly in the light of spirit, because light gets enlightened, Spirit gets enlightened. And you start seeing yourself clearly, understanding what you have. Then you know how to cure yourself, improve yourself."

- Shri Mataji Nirmala Devi

"The greatest friend you have is the divine power which is looking after you and doing everything for you."

- Shri Mataji Nirmala Devi

"We achieve self-knowledge through the Kundalini. Now the journey starts towards God knowledge. Without self-knowledge one cannot know about God as actualized knowledge."

- Shri Mataji Nirmala Devi

"The biggest Guru Mantra is, never share your secrets with anybody. It will destroy you."

- Chanakya

"We should not feel Pride in our charity, austerity, valor, spiritual knowledge, modesty and morality for the world is full of the rarest gems".

- Chanakya

"The fragrance of flower spreads only in the direction of the wind. But the goodness of a person spreads in all directions."

- Chanakya

"Before you start some work, always ask yourself three questions- why am I doing it, what the results might be and will I be successful. Only when you think deeply and find satisfactory answers to these questions, go ahead."

- Chanakya

"Books are as useful to a stupid person as a mirror is useful to a blind person."

- Chanakya

"Education is the best friend. An educated person is respected everywhere. Education beats the beauty and the youth."

- Chanakya

"These are four ways of making someone do a task, stated as "Saam, Daam, Dand, Bhed."

- Chanakya

[Saam: to advice and ask, Daam: to offer and buy, Dand: to punish, Bhed: exploiting the secrets]

"Genius is one percent inspiration and ninety nine percent perspiration."

- Thomas Edison

"I have not failed. I've just found thousand ways that won't work."

- Thomas Edison

"I seem to have been only like a boy playing on the seashore and diverting myself in now and then finding a smoother pebble or a prettier shell than ordinary, whilst the great ocean of truth lay all undiscovered before me."

- Isaac Newton

"The black holes of nature are the most perfect macroscopic objects there are in the universe: the only elements in their construction are our concepts of space and time."

- Subramanyam Chandrashekhar

"Science without religion is lame, religion without science is blind."

- Albert Einstein

"A man who dares to Waste one hour of time has not discovered the value of life."

- Charles Darwin

"Nothing in life is to be feared, it is only to be understood. Now is the time to understand more, so that we may fear less."

- Marie-curie

"You cannot teach a man anything; you can only help him discover it in himself."

- Galileo

"Imagination is more important than knowledge."

- Albert Einstein

"Equipped with his five senses, man explores the universe around him and calls the adventure science."

- Edwin Powell Hubble

"One, remember to look up at the stars and not down at your feet. Two, never give up work. Work gives you meaning and purpose, and life is empty without it. Three, if you are lucky enough to find love, remember it is there and don't throw it away."

- Stephen Hawking

"Our virtues and our failings are inseparable like force and matter. When the separate, man is no more."

- Nikola Tesla

"The day science begins to study non-physical phenomena it will make more progress in one decade than in all the previous centuries of its existence."

- Nikola Tesla

"The scientists today think deeply, instead of clearly. One must be sane to think clearly, but one can think deeply and be quite insane."

- Nikola Tesla

"If your hate could be turned into electricity, it would light up the whole world."

- Nikola Tesla

"If you want to find the secrets of the universe, think in terms of energy, frequency and vibrations."

- Nikola Tesla

"Peace can only come as natural consequences of universal enlightenment."

- Nikola Tesla

"An eye for an eye only ends up making the whole World blind."

- Mahatma Gandhi

"Where there is love there is life."

- Mahatma Gandhi

"In a gentle way. You can shake the world."

- Mahatma Gandhi

"Hate the sin, love the sinner."

- Mahatma Gandhi

"The future depends on what we do in the present."

- Mahatma Gandhi

"Earth provides enough to satisfy every man's needs, but not every man's greed."

- Mahatma Gandhi

"Nobody can hurt me without my permission."

- Mahatma Gandhi

"Happiness is when what you think, what you say, and what you do are in harmony."

- Mahatma Gandhi

"Weak can never forgive. Forgiveness is an attribute of the strong."

- Mahatma Gandhi

"The season of failure is the best time for sowing the seeds of success."

- Paramhansa Yogananda

"Let my Soul smile through my heart and my heart smile through my eyes, that I may scatter rich smiles in sad hearts."

- Paramhansa Yogananda

"Remain calm, serene, always in command of yourself. You will then find out how easy it is to get along."

- Paramhansa Yogananda

"Forget the past. The vanished lives of all men are dark with many shames. Human con- duct is ever unreliable until man is anchored in the Divine. Everything in future will improve if you are making a spiritual effort now."

- Paramhansa Yogananda

"True wisdom: understanding how the One Consciousness becomes all things."

- Paramhansa Yogananda

"What counts in life is not the mere fact that we have lived. It is what difference we have made to the lives of others that will determine the significance of the life we lead."

- Nelson Mandela

'Quotes' by - Pramod Sonar

"Science is a big toy given by God to humans, for his intellectual development, entertainment, enjoyment, and evolution."

"Always be Alert, Awake, Aware, Attentive, and Active for your integral development."

"When you are peaceful and joyful your inner innate divine beauty is projected, it shines."

"Being one with Parabrahman, experiencing oneness, union of your divine Soul with the Supreme Soul is the highest activity of divine friendship. God is our eternal friend."

"Everyone and everything, is independent, interdependent, interconnected and integrated. All is One and One is all."

"Those who dare to look at their own darkness see the light"

"Everything is recreated in newness from moment to moment, it is a great miracle."

"For the change you want, do dharma and karma for change."

"Deep meditation practice is to witness the witnesser, observe the observer, see the seer, know the knower, and enjoy the beauty of enjoyer."

"Zero-point & Infinity co-exist. Infinite possibilities exist everywhere."

"Remember what you have forgotten about your "True Self."

"God has created everything in this universe with a purpose. Each of his creation is unique, wonderful & beautiful. So, you are that purpose. The meaning of life is to find one's own purpose, and to live and enjoy a purposeful life to give its meaning."

"Divinity is immeasurably small, fine, and subtle with infinite potency, present everywhere. It is Akhand (whole, unbroken, uninterrupted, complete), entire cosmos is one. Divinity is most sacred and secret."

"Science can never develop an instrument for measuring and knowing Paramchaitanya (Supreme divine sentient spiritual energy), because God has already created this instrument as human being."

"Absolute pure awareness is joyful enjoyment. Awareness increases enjoyment which increases awareness."

"Being already God is a wonder, becoming like God is greatness, that's why God loves his children most those who devotedly try to become great like him."

"Celebrate all differences, variegatedness, uniqueness of each manifestation of nature in its pristine Beauty."

"Observe and witness your true Self being nurtured, grow, and evolve in the true Spirit of humanity and divinity, experiencing and enjoying beauty of life in love, light, and joy of God."

"Life is divine beauty to be enjoyed naturally moment by moment, knowing 'Joy begets Joy'."

"Do not compete but be unconsciously competent."

"Be aware of awareness, settle in your awareness, submerge your mind & intellect in awareness, enjoy beauty of your awareness resting on your Soul, witness is the witnessing beauty of your Soul in enjoyment."

"From carbon the world has got two great magnificent and beautiful availabilities, one is diamond which shines in black coal mine and second is living creatures to a superhuman who enlightens life and spreads Divinity, and Divine Glory."

'Om' Mahaguru! Let my feet and body be with the fear of 'Mahaprabhu' ('The Almighty Lord'); Let my hands and heart be with the compassion and love of 'Mahaprabhu'; Let my eyes, ears, intellect, and mind be with the understanding of 'Mahaprabhu'; and let my consciousness, awareness, spirit, and breath be like 'Mahaprabhu'; 'Om Jai'.

"Understanding the 'Supreme Understanding': Understand that the understanding you understand is not the understanding of the 'Supreme Understanding' which understands everything. Understand this 'Supreme Understanding' by its grace in your wisdom Understanding. This is Understanding the 'Supreme Understanding."

"Peace is when you are established in your divine pristine Beauty of your Soul. Love emerges when you are at peace with Beauty. Love is the fragrance of Beauty which spreads spontaneously, sharing and spreading Joy everywhere. Miracles happen from Beauty. Beauty is one, unified, is everywhere in the entire Cosmos. Experience Beauty of Enjoyment of Beauty."

"Your greatest contribution to this world is to get your self-realization and spread Divinity."

"Always be in enjoyment of your innate inner Beauty of your Soul."

"Life is Blooming everywhere, there is Beauty everywhere, there is Joy everywhere. Relish this Joy together."

"Do not trust, believe, or have faith on any spiritual knowledge written or said by a spiritual personality. But with your open mind, heart, and wisdom understanding observe, introspect, and analyze the reality and truth in knowledge. Then after finding real spiritual knowledge accept, imbibe, and practice to live and act for your spiritual growth and upliftment and for the enjoyment of all. Always trust, believe, and have faith on the real spiritual divine eternal knowledge of truth."

"Maintain your peace & quietude, always be humble, polite, kind, compassionate and wise in your behavior and action. Be simple. Simplicity creates wonders and miracles."

"To Love it does not require any energy, in fact it itself energizes us and fills us with vitality, bliss & Joy. This eternal Joy you must share, thus it increases exponentially. Love is the essence of all."

"Beauty & Truth are foundation, Peace is the axis, Love, Bliss, & Compassion is the periphery, Joy is the fountain, Happiness & Contentment are the fruits, Forgiveness is the protection, Tolerance & Forbearance are the shields, and Non-Violence is the weapon of a wise Man."

"You must change and bring transformation daily for your betterment and Spiritual Ascent."

"One must selflessly engage oneself in the great service of humanity, and nature, and you will effortlessly experience divine wonders, love, peace, bliss, happiness, joy and beauty."

"In attachment, there is nothing. In detached unconditional love & compassion, there is everything."

"For the freedom of individual Soul, God has created Heaven & Hell and the Universal Laws of Nature."

"The Universal all-pervading divine spiritual power and energy known as 'Kundalini' which is creative, sustaining, nurturing, destructive (de-constructive), transformative and life-giving power of divine. 'Kundalini' which is latent power within us gets itself actualized when a 'Yogi' works creatively as an expression of divine beauty, and with love and compassion creates for the enjoyment of all. For life is creation for Creation in constant newness."

‘MahaAtmanubhuti’

The Great Self Realization

Concentration - Meditation - Liberation (Dharana - Dhyana - Samadhi)

Concentration (Dharana):

Concentration means the ability to give all your attention or effort to something. The ability to think carefully about something you are doing and nothing else. Direction of attention to a single object. Focus all your attention on your task. Attention control refers to an individual’s capacity to choose what they pay attention to and what they ignore. Primarily mediated by the frontal areas of the brain including the anterior cortex, attentional control is related to other executive functions such as working memory. The objective of concentration in meditational practices is to develop a single-minded powerful attention directed at some object: an image, a breath, a word, or phrase. Continually returning one’s attention to this object develops one’s ability to remain calm, focused, and grounded. Focusing your mind is an art. For deep concentration, your body must be relaxed, releasing all tensions and worries and your breathing must be balanced. You must be enthusiastic and interested in the Act of concentration. It is a dedicated devotional Practice. Be focused in the moment. Can you think of any task that can be performed perfectly without giving it your full attention? Many activities, playing sports, music, art, dancing, reading etc. and mainly Meditation require high levels of concentration. When you are mindful at will, your ability to concentrate naturally increases. Mindfulness picks the objects of attention. Concentration does the actual work of holding the attention steady on that chosen object, both are simultaneously important for meditation; concentration is a wholesome one- pointedness of mind. True concentration is free from contaminations; it is when the mind is calm, quiet, clear, pure, serene, and divine. It is a state in which the mind is gathered-together and thus gains power & intensity. Mindfulness is the intellectual understanding faculty which brings great wisdom, concentration is the tool, laser like focus to bring wisdom to practice. If your body and mind are pure and you practice concentration devotedly and faithfully, your mind can be made a searchlight of infinite power. There is no limit to its scope. "If, therefore, thine eye be single, thy whole body shall be full of light." - said Jesus Christ.

The faculty of concentration is innate in every living creature. Among animals, we see a tiger or lion gathering his strength by a moment of absolute stillness before he springs upon his prey. That automatic, instinctive power we all possess, but with the majority of people it is not cultivated, and we never shall have the full use of it until we gain conscious command over our mental and spiritual forces. When our scattered mental forces are gathered up and focused, the mind becomes like a bright searchlight, by means of which we investigate the latent powers of our innermost being. As we grow more awareness of these hidden forces and learn to use them well, we become more proficient in life. One must set higher goals and aims in life and use body,mind and spirit in co-ordination to achieve one's pointed purpose.

Mindful Concentration is the greatest tool to make 'Impossible' to 'I Am Possible'; to make everything possible. Concentration means wholeness, unity and equilibrium. "Shri Krishna" declares in the Gita! "O Arjuna, the practice of Yoga is not for him who eats too much or who does not eat at all, nor for him who sleeps too much or who keeps awake in excess. He who is moderate in eating and recreation, moderate in his efforts in work, moderate in sleep and wakefulness, his practice of Yoga destroys all misery."

Concentration is a definite cure for all manner of mental disturbances. As we focus our mind on a constructive principle, uneasiness, restlessness, worry, the attitude of self-depreciation, all these ailments are crowded out of our system. Concentration is an art which we must learn by degrees and directing the mind toward that which is positive, creative, constructive, and helpful. Through mastery of concentration, one gains access everywhere, from the atom to Infinite. Concentration implies great Self-control, strength of mind, and strength of character. "Shri Krishna" in Gita gives a wonderful picture of the concentrated mind. "As a lamp placed in a windless spot does not flicker, the same simile is used to define Yogi of subdued mind practicing union with the Self". "When the mind is completely subdued by the practice of Yoga, and has attained serenity in that state, seeing Self by the Self, he is satisfied in the Self alone".

There is a danger in the development of the power of concentration —the danger of concentrating the mind upon an object and then being unable to detach it at will. So, along with the development of concentration, we must develop the power of detachment also. We must learn not only to attach the mind to one thing exclusively, but also to detach it at a moment's notice and place it upon something else.

Meditation (Dhyana):

Meditation is the act of giving your attention to only one thing, remaining in a silent and calm state It is the act of thinking about something very carefully and deeply for a long time, focusing the mind on a particular object, thought or activity - to train attention and awareness, and achieve a mentally clear and emotionally calm and stable state. Meditation is practically an individual experience and is very difficult to define. In the Vedas, Dhyana means meditation as part of the path towards enlightenment and, self-realization. Meditation may be used with the aim of reducing stress, anxiety, depression, and pain, and increasing peace, perception, self-concept, and well-being, a state of mental silence. Meditation is a precise technique for resting the mind and attaining a state of consciousness that is totally different from the normal waking state. It is the means for fathoming all the levels of selves and finally experiencing the center of consciousness within. In meditation, the mind is clear, relaxed, and inwardly focused with concentration. You are fully alert, awake, and aware, the mind is silent and no longer distracts as meditation deepens.

Meditation is a systematic technique for taking hold of and concentrating to the utmost degree our latent mental power. It consists in training the mind, especially attention and the will, so that we can set forth from the surface level of consciousness and journey into the very depths. Jesus said succinctly, "By their fruits, ye shall know them." If you want to know how people have progressed on the spiritual path, just watch them in the little interactions of everyday life. Are they patient? Cheerful? Sensitive to the needs of those around them? Are they free from compulsive likes and dislikes? Can they work harmoniously with others? If so, they are evolving. "Our knowledge is as deep as our actions." In the Katha Upanishad, we find a brilliant simile likening the mind to a chariot. Untrained horses can break away and run where they will, here and there, perhaps leading us to destruction, and what can we do about it? But trained horses -horse lovers know the delight of this - respond to even a light touch of the reigns. Similarly, the mind well trained in meditation respond to a light, almost effortless touch. We are thinking in full freedom. The Buddha said, "There is nothing so obedient as a disciplined mind- and there is nothing so disobedient as an undisciplined mind." The one-pointed mind, once we have obtained it, gives us tremendous loyalty and steadfastness. Such people are capable of sustained endeavor. We must develop voluntary control over our attention. We must know how to put it where we want. Divided attention can lead to physical exhaustion. What motivates us receives our attention, and whatever has our attention is what we see. In Meditation concentration becomes consecration, we plunge deeper into reality and closer to the Lord. Thoughts have a powerful imprint on the mind. The Buddha said, "All that we are is the result of what we have thought." Jesus Christ pointed out that just thinking about an action can affect our consciousness almost as much as the actual performance. The mystics say our world is upside down! To be secure everywhere is the mark of sophistication, to be unshakable is the mark of courage, to be permanently in love with every person is the mark of masculinity or femininity, to forgive is the mark of strength, to govern our senses and passions is the mark of freedom. When we stimulate the senses unduly, vitality flows out through them like water from a leaky pail, leaving us drained physically, emotionally, and spiritually. Those who indulge themselves in sense stimulation throughout their lives often end up exhausted, with an enfeebled will and little capacity to love others. But when we train the senses, we conserve our vital energy, the very stuff of life.

People have fire of conflict, anger, jealousy etc. within oneself—the fire, which takes away our peace and leaves us in pieces. Whenever we are in conflict, our peace, our ease, and our serenity are disturbed and this conflict is the fire, which ravages our well-being. The source of the conflict is choice. Human being has a choice,

| | MEDITATION | |

| | CHAKRA MEDITATION | |

and this choice is the substratum, the basis of this conflict. The choice is to do or not to do. Every conflict arises out of a certain choice, but all choices do not lead to conflict.

The Lord Krishna says lift yourself by Your Self. A man should uplift himself by his own Self so let him not weaken this Self. For, this self is the friend of oneself, and this self in the enemy of oneself. Do not condemn yourself, because the moment you start condemning yourself you are unconsciously becoming an enemy to yourself. Your mind itself becomes your enemy. When you see with love, with friendliness, with care, without judgement, you become a friend to your own Self. Vedanta says it is not absence of thoughts, which is moksha. It is not that you must go beyond thoughts. For a wise person, wherever the mind goes, he is in Samadhi. When you start witnessing thoughts, you are not the thoughts. You are the observer. The thoughts are observed. You are in deep silence. The yogi should constantly practice concentration of heart, retiring into solitude, alone with the mind and body subdued, with the heart serene and fearless, with the mind controlled, and ever thinking of "The Lord". When the completely mastered mind rests serenely in the self- alone, free from longing after all desires, then is one called steadfast in the self. The state of detachment from the union with pain is called Yoga. Thus, always keeping the mind steadfast, the Yogi of subdued mind attains the peace residing in "The Lord", the peace that culminates in Moksha, Nirvana. An Awakened person, irrespective of the surrounding conditions will be joyous, effective, creative, and celebrative, abandoning without reserve all desires born of Sankalpa, and completely restraining, by the mind alone, the whole group of sense from their objects in all directions.

The Supreme bliss comes to that yogi of perfectly tranquil mind, with passions quieted, brahman- become, and freed from taint. With the heart concentrated by yoga, with the eye of evenness for all things, he beholds the self in all beings and all beings in the self. He who perceives pleasure or pain everywhere, by the same standard as be applies to himself, that yogi is regarded as the highest.

Yoga Jignyasu - One, who has got this commitment towards Yoga; One who, is an enquirer of Yoga.

Shabda Brahma Iti Vartate - He goes beyond the verbal meaning of the Veda. The Vedas talk of freedom. Just the word freedom is not freedom. Freedom means beyond the word. Such a person doesn't stop at the word freedom, but freedom becomes his experience. It will be his Aparoksha Anubhuti. Here "The Lord" uses the beautiful expression "Shabda Brahma" - That which goes beyond the word Brahma. This refers to the Veda, the central message of which is freedom, and "Lord Krishna" says a yogi goes beyond the verbal meaning of the word freedom. One should appreciate the distinction that there can be a verbal meaning and existential knowing. So often there is an illusion that "I know". This illusion can itself become a big stumbling block in knowing. This is colorful ignorance. A person may talk of 'freedom' but deep within he may be totally shackled. A yogi goes beyond this deadly trap of verbal understanding. "Lord Krishna", says of all yogis, he who with the inner self is merged in me, is considered by me the most steadfast. The "separate self" is merged with the "unified self", or when the 'individual' gets merged with the 'total', such a yogi is the most steadfast one. A Yogi anchored in this vision goes through the ultimate flowering of consciousness. Hence Meditation is the space in which this ultimate flowering happens. In such a space, there is an experience of poetry and wonderment of Oneness. In Shiva Sutras, there is a verse which says "Vismayaha Yoga bhoomika", which means that the inner wonderment is the very basis of Yoga. When a Yogi experiences this oneness, the world around him becomes poetry and dance.

"Vismaya Yoga Bhumika"- Vismaya means wonderment, astonishment, amazement, curiosity. Just look at the small children around and look at the wonder on their faces. A small child is curious and always wondering, asking questions. As we grow, we lose that child in us, we lose the wonder. We look around - look at the vast sky - white clouds floating - the sun, moon, stars - the rivers, mountains, oceans - different colors - different sounds – birds, trees, fruits - different species and so much more... The only thing we can do is a wonder, if only we dropped the false front of maturity. We are thinking beings, but we are thinking a bit too much. It's now Time to Stop and be in Wonder, be in total Amazement, be in Joy. If there is no wonder, how could one become a Yogi? A Yogi is like a small child - Innocent, Amazed, and Natural. Through meditation, you remove layers of ignorance. You meet the small child seated in our heart.

Pranayama helps us to get balanced and integrated. Pranayama is not about inhaling & exhaling. That is happening anyway without our awareness all through our life. It is about being aware of our body, energy, and the breath and how the Prana (vital life force) flows in through our breath being in touch with our life force energy. It is the understanding and experience of oneness. This oneness is the "Udyamo Bhairava" (Shiv Sutra) - Meditation happens... Body- Mind - Spirit - Soul all aligned, all superficial layers get dropped. That is when Vismaya happens, and then one becomes a Yogi.

Patanjali Yoga-Sutras - Noblest of sages is "Patanjali" who gave 'Yoga' for serenity and sanctity of mind, grammar for clarity and purity of speech, and medicine for perfection of health. Where there is Yoga, there is prosperity and bliss with freedom. Yoga is an art, a science, and a philosophy. It touches the life of man at every level, physical, mental, and spiritual. It is a practical method for making one's life purposeful, useful, and noble. It deals with man's development as a whole in thought, speech, and action. In Patanjali's Yoga Darshana, Darshana means "vision of the Soul" and mirror. The effect of Yoga is to reflect the thoughts and actions of the aspirant as in a mirror. The Ultimate effect of Yoga is to experience the effortless, indivisible state of the Seer. Dharma is the seed of Yoga & kaivalya (Emancipation) is its fruit. Kaivalya is the state, which is motiveless and devoid of all worldly aims and qualities of nature.

Patanjali Ashtanga Yoga (The eight limbs of Yoga) - The eight limbs are Yama, Niyama, Asana, Pranayama, Pratyahara, Dharana, Dhyana and Samadhi, sequence from outer to the inner.

1. **Yama** - Abstinences, external disciplines. There are five Yamas. 1)Ahimsa: Non-Violence, non-harming other living beings. 2) Satya: Truthfulness, non-falsehood 3) Asteya: Non- stealing 4) Brahmacharya: Chastity, continence marital fidelity, restraint 5) Aparigraha: non- avarice, non-possessiveness, non-covetousness. Yama - (Attitudes toward our environment).
2. **Niyama** - Virtuous habits and observances. Attitude toward ourselves. There are five Niyamas - 1) Shaucha: Purity, cleanliness, clearness of mind, speech, and body 2) Santosha: contentment, acceptance of others, acceptance of one's circumstances, optimism for Self.

3) Tapas: persistence, perseverance, austerity, asceticism, self-discipline. 4) Svadhyaya: Study of Vedas, sacred scriptures, study of self, self-reflection, introspection of thoughts, speech, and actions, 5) Ishvarapranidhana: Contemplation of the Ishvara (God/Supreme being, Brahman, True Self, Unchanging Reality), Surrender to God.

3. **Asana (Physical Postures)** - Is a posture that one can hold for a time staying relaxed, steady, comfortable, and motionless. The meditation posture should be steady and comfortable. In the Yogic view, the body is a temple of Spirit - Soul.
4. **Pranayama** – It is the control of the breath, from the Sanskrit 'Prana' - Breath and 'Ayama' – Restraint. The practice of consciously regulating the breath (inhalation, the full pause, exhalation, and the empty pause).
5. **Pratyahara**- In Sanskrit 'Prati' - (against or Contra) and 'ahara' (bring near, fetch). Pratyahara is drawing within one's awareness. It is a process of retracting the sensory experience from external objects. It is a step of self-extraction and abstraction. Pratyahara is not consciously closing one's senses or eyes to the sensory world; it is consciously closing one's mind processes to the sensory world. Pratyahara empowers one to stop being controlled by the external world, fetches one's attention to seek self-knowledge and experience the freedom innate in one's inner world. Pratyahara marks the transition of Yoga experience from the first four limbs of Patanjali Astanga Yoga, that perfect external forms, to the last three limbs that perfect the yogin's inner state, moving from outside to inside, from the outer sphere of the body to the inner sphere of the spirit.
6. **Dharana** – It means concentration, introspective focus and one pointedness of mind. The root of the word is 'Dha' (Dhr) meaning, "to hold maintain, keep". Dharana is holding one's mind onto a particular inner state, subject, or topic of one's mind. The mind is fixed on a mantra, or one's breath, or on chakras, any place, or an object one wants to observe, or a concept/idea in one's mind, on a "Deity", Divinity. Fixing the mind means one-pointed focus, without drifting of mind, and without jumping from one topic to another.

7. **Dhyana** – It means "contemplation, reflection and profound abstract meditation. Dhyana is contemplating, reflecting on whatever Dharana has focused on. Focused on Aradhya Devata (Personal Ideal deity), Dhyana is its contemplation. If concentration was on one object, Dhyana is the non-judgemental, non-presumptuous observation of that object. If the focus was on a concept / idea, 'Dhyana' is contemplating that concept / idea in all its aspects, forms, and consequences. Dhyana is uninterrupted train of thought current of cognition, flow of awareness: Dhyana is integrally related to Dharana, one leads to other. Dharana is a state of mind, Dhyana the process of mind. Dhyana is distinct from Dharana in that the meditator becomes actively engaged with its focus. Patanjali defines contemplation (Dhyana) as the mind process, where the mind is fixed on something, and then there is "a course of uniform Modification of knowledge." Adi Shankara, in his commentary on Yoga Sutras, distinguishes Dhyana from Dharana, by explaining Dhyana as the Yoga state when there is only the "stream of continuous thought about the object, uninterrupted by other thoughts of a different kind for the same object"; Dharana, states Shankara, is focussed on one object, but aware of its many aspects and ideas about the same object. Shankara gives the example of a yogin in a state of Dharana on morning sun may be aware of its brilliance, color and orbit; the yogin in dhyana state contemplates on Sun's orbit alone for example, without being interrupted by its color, brilliance or other related ideas.
8. **Samadhi** - Samadhi literally means "putting together, Complete Integrating, joining, combining with, union, harmonious whole, trance". Samadhi is oneness with the subject of meditation. There is no distinction, during the eighth limb of Yoga, between the actor of meditation, the act of meditation and the subject of meditation. Samadhi is that spiritual state when one's Mind is so absorbed in whatever it is contemplating on, that the mind loses the sense of its own identity. The thinker, the thought process, and the thought fuse with the subject of thought. There is only oneness, Samadhi, Enlightenment.

The ultimate effect of following the path laid out by Patanjali is to experience the effortless, indivisible state of the Seer. There are four most important aspects for a Yogi. Samadhi (based on contemplation), Sadhana (on practice), Vibhuti (on properties and powers), Kaivalya (on emancipation and freedom).

The word Samadhi is made up of two components. 'Sama' means level, alike, straight, upright, impartial, just, good & virtuous, and 'adhi' means over and above, the indestructible seer and then diffusing its essence, impartially and evenly, throughout every particle of the intelligence, mind, senses, and body. Through the discipline of Yoga, both actions and intelligence go beyond the qualities (The Three Gunas Rajas, Tamas & Sattva) and the seer comes to experience his own soul with crystal clarity, free from the relative attributes of nature and actions. This state of purity is Samadhi. Yoga is thus both the means and the goal. Yoga is Samadhi and Samadhi is Yoga. There are two main types of Samadhis. Sabija or Samprajnata Samadhi is attained by deliberate effort, using for concentration an object or idea as a 'seed'. Nirbija samadhi is without seed or support. Freedom, that is direct experience of Samadhi, can be attained only by disciplined conduct and renunciation of Sensual desires and appetites. This is brought about through adherence to the 'twin Pillars' of Yoga, Abhyasa and Vairagya. Patanjali defines yoga as the restraint of Chitta (Consciousness). Chitta has three components: mind (manas), intelligence (buddhi) and ego (ahamkara) which combine into one composite whole. 'Self' represents a person as an individual entity. Its identity is separate from mind, intelligence, and ego.

"MahaPrabhu", "God", "Paramatman" or "Purusha Vishesan", is known as the "Universal Soul", the seed of all. The individual Soul, jivatman or Purusa, is the seed of the individual Self. The Soul is therefore distinct from the Spirit Self. Soul is formless, while Self assumes a form. The Soul is an entity, separate from the body and free from the spirit self. Soul is the very essence of the core of one's being. Like mind, the soul has no actual location in the body. It is latent, exists everywhere. The moment the Soul is brought to awareness of itself, it is felt anywhere and everywhere. Unlike the Spirit Self, the Soul is free from the influence of nature, and is thus universal. The Soul perceives spiritual reality and is known as the Seer (Drishta).

Non-attachment does not mean drawing inwards and shutting oneself off but involves carrying out one's responsibilities without incurring obligation or inviting expectation. It is between attachment and detachment, a step towards detachment. Detachment brings discernment: seeing each and everything or being as it is, in its purity, without bias or self-interest. It is a means to understand nature and its potencies. Once nature's purposes are grasped, one must learn to detach oneself from them to achieve an absolute independent state of existence, where in the soul, radiates its own light.

Mind, intelligence, and ego, revolving in the wheel of desire (kama), anger (krodha), greed (lobha), infatuation (moha), pride (Mada) and malice (Matsarya), tie the sadhaka to their imprints; he finds it exceedingly difficult to come out of the turmoil and to differentiate between the mind and the Soul. Practice of yoga and renunciation of sensual desires take one towards spiritual attainment.

Practice demands four qualities from the aspirants: dedication, zeal, uninterrupted awareness, and long durations (Patience). Renunciation also demands four qualities: disengaging the senses from action, avoiding desire, stilling the mind, and freeing oneself from cravings. Practitioners are also of four levels, mild, medium, keen, and intense. They are categorized into four stages: beginners; those who understand the inner functions of the body; those who can connect the intelligence to all parts of the body; and those whose body, mind, spirit Self and Soul have become one.

As the Sadhaka intensifies his effort with faith and vigour and uses his previous experience as a guide to proceed from the state of void or loneliness, towards the non-void state of aloneness or fullness, where freedom is absolute. The Sadhaka experiences Nirbija Samadhi or Dharma Megha Samadhi.

In the practice of Yoga, first and foremost, Patanjali outlines the method of surrender of oneself to God (Ishvara). This involves detachment from the world and attachment to God. Patanjali defines God as the Supreme Being, totally free from afflictions and the fruits of action, in Him abides the matchless seed of all knowledge. He is first and Foremost amongst all masters and teachers, unconditioned by time, place and circumstances. His symbol is the syllable 'Aum' "Om". This sound is divine: it stands in praise of Divine fulfilment; "Om" is the universal sound (Shabda Brahma). It is the seed of all words and sound. "Om" represents communion with God, the soul and with the Universe. "Om" is known as Pranava, or exalted praise of "The Almighty Lord". God is worshipped by repeating or chanting "Om" ("AUM"), because sound vibration is the subtlest and highest expression of Nature. Mahat belongs to this level. Even our innermost unspoken thoughts create waves of sound vibration. So "Om" represents the elemental movement of sound, which is the foremost form of energy. "Om" is therefore held to be the primordial way of worshipping God. At this exalted level of phenomenal evolution, fragmentation has not yet taken place. "Om" offers complete praise, neither partial nor divided: none can be higher. Such prayer begets purity of mind in the sadhaka and helps him to reach the goal of Yoga. "Om" repeated with feeling and awareness of its meaning, overcomes obstacles to Self-Realization.

In Sadhana of a Sadhaka, the journey from Yama to Pratyahara, the first five limbs of Patanjali Yoga Sutra ends in the sea of tranquility, which has no ripples. If Chitta is the sea, its movements (Vrittis) are the ripples. Body, mind, and consciousness are in communion with the Soul; they are now free from attachments and aversions, memories of the place and time. The impurities of body and mind are cleansed, the dawning light of wisdom vanquishes ignorance. Innocence replaces arrogance and pride, and the seeker becomes the Seer.

Cosmology of nature: In Samkya philosophy, the process of evolution and the interaction of spirit and energy-matter, essence and form are carefully explained. To follow nature's evolution from its subtlest concept to its grossest or most dense manifestation, we must start with root nature, Mula-Prakriti. At this phase of its development, nature is infinite, attributeless and undifferentiated. We may call this phase 'noumenal' or alinga (without mark): it can be apprehended only by intuition. It is postulated that the qualities of nature, or gunas, exist in Mula-Prakriti in perfect equilibrium; One-third Sattva, one-third rajas and one third tamas. Root nature evolves into the phenomenal stage, called linga (with mark). At this point, a disturbance or redistribution takes place in the gunas, giving nature its turbulent characteristic, which is to say that one quality will always predominate over the other two (though never to their entire exclusion). The first and most subtle stage of the phenomenal universe is Mahat, cosmic intelligence. Mahat is the great principle, embodying a spontaneous motivating force in nature, without subject or object, acting in both creation and dissolution. Nature further evolves into the stage called a visesa (universal or non-specific) which can be understood by the intellect but not directly perceived by the senses. To this phase belongs to the subtle characteristics of the five elements, which may be equated with the infra-atomic structure of elements. These may be explained at a basic level as the inherent quality of smell in earth (Prithvi), of taste in water (aap/Jal), of sight or shape in fire (tej/Agni), of touch in air (vayu), and of sound in ether (akasha). The 'I' principle is also in this group (Individual Ego). The final stage, visesa, in which nature is specific and obviously manifest, includes the five elements, the five senses of perception (ears, eyes, nose, tongue and skin), the five organs of action (arms, legs, mouth, generative, and excretory organs), and lastly the mind, or the eleventh sense. So, in all, there are twenty four principles (tattvas) of Nature, and a twenty fifth: Purusha, Atman, or Soul. Purusha permeates and transcends nature, without belonging to it. Purusha has spirit self. Atmatattva: It interacts with the Prakriti, with this interaction there is a play of Spirit and Energy which is witnessed by the Soul (Atman). Spirit and Energy are interconnected by Cosmic Intelligence, Supreme Understanding. When Purusha stirs the other principles into activity, it is the path of evolution. Its withdrawal from nature is the path of involution.

If Purusha interacts virtuously with the properties of nature, Bliss is experienced; for such a Purusha, Prakriti becomes a heaven. If wrongly experienced, it becomes a hell.

Purusha, is the Seer or the Soul, is absolute pure knowledge. Unlike nature (Prakriti), which is subject to change, purusha is eternal and unchanging. Free from the qualities of nature, it is an absolute knower of everything. The seer is beyond words, and indescribable. It is the intelligence, one of nature's sheaths, which enmeshes the seer in the playground of nature and influences and contaminates its purity. As a mirror, when covered with dust, cannot reflect clearly, so the Seer, though pure, cannot reflect clearly if the intelligence is clouded. The aspirant who follows the eightfold path of Yoga develops discriminative understanding, Viveka, and learns to use the playground of nature to clear the intelligence and experience the Seer. Everyone has an inborn desire to develop sensitivity and maturity in intelligence. That is why God has provided the Principles of Nature - so that the seer can commune with them and make the fullest use of them for his intellectual and spiritual growth. Nature is there to serve its Master, the Seer, Purusha or Atman (Soul), the inner being of man/woman.

Patanjali speaks of the seven states of understanding or wisdom (Prajnya) that emerge from the release of nature's contact with the seer. First, let us identify the seven corresponding states of ignorance or avidya:

1) Smallness, feebleness, insignificance, inferiority, meanness ...
2) Unsteadiness, fickleness, mutability ...
3) Living with pains, afflictions, misery, agony...
4) Living with the association of pain.
5) Mistaking the perishable body for the Self.
6) Creating conditions for undergoing sorrow.
7) Believing that union with the Soul (Yoga) is impossible and acting as though that were so.

The Seven States of Wisdom are:

1) Knowing that which must be known.
2) Discarding that which is to be discarded.
3) Attaining that which must be attained.
4) Doing that which has to be done.
5) Winning the goal that is to be won.
6) Freeing the intelligence from the pull of the three gunas of nature.
7) Achieving emancipation of the Soul so that it shines in its own light.

These seven states of wisdom are interpreted as right desire, right reflection, disappearance of memory and mind, experiencing pure sattva or the truth (reality), indifference to praise and blame, reabsorption of phenomenal creation, and living in the vision of the Soul. They may be further simplified as:

1) Understanding the body within and without.
2) Understanding energy and it uses.
3) Understanding Mind.
4) Consistency of Will.

5) Awareness of Experience.
6) Awareness of pure quintessence, sentience, and Beauty.
7) Understanding that the individual spirit Soul, jivatman, is a particle of the 'Universal Spirit Soul', 'Paramatman'.

The seven frontiers of awareness also correlate with the five sheaths or Koshas of the Body. Consciousness is the sixth, and the inner Spirit -Self, the seventh.

Patanjali describes the seven states of awareness as:

1) Emerging consciousness (Vyutthana Chitta)
2) Refraining Consciousness (Nirodha Chitta)
3) Sprouted Consciousness (Nirmana Chitta)
4) Tranquil Consciousness (Shanta / Stheer Chitta, Prasanna chitta)
5) One-pointed attention (Ekagra Chitta)
6) Rent, fissured consciousness (Chidra Chitta)
7) Pure Consciousness (Paripakva, Divya Chitta).

It is also possible to consider physical, physiological, ethical, neurological, emotional, intellectual, and spiritual domains as the seven states of Awareness. When one rests on the vision of the Soul, divinity is felt in this empirical state. Bringing the intelligence, buddhi, to a refined, tranquil steadiness is Dharana. When this is achieved, buddhi is re-absorbed by a process of involution into the consciousness, Chitta, whose inherent expression is a sharp awareness but without focus. This is Dhyana. Buddhi is the activator of Pure Chitta. The Blending of Awareness and tranquility brings about a state of Virtue, which is a powerful ethic, or Shakti of the Soul, the culmination of Intelligence and Consciousness. This culturing of intelligence is an evolution and virtue is its special quality. Maintenance of this civilized, cultured, virtuous state leads to a perfect propriety, wherein the intelligence continues to be refined and the sadhaka moves ever closer to the spiritual zenith of 'Yoga'.

Intelligence and consciousness of a Yogi now rise to the levelof the Soul. As honey tastes the same from whichever side of the honeycomb it is taken, so, in the Yogi, the body cells, senses, mind, Intelligence, consciousness and conscience equally reflect the light of the Soul. All parts of the Seer appear as the Soul. This is Kaivalya.

It comes when the powers which attract the misguided, but distract the yogi's consciousness, are renounced. Kaivalya means eternal emancipation. It is a release from Karma: the consequences and obligations of our actions. Kaivalya is an absolute, indivisible state of existence. In it, the Yogi is stripped of thoughts, mind, intellect, and ego, and freed from the play of the gunas of nature, Sattva, Rajas and tamas. He becomes a Gunatitan, a pure, flawless person. Kaivalya is the crowning of the Yogic Sadhana, a state of fullness of the Soul and of unique aloneness.

"Yogah Chittavritti Nirodhah": Yoga is the cessation of movements in the consciousness. Yoga is defined as restraint of fluctuations in the consciousness. It is the art of studying the behavior of consciousness, which has three functions: Cognition, conation or volition, and motion.

This vital Patanjali Yoga Sutra contains the definition of Yoga: the control or restraint of the movement of consciousness, leading to their complete cessation. Chitta is the vehicle which takes The Mind (manas) towards the Soul (atma). Yoga is the cessation of all vibration in the seat of consciousness. It is extremely difficult to convey the meaning of the word chitta because it is the subtlest form of cosmic intelligence (mahat). Mahat is the great principle, the source of the material world of nature (Prakriti); as opposed to the soul, which is an offshoot of nature. The principles of Purusha and Prakriti are the source of all action, volition, and silence.

'MahaGunaDharma'

Glorious Spiritual Personality Qualities

The Integral Global Personality Development:

The Personality of a person is the inner, innate potential of his spirit, the fragrance of which spreads like a bloomed flower. The lion stands as a king of the jungle naturally and spontaneously, governed by nature without any elections or support. As so, you must sit on a throne, the seat of your Soul in your heart governed by nature and rule your kingdom as a King. Life is to weave the beautiful fabric of character and personality. Spiritually uplift and evolve yourself and enjoy the blossoming, blooming, shining, and sweetness of fruits of your life. Your personality must be felt by your presence and must be very attractive, magnetic, and impressive, no matter what your position may be in this material world. Although all human beings have most of the physical and mental resources and possess powers of various sorts, very few are masters in using these resources and powers they have, to develop their personality.

"He who is full of faith and virtue (moral goodness) possessed of repute and wealth, in whatever land he travels is everywhere respected," spoke the Buddha.

You should continuously introspect your improvements in personality development. To improve is to change, to be perfect is to change often. You must change your old uncreative habits and ways. You must workout new fresh better ideas and must aim towards perfection, always there are ways to improve yourself. "Where there is a will there is a way".

Many of the great rich moments in your life come from your inner hidden potentialities and capabilities. You have immense capabilities and potentialities which most people are unknown of. Many of you spend time going nowhere and lead a frustrated life full of illusion. This happens because you have not tried to explore yourself, your innate energies, and potencies. Most of you fail to cope up with problems created by our environment. Our self-concept that of ego of 'I-ness' and 'me', associated with whatever you do has tremendous influence on the way you think and act as whole. Our overall self-concept in fact tends to be an organized cluster of many selves. It helps to explain why we do not always act consistently. It is a common practice to identify our body images (how we perceive and feel about our body) our self-image (the self we see ourselves to be) our ideal self (the self we had like to be) and our social self (the way we feel others see us). Our tendency to see and act in a consistent manner is also strengthened by our self- esteem, the present evaluation of ourselves and the resulting feelings of worth associated with our self- concept. Self-awareness and mental training can help us to achieve miracles in our lives. We can thus overcome our mental block and self-doubts and tap our inner reservoir of energy to control our actions and environment without deliberate effort.

The amazing impact of this over destiny can hardly be over emphasized. Latest psychological research shows that an individual emotional quotient (EQ) contributes much more vibrantly to one's productivity and success in life than even much researched intelligence quotient. Daniel Goleman, on emotional intelligence states "what factors are at play when people of high IQ flounder and those of modest IQ do surprisingly well? I would argue that the difference quite often lies in the abilities called emotional intelligence, which include self-control, zeal and persistence, and the ability to motivate oneself. These skills can be taught to children giving them a better chance to use whatever intellectual potential the genetic lottery may have given them. These are the times, he further maintains when the fabric of society seems to unravel at even greater speed when selfishness, violence, and a meanness of spirit seem to be rotting the goodness of our communal lines. This is a growing evidence that fundamental ethical stances in life steam from underlying emotional capacities. For one impulse is the medium of emotion; the seed of all impulse is a feeling bursting to express itself in action. Those who are at the mercy of impulse— who lack self-control— suffer a moral deficiency. The ability to control impulse is the base of will and characters. By the same token, the root of altruism lies in empathy; the ability to read emotions in others. If there are two moral stances that our times call for, they are precisely these, self-restraint, and compassion.

Unravel your emotional tendencies and move easily through the maze of your own mental world. Prepare and practice your response to physical and psychological problems in the world of varying possibilities; so that if they do occur, you can respond to them completely and confidently. Understanding the interplay of brain structures that rule out moments of rage and fear or passion and joy reveals much about how we have learnt the emotional habits. The incredible power of your self-image has an amazing impact on your destiny. You must enable yourself to drift into a voyage of self-discovery and improvement which is the dire need of the hour. The present scenario of heightened technological and social changes has intensified that challenge of self-direction more than ever before. The need to learn more about ourselves and our world as means of directing our lives more efficiently is especially true in a democratic society like ours, where we enjoy a greater personal freedom and take greater pride in personal achievements than people in more traditional societies. Precisely for this very reason, we tend to be more vulnerable to psychological insecurity, confusion, and loneliness etc. Therefore, explore and unfold your mental mysteries to make your life happy and joyous.

Each one of us is born with uniqueness, an exclusive self which gives us our identity, the essence of our survival, the one that often says in so many ways, "Me, me, I want, I need affection, affirmation, power, recognition, security, achievements etc. We each have a dominant set of motivations and needs that shape our personality and behavior, based on what matters most to us, and what seems to be the best way to achieve that gratification of our inner desire. Everyone wants to be an achiever, whose theme song is "Climb every mountain". An internally motivated person with high self-set standards of excellence and goals are strongly driven by achievements. Attraction is the most important aspect or factor in this world. Personality is the one which attracts the most. That is why, most of the persons irrespective of their age and physical outlook have outstanding personality and attract people. You are what you attract. This inner, innate power of attraction is to be developed and maintained. This attraction brings you friendship with the people without any barriers whatever. You develop friendship with beautiful people and establish mutual bonding. It is a bonding of mutual love and attraction, giving joy to everyone.

Personal magnetism - personality of man is what really impresses immensely. Personality of man is of real gravity than his intellect, his words etc. The man who influences, who throws his magic, as it were, upon his fellow beings, is a dynamo of power, and when that man is ready, he can do anything and everything he likes, that personality put upon anything will make it work. In the philosopher, it is a faint personality that influences, in the great prophets, it is tremendous. In the former we touch intellect, in the latter we touch life.

The secret of all education is to develop the real knowledge of strengthening personality and practice it. The finest is our spirit and the grossest is the body. We also know that the greatest power is lodged in the fine, not in coarse. It is the fine that is really the seat of power, a source of Power. We can perceive thoughts only after they develop a great deal or after they become actions. We constantly complain that we have no control over our action, over our thoughts. But if we can get control over the fine movements, if we can get hold of thoughts at the root, before it has become thought, before it has become action, then it would be possible for us to control the whole. Develop method to analyze, investigate, understand, and finally grapple with those finer powers, the finer causes, then alone is it possible to have control over ourselves. The man who has control over his own mind assuredly will have control over every other mind. Know the secret of every mind. He who knows one lump of clay has known all the clay in the universe.

The need of the modern era is development of the integral personality. A modern human being must integrate within himself all essence and qualities, powers, and energies to fulfil his objectives and desires. The following are a few of the main qualities and essence to be developed and integrated to be a Glorious Personality. Qualities are physical health, mental health, emotional security, self-balancing, efficiency of work, self-control, quality and ways of doing work, activity, capacity to impress, confident responsibilities, constructive nature, positive attitudes, scientific vision, self-study nature, liberation from enigma, clarity, disclosure, self-confidence, self-image, creativity, decision power, great significant desire, balancing of all energies and qualities, purity, wisdom, innocence, beatitude, intelligence and skills, satisfaction, virtues, self-guidance, compassion, love, collectiveness, divine diplomacy, steadfastness, forgiving nature, truthfulness, joyous nature and many other good essential qualities. "Mahaprabhu" "The Almighty Lord" is all perfect, all powerful, the real personality of godhead. Complete surrendering unto The Lotus Feet of "The Lord", is the real beginning of one's glorious integral personality development.

MahaGunaDharma:

Glorious Spiritual Personality Qualities:

Patanjali's eightfold path of yoga, the first two steps of moral do's and don'ts "Yam and Niyama" are the foundation on which the Yogi begins to build his spiritual life. They harmonize body and mind with the divine laws of nature, or creation. The cosmic order (rita) that upholds the uni- verse is not different from the moral order that rules man's destiny. He who is unwilling to observe the universal moral precepts is not seriously determined to pursue truth.

In Bhagavad Gita 26 Soul qualities that make man God like are:

1) Fearlessness
2) Purity of heart
3) Steadfastness
4) Almsgiving
5) Self-restraint
6) Religious rites
7) Right study of scriptures
8) Self-discipline

9) Straightforwardness
10) Noninjury (Ahimsa)
11) Truth
12) Absence of wrath
13) Renunciation
14) Peaceful
15) Absence of fault finding
16) Compassion to all beings
17) Absence of greed
18) Gentleness
19) Modesty
20) Absence of restlessness
21) Radiance of character
22) Forgiveness
23) Patience, fortitude
24) Purity of body and mind
25) Non-hatred
26) Lack of conceit.

Cultivation of virtue is Central to the practice of Yoga as per the Vedas. It is also important to uphold Dharma and live righteously. The above divine qualities lead to ethical behavior, virtue, and liberation. Persons who have listened and internalized from the instructions of the learned Guru will be like Gods on Earth. 'That man whose hair stands on ends at the mere mention of the name of God, and from whose eyes flow tears of love he had indeed reached his liberation,' said Ramakrishna Paramhansa. Each person is potentially divine, and the goal of human life is to manifest that divinity in one's life. A person is called divine, when this divinity shines through his / her thoughts, speech, and actions. The qualities which help us manifest this inner divinity are called the divine qualities. These divine qualities free us from all our limitations and bondages. On the other hand, the qualities, which block our divinity create confusion and ignorance are called the demonic qualities. These demonic qualities, in turn, lead us toward miserable life and to our destruction. Such demonic qualities make us slaves of our weaknesses.

‘MahaSatsang – MahaUtsav’

Great Spiritual Collective Joyous Celebrations

Art-Music-Creativity-Singing-Dancing Wellness-Wellbeing

Mahasatsang:

Spiritual Satsang collective celebration is the most beautiful, blissful, and Joy sharing for the spiritual upliftment of Individual Sadhaka and the Collectivity as a whole. Sanskrit meaning of ‘Sat’ means true, truth, reality and ‘Sang’ means company or association, companionship of good divine natured people. Divine companionship is togetherness with the Sadguru (Spiritual Master). Collectivity of good righteous seekers of truth is to experience love, peace, bliss, happiness, joy, and beauty. In Mahautsav collective joy celebration, we celebrate our differences and uniqueness, we transcend different cultures and enjoy the beauty of creativity, art, music, wisdom, goodness and divine qualities and potencies of each other by sharing, caring, singing, and dancing. Happiness will not leave from where there is association with self-realized beings and with Sadguru. For the one whose association improves, everything indeed improves. Everything indeed gets ruined, for the one who gets into bad or harmful associations. Satsang is association with the Self and to understand what this world is and what it is not. Satsang is a sacred gathering for spiritual discourse. It is for the enjoyment of everyone’s freedom in loving friendliness. People who believe in God will be worshipping God in one way or the other.

Navavidha Bhakti:

There are nine types of bhakti ways of worshipping God in devotion.
Shloka from Shrimad Bhagwat Purana-

“Shravanam Kirtanam Vishnoh Smaranam Paadasevanam” |
“Archanam Vandanam Daasyam Sakhyam Aatmanivedanam” ||

The above shloka is told by Bhakta Prahlada, one of the greatest devotees of "Lord Vishnu". As per the above shloka, there are 9 types of Bhakti Marg (Devotional Path).

1. **Shravanam** - Hearing the names and glories of "The Lord". Hearing and listening the greatness of God with great interest in Satsang with other devotees.
2. **Keertanam** - Chanting the glories of "The Lord". Singing Bhajans (devotional songs) for pleasing "The Lord". Devotees can also dance in divine ecstasy while singing and playing music.
3. **Smaranam** - Remembering "The Lord". Smaranam is the constant remembrance of God. It is an advanced stage of Shravanam and Kirtanam.
4. **Padasevanam** - Serving the Lord's Lotus feet. To bow down to the great Lord keeping all our ego and attitude aside and asking "The Almighty Lord" to take care of us. By doing padasevanam, you are saying God that you are keeping your life at his feet.
5. **Archanam** - Worshipping the Lord. Archanam worship combines an external ritual with internal devotion, meditation. Archana can be done by offering flowers, fruits, leaves, food or even water to "The Lord". Bhavana (your heartily belief) is important.
6. **Vandanam** - Offering obeisance unto the Lord. It is an expression of gratitude to God. Whatever you are is all given by God. Vandana bhakti means saying thanks to God for all the things he has given. Be always grateful to God.
7. **Daasyam** - Serving 'The Lord' as his servant. In Daasya Bhakti, consider God as your Swami, Father, Mother, Mahaguru and everything to you, so what all you do, you will do to please God. This kind of Service, Seva and all kind activities will bring you close to God which leads to Moksha.
8. **Sakhyam** - Developing friendliness with God. God is our eternal friend. In sakhya bhakti, you consider God as your friend. So, in this form of bhakti, you will share all your happiness, sorrows, and every moment of your life with God. You always feel that God is with you in every point of your life.
9. **Aatma Nivedanam** - Total surrender of oneself to "The Lord". In Aatma Nivedanam, you should offer everything

to God including your body, mind, and soul. You should not have any personal and independent existence. You should leave all your karmas, dharmas and offer yourself to God. In Bhagavad Gita, lord Krishna says,
"Sarva Dharma Pari Tyajya Maamekam Sharanam Vraja..."
Which means leave all your karmas & dharmas and surrender to me totally and I will liberate you from all your sins.

Navavidha Bhakti comprises the nine ways to express devotion for "The Lord" which leads to moksha or liberation. Bhakti means faithfulness, love, and devotion to God. By complete devotion, one enters the Divine Kingdom of God. Bhakti is like nectar (Amrita), which when one drinks, leads to the experience of ultimate bliss (Sat-Chit-Ananda), which is not subject to change. All the desires of the devotee are fulfilled. Devotee transcends all the worldly bondages and becomes free from all Illusions. Complete surrendering unto the Lotus feet of "The Almighty Lord" "Mahaprabhu" is the first step of bhakti, when devotee becomes egoless. Bhakti is endowed by God's grace. Whatever work you do in your daily life, do it as a devotional service to "The Lord". All the creativity, art, music, singing, dancing when done as a devotional service to "The Lord" gives us real happiness and joy. We experience pure Bliss and enjoy the Nectar of Divinity. Devotees Dance and sing the praises of the lord's magnificence and omniscience with heartfelt devotion. It is said that Keertanam is the only way to achieve salvation in this KaliYuga.

Nataraja - "The Lord" (or King) of dance; is a depiction of "God Shiva" as the Cosmic Dancer. Shiva dancing in an aureole of flames, lifting his left leg and balancing over a demon or dwarf (Apasmara) who symbolizes ignorance. The two most common forms of Shiva's dance are the Lasya (the gentle form of dance) associated with the creation of the world, and the Tandav (the violent and dangerous dance) associated with the destruction of weary worldviews - weary perspectives and lifestyle. In essence, the Lasya and the Tandava are just two aspects of Shiva's nature; for he destroys for to create new, tearing down to build again. Deconstruction and transformation are essential to bring newness, bliss, and joy. It is the Beauty of the "Lord Shiva".

Dancing on the dwarf also symbolizes the passage of spirit from the divine Lord into material world. The Stoic face of Shiva represents his neutrality thus being in perfect balance. This dance is called Aananda Taandavam - the Dance of Bliss. The surrounding flames represent the manifest universe. The snake swirling around his waist is Kundalini (The divine sentient cosmic energy), the Shakti or divine force thought to reside within everything. (This also parallels the cords of life worn by the Brahmins to represent the second rebirth) Dwija (The newly born divine spirit in the heart of the devotee of "The Almighty Lord".)

Apasmara was a dwarf who represented Ego, ignorance, and epilepsy during the Tandava by God Shiva in the form of Nataraja, Apasmara was crushed by the right foot of Shiva and was killed. Apasmara is also a neurological disorder described in Ayurveda.

All the negativities, shadaripu's, ego, ignorance and disorders are destroyed by the grace of "Lord Shiva".

"The Lord Shiva" bestows many boons, blessings, bliss, and divine Joy on his sincere and truthful devotees.

| | Nataraja Dancing | |

| | Musical Bhajan Singing & Dancing | |

| | Beautiful Art | |

| | Traditional Garba Dance Joyous Celebration | |

Divine Classical Music - The roots of the classical music of India are found in the Vedas and in the ancient Natyashastra. The Indian classical music has two foundational elements, Raga and Taal. The Raga based on Swara (notes including microtones) forms the fabric of a melodic structure, while the Tala measures the time cycle. The Raga gives an artist a palette to build the melody from sounds, while the Tala provides them with a creative framework for rhythm improvisation using time.

The earliest Indian thought combined three Arts, Syllabic recital (Vadya), Melos (Geeta) and Dance (Nruttya). Sangeet became a distinct genre of art. There are different combinations of Swaras. Ragas contain melodic content, form, rhythm, and metric organization. It embeds musical meter. For example, the Gayatri

Mantra contains three metric lines of exactly eight syllables, with an embedded ternary rhythm. In the ancient traditions of India, two musical genres appeared, namely Gandharva (formal, composed, ceremonial, music) and Gaana (informal, improvised, entertainment music). The Gandharva music also implied celestial, divine associations, while the Gaana also implied singing. The classic Sanskrit text Natyashastra is at the foundations of the numerous classical music and dance traditions of India. Ancient Sanskrit text Sangitaratnakara literally means "The Ocean of Music and Dance". Sarangadeva, mentions and discusses ragas and talas. "MahaSaraswati" is the Goddess of music and knowledge as per the Vedas.

Music was born of our reverence for nature, and its Godly associations. An art of singing-music and Dancing is a Bridge to The Divine. 'Om' is the first sound of creation, with which all the ancient Vedic prayers start and end, as if emulating the sacred process of creations through sound. It is sacred means to interact with the creative principle of life; it has the potential to play the role of a bridge between the musicians and the divine, the higher aspect of life. It's a journey seeking that connection with the source and destiny of all life. Vedic shlokas or hymns, sung in specific musical and rhythmic patterns. Classical music influences our body, mind, and moods.It also enriches our Soul. Singing is the act of producing musical sounds with the voice and augments regular speech by the use of sustained tonality, rhythm, and a variety of vocal techniques. The singer must have Madhura Aawaj, a sweet, pleasant smooth and gentle voice.

‘MahaBhajans – MahaAartis’

Sublime Divine Harmony

The spiritual influence of Bhajans and Aartis is connected to many elements of music, with the melody and the harmony of bhajan, with its arrangements, with the depth of music and text synthesis, with its interpretation, with sincerity and expressiveness of performance. In the genre of Bhajans, there is a sub-genre of Kirtans-repetition, glorification of the name of God. They are performed under the accompaniment of various musical instruments and simply with the clapping of hands. Performers in the process of singing are immersed in a joyous sublime state, they do not get tired, but on the contrary, they are enthusiastic and inspiring. The secret is in the word - in the name of God. It is the main influencing and elevating element, it immerses the performer, and the listeners in the inner spiritual atmosphere of high feelings. This requires faith and love for God, desire and interest in spirituality and one’s spiritual development.

Sanskrit is a language, with most accurate deep compliance of the sound of every word with the subject, concept or the quality which means it. It corresponds with the truth. Every object, concept or feeling has its own vibration in the subtle world and in the higher worlds. It corresponds to the certain sound vibration - to a word on the Earth. Sanskrit is the oldest language, the language of Yogis, Mahatmas, the Vedic teachings, it is closest to such a harmonious correspondence of vibrations. Each letter has a universal spiritual meaning. Every word and especially thought expressed in Sanskrit deeply penetrate the subtle spiritual nature of man. They concern our spiritual centers and heart and cause a response in a form of a feeling and/or understanding. And then there is a process that is described by a proverbial expression. “When a man does one step towards God, God does ten steps towards him”.

A man’s readiness to perceive subtle, spiritual vibrations is manifested in the increase of sensitivity and retirement of his perceiving apparatus, in aspiration towards profound and high feelings towards God, and God steps forward to meet him and give a man what he desires to. If a person is ready, he shows interest in spiritual things, tries to feel, and see a high spiritual content in everything, and looks for spiritual meaning. A step to God with reference to Bhajans and music is when a person begins to listen to the Bhajans, to sing them, to listen to songs with spiritual texts, to listen to deep music, to reinterpret it, to put spiritual content in it, to listen to plainly beautiful songs that touch and inspire his soul, as well as reconsidering the content of these songs. In a human's soul, new higher, more subtle feelings are born. Sometimes they capture the soul so strongly and unexpectedly, that a man realizes, that they are of a different level, of a different quality, and they cannot be compared to anything from the previous period of his life.

Subtle vibrations of the sound of music, words, spiritual meanings found an echo in one's soul, they resonate with the high vibrations of spiritual centers and a person has strong feelings of no resemblance to anything-his own soul answers him sublimely and repeatedly. All these vibrations harmonize his spiritual centers, consistently entering in to, resonance with the corresponding centers. In this case, not only harmonization occurs, but also the energy saturation of centers. The same process occurs when one reads Mantras. Mantras, repeated in daily life, gradually harmonize, and imbue the subtle bodies with spiritual energy.

The emergence of high feelings is the answer of God to a man. This is the answer of Aatma - the particle of God in the soul of a man. The Spiritual Master leads us on the atomic plane; he tries to awaken us spiritually and inspires us to take steps towards God.

Bhajan means reverential spiritual devotional song for divine, God. Bhajans are prayers in song. Aarti is a ceremony in which lights are lit and offered up to Gods. Aarti is singing of hymns in praise of God. It is a worship of God. In Sanskrit, Aarti means something that removes darkness.

In Marathi language, it is also known as Mahaneeranjana. Aarti ceremony is symbolical offering to "The Lord". Aarti is devotional song in praise of "The Lord". It is an expression of love, gratitude, prayers, desires etc. Just as the lighted wick provides light and chases away darkness, the Vigilance of an individual can keep away the influence of the material world.

The universal Aarti "Om Jai Jagdish Hare" in praise of "The Almighty Lord" "Mahaprabhu" is very common revered Aarti in India. There are many Aartis in praise of deities which elevate us spiritually.

'Om Jai Jagdish Hare' Aarti: | Meaning:

Om Jai Jagdish Hare
Swami Jai Jagdish Hare
Bhakt jano ke sankat
Daas jano ke sankat
Kshan mein door kare
Om Jai Jagdish Hare

Joh dhyave phal paave
Dukh bin se mann ka
Swami dukh bin se mann ka
Sukh sampati ghar aave
Sukh sampati ghar aave
Kasht mite tann ka
Om Jai Jagdish Hare

Maat pita tum mere
Sharan padhon kiski
Swami sharan padhon kiski
Tum bin aur na duja
Prabhu bin aur na duja
Aas karoon kiski
Om Jai Jagdish Hare

Tum pooran paramatma
Tum antaryami
Swami tum antaryami
Paar brahm parmeshwar
Paar brahm parmeshwar
Tum sabke swami
Om Jai Jagdish Hare

Tum karuna ke saagar
Tum paalan karta
Swami tum paalan karta
Main moorakh khalkhami
Main sevak tum swami
Kripa karo bharta
Om Jai Jagdish Hare

O Lord of the entire universe
Mighty Lord of the entire universe
The sorrows of devotees
The sorrows of followers
In an instant, thou please eliminate them
O Lord of the entire universe

He who is immersed in devotion
Sadness ceases from his mind
Lord, sadness ceases from his mind
Joy and prosperity will enter the home
Joy and prosperity will enter the home
The problems of the body will go away
O Lord of the entire universe

You are my mother and father
Whom should I take refuge with
Lord, whom should I take refuge with
There is no one else but you
Lord, there is no one else but you
For whom should I wish
O Lord of the entire universe

You are the greatest soul
You are the omnipotent master
Lord, you are the omnipotent master
Perfect, absolute, and supreme God
Perfect, absolute, and supreme God
You are the Lord of everyone
O Lord of the entire universe

You are an ocean of mercy
You are the protector
Lord, you are the protector
I am a simpleton with vain desires
I am a servant, and you are the Lord
Grant me thy divine grace
O Lord of the entire universe

Vishay vikaar mitaao	Remove faults from the mind
Paap haro deva	Please defeat evil, O Lord
Swami paap haro deva	Lord, please defeat evil
Shradha bhakti badhao	Grow my faith and devotion
Shradha bhakti badhao	Grow my faith and devotion
Santan ki seva	So, I can serve the saints
Om Jai Jagdish Hare	O Lord of the entire universe
Tann, mann, dhan sab hai tera	Body, soul, wealth, everything is yours
Swami sab kuch hai tera	Lord, everything is yours
Swami sab kuch hai tera	Lord, everything is yours
Tera tujhko arpan	I'll give everything yours back to you
Tera tujhko arpan	I'll give everything yours back to you
Kya lage mera	Nothing is mine
Om Jai Jagdish Hare	O Lord of the entire universe
Om Jai Jagdish Hare	O Lord of the entire universe
Swami Jai Jagdish Hare	Mighty Lord of the entire universe
Bhakt jano ke sankat	The sorrows of devotees
Daas jano ke sankat	The sorrows of followers
Kshan mein door kare	In an instant, thou please eliminate them
Om Jai Jagdish Hare	O Lord of the entire universe

'Omkar Swaroopa'- Abhang

Omkaara swaroopa, sadguru samartha
Anthacha natha, tuja namo
Tuja namo, tuja namo, tuja namo

Namo maayabaapa, gurukripa dhana
Todia bandhana maayamoha
MohajaaLa maajhe koNa neerakshir
TujaviNa dayaaLa sadguru raaya

Sadguru raaya maajha aananda saagara
Trailokya aadhaar guru raava
Gururaava swami asey swayamprakaasha
Jyaa puDey udaasa chandraravi
Ravi, shashi, agni, neNti jya roopa
Ravi, shashi, agni, neNti jya roopa
Swaprakasharoopa neNe vede

Eka janardhani, guru parabrahma
Tayaache pe naam sadaa mukhi
Tuja namo, tuja namo, tuja namo

Meaning –

Oh, embodiment of Omkara, all powerful sat-Guru,
Lord of all those who are helpless,
Salutations to You!

Salutations to You who are our Mother and Father,
treasure of mercy and grace,
You break the bindings of illusions & worldly temptations,
If not You, my compassionate sat-Guru,
Salutations to You!

My sat-Guru is an ocean of joy and happiness,
He is the support of this Universe and of the three worlds,
My master, my Guru, He is the embodiment of light,
In front of Him, even the sun and the moon appear as dull,
He is Himself in the form of the sun and the moon,
He is both the Light and the Vedas,
Salutations to You!

My Guru verily is parabramha,
His name always dwells in my mouth,
Salutations to You!

MahaPrarthana – MahaStuti - MahaPratidnya (dhrudha vachan)

The Great Prayers – Praises - Affirmations

Prayer - A solemn request for help or expression of thanks addressed to God or deities. The act or ceremony of speaking to God. Act of devotion, invocation, worshipping. A Spiritual communion with God, as in Thanksgiving, adoration, or confession. Prayer is an invocation or act that seeks to activate a rapport with an object of worship through deliberate communication. Prayer can be performed alone or with group collectively. In Sanskrit, prayer means Prarthana, recitation of timeless verses. Prayers can be directed to fulfilling personal needs or deep spiritual enlightenment, and for the benefit of others. Ritual invocation is part and parcel of the Vedas. Prayer is performed with the palms of hands and joined together in Pranam with head slightly bowed down.

MahaPrarthana (Prayers) -

> "Om Gam Ganapatayei Namaha" "I bow to Lord Shri Ganesha who is the remover of all obstacles. I pray for blessings and protection."
>
> Vakra - Tunndda Maha – Kaaya, Suurya - Kotti Samaprabha |
> Nirvighnam Kuru Me Deva, Sarva - Kaaryeshu Sarvada | |

Salutations to Lord Shri Ganesha, who has a curved Trunk, who has a large body and whose splendor is same as million suns; O Deva, please make my undertakings free of obstacles, by extending your blessings in all my works Always!

> Om Bhuur-Bhuvah Svah, Tat-Savitur-Varennyam
> Bhargo Devasya Dhimahi, Dhiyo yo Nah Prachodayaat | |

Om, Pervading the Bhu Loka (Earth, consciousness of the physical plane), Bhuvar Loka (Antariksha, The Intermediate space, consciousness of Prana) and Swar Loka (Sky, Heaven, consciousness of the divine mind), that Savitur (Savitri, divine essence of the Sun) which is the most adorable, I meditate on that Divine Effulgence, may that awaken our intelligence (spiritual consciousness)

Karagre Vasate Lakshmi, Karamadhye Saraswati
Karamoole Sthitha Gauri, Prabhate Kar Darshanam
Samudra Vasane Devi, Parvatha Sthana Mandithe,
Vishnu Patni Namasthubhyam Pada Sparsham Kshamasva Maye

Brahma Muhurte Chotthaya Chitayedatmano
Hitam Smaranam Vasudevasya Kuryat Kalimalapaharam

Santhkumara, Sanaka, Sananthana, Sangathane
Apyasoori Pingalow Cha, Saptha Swara, Saptha Rasa
Thaani, Kurvanthu Sarve Maam Suprabhatam

Satharnva Saptha Kulachalaschya, Sapthárshayo
Dweepa Pavanani Saptha, Bhooradhi Kruthwa,
Bhuvanai Saptha, Kurvantu Maam Suprabhatam.

Bhano, Bhaskara Marthanda, Chanda Rasmai,
Divakara, Ayur, Arogyam, Buddhim, Shree Yamascha Dehi

Shubham Karoti Kalyaanam, Aarogyam Dhana Sampadaa
Shatru Buddhir Vinaashaaya, Dipa Jyotir Namostute

Yaani Kaani Cha Paapaani Janmaantara Kritani Cha
Taani Taani Vinashyanti Pradakshina Pade Pade

Brahmaarpanam Brahma Havih, Brahmaagnau
Brahmanaahutam, Brahmaiva

Gange Cha Yamune Chaiva Godavari Saraswati
Narmade Sindhu Kaveri Jalesmin Sannidhim Kuru

Saraswati Namastubhyam Varade Kaamaroopini
Vidyaarambham Karishyaami Siddhirbhavatu Me Sadaa

Sarve Bhavantu Sukhinaha Sarve Santu Niraamayah
Sarve Bhadrani Pashyantu Ma Kaschit Duhkha Bhag Bhavet

Karacharana Kritham Vaa Kaayajam Karmajam Vaa
Shravan Nayanajam Vaa Maanasam Vaa Aparaadham
Vihitham Avihitham Vaa Sarvam Etat Kshamasva
Jaya Jaya Karunaabbdhe Shri Maha Deva Shambho

Raamaskandham Hanumantam Vainateyam Vrkodaram
Shayane Yah Smarennityam Duh Swapnam Tasya Nashyati

Anaayaasena Maranam Vinaa Dainyeno Jeevanam
Dehi Me Kripayaa Krishna Tvayi Bhaktim Achanchalam

Gurur Brahma Gurur Vishnuh Gurur Devo Maheshwarah;
Guru Sakshat Para Brahma Tasmai Shree Guruve Namaha

Dhanvantarim Garudmantam Phanirajam Cha Kaustubham,
Achyutam Camritam Chandram Smaredausaadhakarmani

Labhastesam Jayastesam Kutastesam Parabhavah Esam,
Indee Varasyamahah Hridayastho Janardanah

*****

Raghupati Raghav Rajaram, Patit Pavan Sitaram,
Sitaram, Sitaram, Bhaj Pyare Tu Sitaram,
Ishwar Allah Tero Naam, Sabko Sanmati De Bhagavan

*****

Buddham Sharanam Gacchami
Dhammam Sharanam Gacchami
Sangham Sharanam Gacchami

*****

Namo Arihantanam, Namo Siddhanam,
Namo Ayariyanam, Namo Uvajjhayanam,
Namo Loe Savva Sahunam

(I bow to the liberated ones, I bow to the perfected ones, I bow to the preceptors, I bow to the teachers, I bow to the saints.

Lord's Prayer - Our 'Father' who art in heaven, Hallowed, be thy name, Thy, kingdom come, Thy, will be done on earth as it is in heaven. Give us this day our daily bread, and forgive us our trespasses, as we forgive those who trespass against us. And lead us not into temptation but deliver us from evil. For thine is the kingdom, and the power and the glory for ever and ever. 'Amen'.

Prayer Of Saint Francis of Assisi -

"Lord", make me an instrument of your peace
Where there is a hatred, let me sow love
Where there is injury, pardon
Where there is a doubt, faith
Where there is despair, hope
Where there is darkness, light And,
where there is sadness, joy
O Divine Master, grant that I may Not
so much seek to be consoled as to console.
To be understood as to understand
To be loved, as to love.
For it is in giving that we receive
And it's in pardoning that we are pardoned And,
it's in dying that we are born to Eternal life.
'Amen'.

Prayer To the Archangel Gabriel -

(Asking him to "intercede for us at the throne of divine mercy."

O blessed Archangel Gabriel, we beseech thee, do thou intercede for us at the throne of divine mercy in our present necessities, that as thou didst announce to Mary the mystery of the incarnation, so through thy prayers and patronage in heaven we may obtain the benefits of the same, and sing the praise of God forever in the land of the living. Amen.

Prayer To St. Michael The Archangel -

St. Michael the Archangel, defend us in battle, be our protection against the wickedness and snares of the devil. May God rebuke him we humbly pray; and do thou, O prince of the heavenly host, by the power of God, cast into hell Satan and all the evil spirits who prowl about the world seeking the ruin of souls, Amen.

Prayer to Allah -

I pray to Allah in the heavens above,
I pray to Allah asking Him for His love,
I pray to Allah to keep us safe and warm,
I pray to Allah to keep us away from harm,
I pray to Allah keep our families safe,
I pray to Allah to keep us all in His embrace,
I pray to Allah so that I have no fear,
I pray to Allah for all that I hold dear,
I pray to Allah for me and for you All,
I pray to Allah that He forgives the wrong that we do,
I pray to Allah in the heavens above,
I pray to Allah asking Him for His love.
'Ameen'.

Guru Vandana

Tvam-Eva Maataa Cha Pitaa Tvam-Eva |
Tvam-Eva Bandhush-Cha Sakhaa Tvam-Eva |
Tvam-Eva Viidyaa Dravinnam Tvam-Eva |
Tvam-Eva Sarvam Mama Deva Deva ||

MahaStuti – (praise)

1. **Shri Ganesh Stuti**

Gajaananam Bhootha Ganaadhi Sevitham,
Kapiththa Jamboo Phala Chaaru Bhakshitham,
Umaa Sutham Shoka Vinnasa Kaaranam,
Namaami Vighneshwara Paada Pankajam.

2. **Shri Vishnu Stuti**

Shanta-Aakaaram Bhujaga-Shayanam Padma-Naabham Suresham
Vishva-Aadhaaram Gagana-Sadrisham
Megha-Varnnam Shubh-Anggam |
Lakshmii-Kaantam Kamala-Nayanam Yogibhir-Dhyaana-Gamyam
Vande Vishnnum Bhava-Bhaya-Haram Sarva-Lokaiaeka-Naatham ||

3. **Guru Stuti**

Om Brahmanandam Parama Sukhadam Kevalam Jnyanamurtim |
Dvandvaateetam Gaganasadrusham Tatvamasyadi Lakshyam | |
Ekam Nityam Vimalamachalam Sarvadheesaakshibhuutam |
Bhaavaateetam Triguna Rahitam Sadgurum Tam Namaami | |
Chaitanyam Shashvatam Shantam Vyomatitam Niranjanam |
Naadabindukalatitam Tasmai Shri Gurave Namah | |
GururBrahma GururVishnu Gurur Devo Maheshvarah |
Guruh Sakshat Parambrahma Tasmai Shri Gurave Namah | |
Dhyanamulam Gurumurtih Pujamulam Guru Padam |
Mantramulam Guru Vakyam Mokshamulam Guru Kripa | |
Chinmayam Vyapitam Sarvam Trailokyam Sacharacharam |
Asitvam Darshitam Yena Tasmai Shri Gurave Namah | |
Yatsatyena Jagat Sarvam Yat Prakashena Bhanti Yat |
Yadanandena Nandanti Tasmai Shri Gurave Namah | |
Om Namah Shivaya Gurave Satchidananda Murtaye |
Nishprapanchaya Shantaya Niralambaya Tejase | |
Akhandamandalakaram Vyaptam Yena Characharam |
Tatpadam Darshitam Yena Tasmai Shri Gurave Namah | |
Ajnanamulaharanam Janmakarmanivaranam |
Jnanavairagya Siddhyartham Guruh Padodakam Pibet | |
Nityam Suddham Nirabhasam Nirakaram Niranjanam |
Nityabodham Chidanandam Gurum Brahma Namamyaham | |

4. **Shri Durga Stuti**

Sarva Mangala Mangalye Shive Sarvaartha Saadhike |
Sharanye Trayambake Gauri Naarayani Namostute | |

Shri Shiva Stuti -

Om Namah Shivaya |
Om Namo Bhagawate Rudraay |
Om Tatpurushaay Vidmahe Mahadevaay Dheemahi
Tanno Rudrah Prachodayat | |
Om Karcharankritam Vaa Kaayjam
Karmjam Vaa Shravanna Yanjam Vaa
Maansam Vaa Paradham |
Vihitam Vihitam Vaa Sarva Metat Kshamasva Jay Jay
Karunaabdhe Shree Mahadev Shambho | |

Shri Krishna Stuti -

Om Krishnaya Namaha |
Om Devkinandanaye Vidmahe Vasudevaye Dheemahi |
Tanno Krishna Prachodayat | |
Om Shri Keshvay Namah | Om Narayanaya Namah |
Om Madhavay Namah | Om Govinday Namah |
Om Vishnave Namah | Om Madhusudnay Namah |
Om Trivikramay Namah | Om Vamanay Namah |
Om Shridharay Namah | Om Hrishikeshay Namah |
Om Padmanabhay Namah | Om Damodaray Namah |
Om Sankarshanay Namah | Om Vasudevay Namah |
Om Pradyumnay Namah | Om Aniruddhay Namah |
Om Purushottamay Namah | Om Adhokshajay Namah |
Om Narsimhay Namah | Om Achyutay Namah |
Om Janardanay Namah | Om Upendray Namah |
Om Haraye Namah | Om Shri Krishnay Namah | |

Purushsuktam –

The word 'Purusha' means 'God Almighty'. This suktam is in praise of the glory of God. Reciting this confers blessings on one's life.

Serenity Prayer:

God, grant me the Serenity
to accept the things, I cannot change.
The Courage to change the things I can,
and the Wisdom to know the difference.

Prayer For Protection from Evil –

Heavenly Father, guide me and direct me as I seek to love strangers the way You love them. Help me take risks in this world which require your protection from the evil one. I want to live "dangerously" for Your glory, "Lord". 'Amen'.

Affirmations - (Dhrudha Vachan / Maha Pratidnya)

Affirmation is a statement of Truth. Affirmations help to change the subconscious mind. Affirmations should be repeated in a quiet space with concentration which allows to change habit patterns and attitudes over which one normally has little control. Affirmations motivate, inspire, and encourage us to take action to realize our goals. To Affirm means "To state something as true". To state positively. To assert as valid or confirmed. To show or express a strong belief in or dedication to imported Idea. Affirmations are sentences aimed to affect the conscious and the subconscious minds, so that in turn, they affect our behavior, thinking patterns, habits, and environment, which inspire, energize, and motivate and feel positive, transforms your inner and external worlds. For Affirmations to be effective, affirm with faith, with positive feelings. Do not affirm absentmindedly. Affirmation meaning "to make steady, strengthen." In self introspection and through meditation you know that your specific Chakra has been affected, and if the residing Deity of the Chakra recedes, the qualities of that Chakra do not maintain themselves without constant attention and nourishment. The Affirmation is used to bring our attention back to the qualities of Chakra so that the Deity returns, helping their qualities to reflourish and act spontaneously within us. Positive Affirmations release you from anxiety, negativity, guilt, fear, and pain. These mantras are simple messages, repeated over again and again they begin to change your thinking and your reality. Your mind is transformed. These sayings start as wishful thinking, but they often end up becoming the reality of your life. Positive affirmations are phrases or mantras that you repeat to yourself, which describe a specific outcome or who you want to be. At first, these affirmations might not be true, but with constant repetition, your subconscious mind will start to believe them. And eventually, these affirmations will become your reality. Affirmations do not work by magic. For the most part, they work due to the power of positive thinking. Daily use of affirmations, prime your brain for change. As per the science of neuroplasticity our brains can be rewired for different thoughts. Kids do this all the time. And they do it quite easily. As we grow older, it becomes tougher and tougher to change our thoughts. We become used to our thought patterns. But with conscious effort, you can "rewire" your brain. One of the best ways to do this is by using positive affirmations. Embrace the power of positive thinking with daily affirmations to help you get inspired! Beat negative thinking by reciting positive affirmations every day. Affirmations can banish negative thoughts. With each breath you let out, you should also release old, negative thoughts that may be plaquing your mental health.

Affirmations can be used for your glorious integral personality development and for your spiritual upliftment and ascent. It is useful to build your self-esteem, self-confidence, social skills, self-love, for setting and achieving esteemed goals of life. It can also be used for empowering yourself, to get motivated, to develop positive habits and attitudes and to develop leadership qualities.

Positive Affirmations:

1) I am happy and grateful to "The Lord". 2) Yes, I can. 3) I believe in myself. 4) My body is a temple of God and I take care of my body. I respect my body and listen to its needs. 5) I have the power. 6) I believe in my skills and abilities. 7) I am a winner. 8) I'm fearless. 9) I use my failures as stepping-stone. 10) I am confident. 11) I dare to be different. 12) My every desire is achievable. 13) I am worthy of love and joy. 14) Positivity is a choice that I choose to make. 15) My commitment to myself is real. 16) I believe in me. 17) I accept myself unconditionally. 18) I am successful. 19) I am a beautiful person. 20) I deserve love, compassion, and empathy. 21) I believe in the person I dream of becoming. 22) I choose faith over fear. 23) I am free of worry and am at peace with who I am. 24) I am a diamond. It is time for me to shine. 25) I am making healthier decisions every day. 26) My body, mind and spirit are in harmony. 27) My thoughts are kind to me because I deserve peace. 28) I have faith in myself and my future. 29) I am a good person who deserves good things. 30) I approve of who I am and that is enough. 31) My life is fortunate and special to me. 32) I deserve and attract amazing experiences. 33) My intelligence and wisdom grow every day. 34) I am on the best path for me. 35) I am here for a reason, and it is clear to me now. 36) Life is guiding and flowing through me. I trust life. 37) I dare to be different. 38) My every desire is achievable. 39) My confidence knows no limits. 40) I have my own abundance, comparisons are

unnecessary. 41) I'm in tune with the universe and it guides me effortlessly. 42) The universe sends me guidance when I need uplifting. 43) I treat others fairly and with love. 44) I openly accept loving spiritual guidance. 45) I feel a deep connection to nature, and it lifts my soul. 46) Inner wisdom shines from me as I grow. 47) Negative self-talk has no place in my life. 48) My body, mind, spirit, and soul are fit and strong. 49) I am grateful to "The Lord" for the things I have. 50) I am a doer and I take action to get things accomplished. 51) I will achieve all my goals. 52) I set clear goals and work to complete them every day. 53) I am focused consistent and will never quit. 54) I have a plan of action to achieve my desires. 55) My goals are my focus. 56) All is well in my world. I am enough. I can easily create a life I love. I make positive choices for myself. 57) My mind is like water. I will change and adjust as needed. 58) I will master distractions and keep my focus on my goals. 59) I must rely upon myself. 60) Blame for failure rests upon my shoulders. 61) When it comes to taking care of myself, I only seek permission from my heart. 62) I am constantly improving. 63) I desire to learn new things. 64) Time is my friend. I finish all the tasks I need to finish. 65) My life is made for joy. I will live with exuberance. 66) Mindfulness will help me get the most from my time. 67) I am not dependent on anyone else. 68) I think only positive thoughts and am always happy and Joyous, no matter what the external conditions are. 69) I am calm, patient and in control of my emotions. 70) The more I give, the more I will receive. 71) My life is an adventure. 72) My strength is stronger than my anxiety. 73) I move beyond stress to peace. 74) I am safe, I trust life, and I trust in myself. 75) I am fearless. 76) I am calm and mindful. 77) I am compassionate with others and myself. 78) I am a positive being, aware of my potential. 79) I love to meet other people and make new friends. 80) Life is beautiful. 81) I am a unique and that's my gift to the world. 82) I only attract positive people because I am a positive person myself. 83) My actions are intentional they bring me closer to goal. 84) I deserve what I want because my wish is pure, and I have the required qualities. 85) I am solution driven. I am not afraid of obstacles. 86) I am capable to accomplishing my tasks and responsibilities. 87) I have unlimited power. 88) I love myself and the circumstances life presents me. 89) Everything is possible. 90) I am talented and intelligent. 91) My work fulfills me. 92) I am enthusiastic, confident, and persistent. 93)

I let go of fearing mistakes and failures. 94) I do not fear, feelings are not facts. 95) I have abundant energy. 96) Balance in life is what I strive for. 97) I will act after thought, not on instinct. 98) Calm is my primary state of being. 99) I am powerful. 100) Doors of opportunity and abundance open to me today. 101) New opportunities come easily to me. 102) There are no limits to what I can achieve. 103) I am optimistic. I think positively and surround myself with positive energy. 104) I will work smarter, not harder. 105) I am a positive influence, and I surround myself with others like me. 106) Time is the most valuable asset and I guard my time carefully.107) Balance is key. I will mix self-care with effort. 108) Positive energy surrounds me. 109) I refuse to be distracted from my goals and vision. 110) The universe provides bountiful opportunities for my success. 111) I have all the power I need to create the success I desire. 112) Every day is filled with new ideas and new possibilities. 113) I am worthy of financial stability. 114) Organization comes naturally to me. 115) I believe in myself. 116) I am prepared for the challenges of the day. 117) I am filled with positive energy. I face the day with calm and patience. 118) I accept myself just as I am. 119) I love myself deeply and unconditionally. 120) I am beautiful. I am enough. I am blessed. 121) My success is inevitable. 122) Everything in my life is working out for my highest good. 123) I am filled with blessings and my heart is open, to receive blessings. 124) My life is ever flowing with abundance, love, bliss, and joy. 125) Something amazing is now happening to me. 126) I am deeply devoted to creating the life of my dreams. 127) I am a radiant magnificent divine being. 128) I manifest miracles in my life. 129) I am life, I am light, I am love, I am joy, I am divine beauty. 130) I fully let go and trust in divine timing. 131) Every day I am moving closer to my dreams. 132) The world needs my light and I'm not afraid to shine. 133) My heart is full of gratitude to "The Lord" for all that I have and all that is coming. 134) I live my truth unapologetically and inspire others to do the same. 135) I trust my inner wisdom to guide me. 136) I will not compare myself to others. 137) I believe in myself. 138) I am feeling healthy and strong. 139) I have the knowledge to make smart decisions. 140) I face every situation with an open heart and open mind. 141) I am happy and content with my life. 142) I am patient and calm and greet the day with ease. 143) I am the architect of my life; I build its foundation and choose its contents. 144) Today, I am brimming with energy and overflowing with joy. 145) My body is healthy; mind is brilliant; my soul is tranquil. 146) I am superior to negative thoughts and low actions. 147) I forgive those who have harmed me in my past and peacefully detach myself from them. 148) A river of compassion washes away my anger and replaces it with love. 149) I have compassion for myself and others. 150) I am guided in my every step by the spirit who leads me towards what I must know and do. 151) I possess the qualities needed to be extremely successful. 152) My business is growing, expanding, and thriving. 153) Creative energy surges through me and leads me to new and brilliant ideas. 154) I am courageous, and I stand up for myself. 155) My thoughts are filled with positivity and my life is plentiful with prosperity. 156) Today, I abandon my old habits and take up new, more positive ones. 157) I am blessed with an incredible family and wonderful friends. 158) Everything that is happening now is happening for my ultimate good. 159) My future is an ideal projection of what I envision now. 160) My efforts are being supported by the Universe and my dreams manifest into reality before my eyes. 161) I radiate beauty, charm, and grace. 162) I am conquering my illness and I am defeating it steadily each day. 163) My obstacles are moving out of my way; my path is carved towards greatness. 164) I wake up today with strength in my heart and clarity in my mind. 165) My fears of tomorrow are simply melting away. 166) I am at peace with all that has happened, is happening, and will happen. 167) My nature is divine; I am a spiritual being. 168) I love and approve of myself. 169) I am too big a gift to the world to waste my time on self-pity and sadness. 170) I focus on breathing and grounding myself. 171) Following my intuition, my heart keeps me safe and sound. 172) I make the right choices every time. 173) I trust myself. 174) I draw from my inner strength and light. 175) Money comes to me easily and effortlessly. 176) Wealth constantly flows into my life. 177) My actions create constant prosperity. 178) I am aligned with the energy of abundance. 179) I forgive myself for all the mistakes I have done. 180) I replace my anger with understanding and compassion. 181) I offer an apology to those affected by my anger. 182) I know my wisdom guides me to the right decision. 183) I take the time to show my friends that I care about them. 184) I am doing work that I enjoy and find fulfilling. 185) I engage in work that impacts this world positively. 186) I believe in my ability to change the world with the work that I do. 187) I choose to fully participate in my day with good work and joy. 188) I am a money magnet and attract wealth and abundance. 189) I compare myself only to my highest self. 190) The past has no power over me anymore. 191) I embrace the rhythm and the flowing of my own heart. 192) All that I need comes to me at the right time and place in this life. 193) I am deeply fulfilled with who I am. 194) I am a powerful creator. I create the life I want to enjoy it.

Affirmation Prayers -

1. Breathing in, Peace. Breathing out, Peace.
2. With every step forward, I am faith-filled and faithful.
3. Attuned to divine Life, I heal and live fully.
4. Centered in divine love, I am a harmonious presence.
5. Centered in God, I am secure, balanced, and peaceful.
6. Within the silence of prayer, I gain a clear sense of direction.
7. By the power of divine Life, I thrive.
8. I welcome every blessing in a spirit of gratitude and generosity.
9. Every beat of my heart radiates the harmonizing power of divine love.
10. I breathe into the healing power of God, the renewing pulse in my body, mind, and spirit.
11. All wisdom is within. I turn within to know all I need to know, in the silence.
12. Celebrating unexpected blessings, I live well today.
13. One with God and one with all, I am a peaceful presence.
14. Dear God, please give me the strength to endure this situation and to find the blessings and lessons that it contains. Please give me the endurance to continue ahead. Please guide my thoughts, words, and actions, so that I walk your path of peace and love. Amen.
15. Today and every day I feel the divine wisdom of the Goddess filling my body, mind and spirit.
16. For today, help me, God, to remember you.
17. Let this be a good day, God, full of joy and love.
18. Beloved God, may I know that Thine unseen, all protecting mantle is ever around me, in joy and in sorrow.

19. God is within and around me, protecting me; so, I will banish the fear that shuts out His guiding light.
20. I know that God's power is limitless; and as I am made in His image, I too have the strength to overcome all obstacles.
21. I possess the creative power of spirit. The infinite intelligence will guide me and solve every problem.
22. God, please make me the innocence.
23. God, please make me the creative knowledge.
24. God, please make me my own master.
25. God, please make me fearless person.
26. God, please make me detached witness.
27. God, please make me a part and parcel of the whole.
28. God, please make me a self-correcting and discriminating person.
29. God, please make me a forgiving and sacrificing person.
30. God, please accept my complete surrender.
31. God, please give me my Self-realization.

‘MahaAdhyatmaSadhana’

The Great Spiritual Practice

Sadhaka (disciple) gains maximum spiritual benefit by performing Adhyatma Sadhana (Spiritual practice) through Satsang with less effort and time. Sadhana is literally “a means of accomplishing something”. It is a spiritual exercise, practice. Everything you do in your daily life for your spiritual upliftment, your integral growth of body, mind, and spirit on the path of spiritual enlightenment, and to achieve Yoga (union) with the Divine is “Adhyatma Sadhana” (Spiritual Practice). Sadhana is a means whereby bondage becomes liberation. Sadhana is a discipline undertaken in pursuit of a higher esteem goal. It is a repeated practice performed with observation and reflection, with study and investigation. The drive for spirituality is inherent in our nature, but the way the spiritual path unfolds is unique to every individual. Spirituality is a worldview and a way of life based on the belief that there is more to life than what meets the senses, more to the universe than just purposeless mechanics, more to consciousness than electrical impulses in the brain, and more to our existence than the body and its needs. The spiritual goals are to purify body - mind - spirit so as to achieve liberation (moksha); to achieve Yoga - uniting individual Soul with the Universal Supreme Soul; to be the true Self, becoming one with the absolute consciousness; to dissolve the knot of the ego, which limits pure consciousness to a body-mind-spirit; realize the true Self; experiencing divine revelation by surrendering and serving to God; to achieve the cessation of suffering by uprooting the mental defilements; see reality for what it is; achieving enlightenment, Nirvana, experiencing union with God, the kingdom of heaven, feel the love of creator; cultivating and sublimating energy cultivate body, mind, and spirit, living in divine harmony; learning the ultimate laws of the universe; know oneself and the creator, live as per the universal laws of nature; by karmic purification become a siddha (a perfect being),achieve salvation; live in harmony and connection with nature; develop knowledge and power to work with invisible divine forces; heal the soul; use spiritual wisdom and techniques for rejuvenation, clearance, cleansing, wellness, wellbeing, healing, treatments, and purification of body, mind-spirit for our overall integral development and spiritual upliftment, transformation, and transcendence. The main aspects of Adhyatma Sadhana (Spiritual Practice) are cessation, sublimation, Dharana (Concentration, Contemplation), Dhyana (Meditation), Samadhi (Union and absorption with ultimate reality, Oneness with Divine). Saadhaka must develop good positive habits, use advanced technics and skills for spiritual upliftment / Ascent and experience transformation to create new experiences.

Regular spiritual practices are very important. They are gifted in solving problems for us. This is what they were made to do. All creativity comes from this. Many a times one experiences stress, worry, anxiety, fear, anger and negative emotions which distract the mind. Spiritual practices help us to put our minds at rest to come back to the present moment and connect with our Source energy the divine source of peace, bliss, love, abundance, happiness and joy. Help us to realign our body, mind, heart, and spirit self with our Soul.

Spiritual Healing & Wellbeing:

Spiritual healing practices are used for our holistic health, mind balance and spiritual well-being. Energy healing system restores the balance and flow of energy throughout our body, mind, and spirit at both gross and subtle levels. Spiritual wisdom and the subtle energy are used with specific techniques to channelize the universal divine spirited energy (ParamChaitanya) to heal our subtle energy centers (Chakras) and our sympathetic and parasympathetic nervous system and related body organs. Breathing and pranic healing techniques are also used. One should accept the spiritual healing techniques which are positive and divine and have faith in them. One must first properly evaluate and take a practical experience of result. Self-healing visualization is best experienced rather than described. The first thing you must do for healing your body, mind, heart, and spirit-soul is to forgive yourself and forgive everyone else and make peace with yourself and the world. Once you fully commit to helping other's you'll understand that people were instruments to aide in your evolution. Focus on the lesson not the person.

Heal the Spirit-Self of the Soul first and then the healing of body, mind, and heart shall follow spontaneously, automatically, and naturally. There are many different self-healing spiritual techniques you can practice by yourself. There are other treatments that involve the transfer of energy through the healer to the recipient. It promotes self-healing by relaxing the body, relaxing tensions, and strengthening the body's own immune system. Healing is natural and non-invasive with the intention of bringing the recipient into a state of balance and wellbeing on all levels. The word 'spiritual' originates from the Latin word 'spiritus' meaning breath of life. The spiritual aspect refers to spiritual energy working at a deep level on our spiritual being. The healing involves the transfer of energy; in other words, it is not from the healer himself or herself, the healer is only the instrument of divine, the healer links with universal divine energy to channel healing for the body, mind, and spirit-soul of the recipient. The Universal divine sentient spiritual energy (ParamChaitanya) can be directed with pure desire and intention. When focused on the human body, via the aura (human energy field), with distance of about one to three feet, it raises the 'Spiritual Vibrations' of the recipient person. Distant healing also can be done with collective healing. For optimum healing, repeated treatments needed to overcome the body's inertia. When people are ill, it is common for them to say that they are 'low in energy'; conversely when people are healthy, we talk about them bursting with energy. Energy is channeled usually via the healer's hands by its conscious sentient motions around the recipient. Divine energy flow increases when the healer and recipient pray from within the heart, and by chanting mantras for specific purpose in mind silently or can be spoken in medium low voice. Healing can also be given as distant healing through attunement and visualization. The effects of healing are alleviation of physical symptoms, reduced pain, lightning of burden, increased vitality, deepening inner peace, sense of connectedness with the universe. The healer senses the energies on the palms of the hands and in the conscious mind. These energies are very subtle and are very low frequency vibrations which carry divine sentient energy and electromagnetic, gravitational fields at very subtle level. Healing from distance with intention, sending thoughts at a distance. A very deep energetic connection is to be established between the healer and the recipient. The healer who is an initiated, activated person by his Guru, who is spiritually balanced and elevated spiritual personality has in him electromagnetic flow, vibrations, in him everything is coherent full of vitality, his energies go beyond the body into his Aura where there is an exchange of energies and vibrations with environment. This allows the recipient to receive healing vibrations with positive intentions. Certainly, many of us can, upon entering an empty room, 'Know' when there has recently been an argument there. We can sense the negative energy through our Aura. Equally, we can sense if someone has good or bad intentions towards us, irrespective of what they are saying or how they are acting to us. For to understand the process of healing, how it works we need to explore our reality in a new way, the quantum nature of things in which everything is interconnected, interdependent, integrated, and independent and works through divine energies. All objects remain interconnected through time and space. Bioelectromagnetic fields around our bodies are entangled with electromagnetic fields in the local environment and with photons (energy) from the rest of the universe.

Energy (photons) and matter (atoms) are different aspects of the same. Another possible reality is that of a holographic model; that despite its apparent materiality, the universe is 3D image projecting from a level of reality beyond time and space. It makes sense not only of all the phenomena encountered in quantum physics and other neurophysiological quandaries, but also paranormal and mystic experiences. It is true what the mystics had been saying for centuries that reality what we see in this material world is 'Maya', an 'Illusion'; that reality is really a vast, resonating Symphony of wave forms, a frequency domain which is transformed into the world as we know it only after it enters our senses. The conscious mind directs a dynamic distribution of parallel virtual States into a single state of focused awareness. This opens the responsibility that one person's mind/brain can cause the probabilistic brain states of another person or object (or other human organs) to preferentially collapse into selected States. This may be how the intention of healing can produce an effect. It is really very difficult to explain the mechanism of something as ethereal as Healing.

'Sit down before fact like a little child and be prepared to give up every pre-convinced notion, follow humbly wherever and to whatever abyss nature leads, or you shall learn nothing.'

-Biologist T.H. Huxley

The fundamental, underlying philosophy of spiritual healing centers on the notion of the connectedness of all at an energetic level, which is now supported by quantum physics. It is considered that healing through the input of thought at an energetic level, can influence the harmony of the mind, body, Spirit Self, and Soul.

The beneficial effects of the spiritual healing matter the most. Spiritualhealing,prayers,Mantra,energymedicines,mentalintention effects, intentional distant healing are dependent on the faith, belief, involvement, pure desire, deep heartily feeling, dedication and harmonious connection between the healer and recipient. The clear flow of divine sentient cosmic energy is to be established. There must be a clear understanding between the healer and the recipient, there must be intense desire, intent to heal and channeling of spiritual energy. It takes a lot of practice, pure intention, and effort to develop Spiritual healing. The benefits are far reaching. The sense of transcendence is experienced in spirituality. Transcendent moments are filled with, peace, bliss, awe, contentment, emotional and spiritual well-being. Self-transcendent emotions such as compassion, awe, gratitude, appreciation, inspiration, admiration, elevation, love, peace and bliss have a particular capability of bonding individuals together. They are linked with higher levels of spirituality. Energy cleansing is not something we do just once. It is an ongoing activity. First clear negative energy. The most effective negative energy clearing practices are conscious walking, dancing, listening to music, mantra chanting, meditation, prayers etc. They are more effective in collectivity.

Paper writing: To manifest your wish, dreams, desires, goals & to get rid of negative thoughts, emotions, and other negativities.

Writing things on paper enables you to manifest works magically to make happen what you want to accomplish. While writing on paper you must have concentration, focus and intense desire for your dreams, wishes, desires, wants, needs, aims and goals to be manifested in your life. Your attention and intention and the energy flow must be towards writing. Let your mind work for you. While writing don't think about how possible or impossible it would be. Write enthusiastically with full interest as if it is manifesting for you. Many people have experienced suddenly that their dream, desires, or wishes are manifested which they had visualized and written on paper long time back and they had forgotten and remembered when it was fulfilled. Focused attention is important while writing. Whatever you put your attention on grows; your energy is concentrated on this one thing. Energy draws more things vibrating at the same rate frequency. The more you focus on something the more whatever you're focused on increases or expands by power. When you write, all your attention is on creating the words that you put down on paper, and back of the words, is the intent or the energy that you're putting into them. That focused energy is why writing things down to manifest works.

Desire, wish and wants, untainted by Doubt must manifest. The thing about desire is once you have it, its fulfilment is also yours. "Therefore, I tell you, whatever you ask for in prayer believe that you have received it, and it will be yours," – **Jesus Christ**

Well, writing works, because in that moment, you're writing down your desire. So, your pure attention is on your desire not on your doubts. Since you're watering your desire with your pure attention, it has no choice but to grow into an actual manifestation, sooner or later. You must have positive attitude while writing desire. Write your manifestations into being on a white paper with a blue ink pen (do not use black ink pen). Identify your desires, wants, needs, write it down on paper, you can also write down in your personal notebook, believe that it's already done. You can use this writing process for anything and everything, big and small. This is a powerful process that works.

There are other ways for getting manifestation working. One is paper burning. Take a sheet of white paper, write down all your dreams, wishes, wants and desires with a blue ink pen with positive attitude and intention with full attention and focus. Fold the paper and keep it for one or two days at an auspicious place or below your pillow. Next day, burn the paper as your desires are released into the Air and Sky (Ether) element and the fire element. Put the ashes to the plants or you can also store for a few days in a glass bottle. Keep the bottle at an auspicious place. Everything happens in its own time, trust the timing, trust your inner-feelings, and energy levels. Intentions have different frequencies which may be guessed from how much time it has taken to burn the paper completely. Longer time it takes to burn means it would take a little more time and your hard work for your desires to manifest. When the paper burns, it unfurls like a flower busting into bloom. It's incredible to observe. Giving voice to your desires open the floodgates to more desires, changes the energy you carry. The things around you change very fast. Do what feels good, do what feels right. Many a times the things you want will manifest quickly. The universe feels your vibrations, intentions, attitudes and your intense heartily desire.

Always think that it is possible. Your dreams are given to you because you have the ability to become the person who manifests them. Give voice to your desires. Your desires are 'holy' and they come to you for a reason. Be inspired by the space between where you are and where you want to be. Choose to be inspired by the path ahead of you. Make dreams big enough that you can grow into them. See above growing into new dreams keeps you young at heart, so every time you grow into one, set a new, bigger one! when you do cool things, more cool things happen. Pay attention towards happening. Don't delay gratification. Whenever you feel from within your heart, write down your desires, wishes and wants on paper. It's pretty and magnificent watching fire claim paper. You'll never be ready. Just start. Make your own magic. Ultimately these dreams and desires are not going to come to fruition just because you burned some paper. Burning paper is the symbolic physical manifestation of igniting the desire and passion, you'll need to see these dreams through to completion absolutely.

Law of attraction works when you write down your dreams, wishes, desires, wants, needs, aims and goals. Law of attraction works on the basis of clean energy and clear intentions. Sit back and think clearly about what you want to attract into your life. Clarify your goal(s). Once you know and feel what you want, hold the pen with paper and write it down. Never, never use the future tense. Always use the present tense- Now, here in this place. The universe knows about your wishes as soon as you write and clearly starts to fulfil them. First believe and you will see that sooner or later your wish is fulfilled. Be patient and persistent in working towards your goals.

Great formula of manifestation:

(Thought, Attention) + (Feeling, Intention) + (Action, Attitude) = Manifestation. Your Intent, Attitude, Attention, Concentration, Intensity and Focus matters much in the work you do and efforts you put in.

To get rid of negative thoughts, emotions, depression, stress, anxiety, and other negativities: With your full attention and clear intention, write the problem with black ink on a paper of any color other than black, repeatedly for three times, and then burn the paper, put it in the toilet and flush it out. All negativities get burnt and flushed. You feel the effect of release and relief. Fire burns the negativities and old past energies.

Salt- Water treatment, foot soaking:

The healing benefits of foot soaks are many. Immersing your feet in a tub of warm water, even without anything extra in it, is a nice way to relax after a long day's hard work. You can also use running water to wash your arms, legs and feet. A foot soak soothes your muscles, hydrates your skin, and can relieve aches and pains due to standing for hours or walking in uncomfortable shoes. It reduces swelling, prevents bacteria from setting between toes and foot fingers. You can also soak your feet in cold water when the weather is hot.

Epsom salt foot soak: A combination of magnesium and sulfate, Epsom salt is a compound that can help flush toxins & heavy metals from your skin's cells, reduce inflammation, increase blood circulation, and ease muscle cramp and joint pain. As your feet absorb the magnesium, pain reducing ions are released, relaxing your muscles and nerves, and helping them function properly by regulating your electrolyte levels. The sulfate targets any harmful substances that need to be eliminated from your body. Epsom salt can also quell foot odor, help heal fungus and smooth dry skin. In a standard size tub, dissolve one cup of Epsom salt in warm water and soak your feet for ten to fifteen minutes. Be present and involved in the treatment. Keep your attention in the process and experience getting cleared and feeling good. You can also repeat Mantra while taking treatment. You can also add some essential oils to your Epsom salt soak treatment. Wash your feet after soaking. Be sure to purchase Epsom salts intended for foot soak. You can also add baking soda 2-3 tablespoons for foot soak. Meditate while soaking.

Salt- Water treatment: (Rock Salt or Sea Salt Can Be Used)

In a standard size tub, fill water to the level so that your feet and ankles will be immersed in water. Add one cup of sea salt in warm or cold water as per weather conditions. Sitting on a chair immerse your feet in salt water and relax. Be conscious and calm your body and mind. You can say mantras for clearance. Meditate for ten to fifteen minutes. You can also say some affirmations to clear your subtle system Nadis and Chakras. Sea salt also represents the Earth element. Elements help us to clear our body imbalances, ailments and ensure the smooth flow of energy throughout our physical body. Sea salt absorbs away toxins and negativities. Our foot is the organ that we use very hard. After the day's work, our feet get tired and fatigue. Sea-salt water treatment is best to remove fatigue, stress, strain. It also cools down our whole body; we gain stability and balance. Helps pull the residue from the body. Removes negative energy caused by emotions. It is better to do this treatment every day or on alternate days after day's work. Foot bathing is a long-standing practice reflexology, our feet have touch points, which are related to the functioning of various organs of our body which helps the body to relax. By soaking feet in salt - water, it stimulates these touch points with thermal energy. Our skin senses are connected by neurons. With muscles including organs, inside the body and when the thermal effect with skin it sends signals to different parts of the body and helps balance the organ functioning. It also stimulates the body's resistance. Helps the digestive system to work better, helps reduce headaches, makes sleep easy overnight. It removes negative energies, lethargy, effects of excessive thinking and bad vibes. It promotes spiritual healing process at very subtle level when you take specific mantras and do meditation and contemplation. With your conscious awareness, you can clear all negative energies and bring you in balance with positive energies. The salt- water remedy is a simple but powerful spiritual remedy to counteract the harmful unseen dark negative energies and drain them out of our system. It helps bring spiritual growth. Rock salt also can be used for this treatment.

While taking the treatment, pray to "The Almighty Lord" sincerely with faith to remove negative energies. Prayer is an important aspect which enhances the effectiveness of this remedy. Sit upright on a chair with feet immersed in the salt water. Keep a distance of at least one to two inches between the feet. Keep the feet in the salt water for ten to fifteen minutes. You can chant Mantra and meditate. After the completion of the treatment have gratitude to "The Almighty Lord" and pray for creating protective aura (sheath) around you.

After finishing, pour the salt water in the toilet and flush. Rinse the bucket with fresh water. Wash your hands and feet with fresh water. You can also use Himalayan salt. Because of its mineral content, Himalayan salt helps regulate cellular water content, balance electrolytes, prevents muscle cramping, improves blood circulation, and lowers blood pressure, also helps skin retain moisture, improves skin's appearance, helps strengthen bones, connective tissues, reduces soreness or pain. The negative ions present in Himalayan salt are associated with the waterfalls, ocean and rivers and help bring balance back to your body, boost brain function, reduce inflammation and improves sleep. Helps balance your body's ionic properties and supply with necessary minerals and boosts your body's metabolism.

Enjoy nature's healing powers with the above healing treatments and experience, peace, bliss, and happiness. It's Joy giving. Foot soaking can also be done in a river, lake or sea which are very much beneficial. After a barefoot walk on mother earth, washing your feet with water helps clear your subtle system.

Osmosis process is activated while taking salt- water treatment.

Salt water has higher density than normal water. Osmosis is the spontaneous net movement of solvent (normal water) molecules through a selectively permeable membrane (our skin, tissue cells and blood cells membranes) into a region of higher solute (salt, minerals) concentration in the direction that tends to equalize the solute concentration on the two sides.

While we are taking foot soak (salt- water treatment) our toxins, waste materials, extra salts and excess of any harmful minerals are removed from our body and are sucked out by salt water. Thus, we feel relief from stress, strain and we experience bliss in our body. It is recommended to drink one to two glasses of water before taking this treatment for more benefit. This treatment must be taken around thirty minutes before evening meals or forty-five minutes after meals for best results.

MahaParivartana

The Great Spiritual Transformation

'Naad-Brahman' Synchronous Resonance Transcendence Art:

The Great Zero-Point Power Transformation. Incredible Turning Point:

Naad-Bindu is Zero-Point. It is a Point of Infinite Possibilities. Amrut Naad Bindu, Point of Divine Nectar. This point has all potencies of creation, sustenance, dissolution, and transformation. It can make anything possible. It can make the Impossible to I Am Possible. It can achieve what you want and fulfill your esteemed desires. It will also enhance your creative skill through visualization and imagination. It is a Point of exploring Eternity in a moment, divine experiencing and working out miracles. Zero-point and Infinity coexist. Zero-point is supremely sacred, secret of all secrets, omnipotent, omniscient, and omnipresent. All divine spirits and energies, its qualities, essence, powers exist in unison, oneness, simultaneously at these zero-points. Zero-point exists everywhere eternally and it works out everything everywhere. It is the only truth, reality beyond all illusions (Maya). It is the presence of "MahaPrabhu" ("The Almighty Lord"). It is beyond all materialistic Nature. It can never be known through physical Sciences. It is the point of infinite possibilities, the creative principle of reality. It is Sat-Chit-Ananda (Truth-Consciousness-Bliss), permanent, unchanging, and eternal, absolute cosmic principle. It creates, maintains, and withdraws within it all creation. The ultimate cause of everything. It is the essence of liberation, essence of spiritual freedom. It can never be seen, though it can be experienced and known through metaphysical divine spiritual knowledge.

Zero-Point is the incredible turning point of our life for transformations we want for our integral physical, mental, and spiritual growth. Zero-Point Spin & Win. In deep meditation, when you reach zero-point, it heals your gross and subtle body system.

Clearing all your nervous system and all your chakras related plexus and glands. Control of Hormones and maintaining Balance. DNA can be reprogrammed and transformed, developing powerful immune system and warding off all negativities, negative thoughts, emotions, and evil spirits. It is experiencing complete transformation of your integral personality, your spiritual development and ascent. It is manifesting your pure desires with certainty, state of excelling or surpassing, going beyond limits. Zero-Point is experiencing the state of being or existence above and beyond the limits of material existence.

Zero-Point is beyond causation and beyond any identity. It is the point of infinity, truth, reality, silence, bliss, joy, and beauty. It is the heart throb of all creation. Everything is transcended at this point. It is the final goal of All Life. It is the point of Turiyatitah (The Highest Transcendental State). It is nonlocal and exists everywhere. It is Supreme Brahman. It is the point of AtmaDarshana, Realization of the Self. It is the point of Renunciation where all Vibrations merge and emerge. It is the Presence in the present. It is the Supreme Understanding, Intelligence and Consciousness. The point of Divine Wisdom and Action. It is the point of union (Yoga) oneness. It is the point of Supreme Dharma and Karma. It is supremely pure in Nature. It is the point of experiencing eternal Beauty, 'Beauty Awakens the Soul to Act. To Love Beauty is to see Light'. It is the the point of BrahmaBhava, BrahmaDyana and BrahmaSthithi. It is Gunatitah beyond the three Gunas of Nature. It is the Heart of all intuition and pure desire.

Zero-point is our own Reality. It is the Source of our Being. It is Eternal. Zero-point interconnects everyone and everything. It is Omnipotent, all powerful and has the ability to create anything. It is Omniscient- All knowing. It is timeless, knows all past, present, and future. It is eternally aware, supreme witness, pure conscious awareness. The Supreme consciousness holds supreme intelligence, thoughts, feelings, desires, emotions, will power, intuition, powers of imagination and visualization, infinite possibilities, choices, all creativity, art, powers of mind and heart, power to synchronize all spirits and energies. Both Spirit and Energy are mutually dependent, mutually consumptive, and mutually change. The Source of Consciousness is supreme luminous, effulgent, pure, pristine, divine awareness innate in Zero Point.

The Divine Sound Vibration: "ॐ"('Om')

'Om' 'ॐ' Meaning - Welcome to the Kingdom of God. It is the Divine Cosmic Sound Vibration reverberating everywhere. If we pronounce it rhythmically, it gives us harmony with Nature. We resonate with the subtle synchronous rhythmic vibrations created by the Lord's divine spirited sentient cosmic energy. The divine sound vibration 'Om' is eternal, omnipresent, omniscient, and omnipotent. It is the Eternal divine music. Thoughts, emotions, feelings, desires, and wants have vibrations. These vibrational waves resonate the energy. We are sending out sound vibrations. These sound vibrations cannot be heard by human ear. Everything is Sound. In the beginning was the Word and the Word was Sound, and that Word is 'Om' "ॐ" ('AUM') The Eternal Word, Eternal Sound. It is the Sound that turns Matter and Energy into Form. What you give out is what you create. If the Sound Changes, the Matter Changes and the Energy Changes. When we think & feel, we create a Sound.

The first sound vibration created was 'Om'. This natural rhythmic sound is always present in nature which is the music of the divine. When we pronounce 'Om' sound in harmony, we get completely balanced with nature and its divinity. It opens the doors to the Heavenly Kingdoms. This also represents Beginning, Present and End of this entire cosmos. It unites us in rhythm with the Lord himself. It makes our gross body, mind, and intellect calm and peaceful. It is a uniting sound vibration which unites us all. It destroys all the anti-life elements and energizes and creates new life elements in us. It enlightens our thought and action. It emancipates Love. It helps us to reach the complete Meditative state of peace, bliss, & Joy. It pulls our Attention inwards to explore our own Nature and The Self. It is Sanjeevani (Benevolence energy) which brings Life Force in a deteriorated matter. It cures and restores our energies and our innate qualities and essence, when used in combination with other vowels and consonants. It is a source of energy. Origin of all languages, primarily Sanskrit and all other languages of the World. It is the binding force of Divine Collective. It leads us to the knowledge of Absolute Truth, bliss, peace, and Joy. It helps us to establish connection with the Lord and ultimately union with the Lord. 'OM' is the beginning of all auspiciousness and worship of the Lord. It also signifies the Form and Formless Nature of Creation of the Lord.

There are various theories of creation and origin. Scientifically these are termed as Big Bang Theory, Oscillation Theory, Steady State Theory, etc. There are also theories of Origin in Religious and Philosophical Scriptures like the Vedas, the Upanishads, the Gita, the Bible, the Koran, etc. The Owner and Creator of this entire cosmos is called "MahaPrabhu" God, The Lord, Allah, Sadashiva, Parmatma, Elohim, Parmeshwar, God Almighty, In Scientific terminology, it is called 'the Supreme Conscious Power'.

The Lord wanted to see himself. Desire is a form of conscious activity and hence has the capability to think and act. Both thinking and action have energy at its core and hence desire has its base in energy. This entire Universe has been created out of the pure desire of God Almighty. This desire took birth as the Primordial spiritual power & energy. This pure Energy is associated with pure consciousness and is the source of all creations of matter, energy forms, objects, life, thoughts, mind, intellect, etc. This pure energy created out of the love of the Lord is the sentient divine energy.

Energy is at the core of all creation, items & concepts. Energy has consciousness and can change form. Energy and consciousness have changed forms to give birth to all forms of material, non-material, living and non-living things in creation.

Evolution, revolving change is the basic principle of this universe where the Energy and Consciousness are transformed to create higher complex Being with higher intellect & awareness to perform more complicated tasks to achieve higher knowledge of reality and Absolute Truth and enjoy in reality the higher pleasures and joy.

It is impossible to know the Domain of God Almighty. He is in Everything, and Everything is in Him. He is Omnipresent. He is the creator of all the Spirits , Energies & Matter. Energy exhibits certain capabilities and characteristics like sensing, precepting, evaluating and performing functions in varying degrees its various elements, objects and living and non-living.

Energy and consciousness co-exist and have a correlation. Energy is the cause and is at the core of all that is existing, and consciousness is an attribute of that existence with its level.

Although in practical life, reliable and Organized Studies and practice of conversion / transformation of consciousness in a Scientific Experimental way are not yet available, a study of the evolution of consciousness in human beings, under special conditions of Meditation shows that individuals can evolve in consciousness. Even activities like moving of objects by thought waves (Telekinesis / Teleporting) performing of tasks by objects (Metal / Wood / Plant / Animal etc.), like telling of future thought reading; warding off evil, etc. indicate towards conversion / evolution of consciousness under special conditions.

The Soul (Spirit Self) is indestructible, unchanging, unique, and absolute in every aspect. It is the Absolute Truth. Universal Conscious Energy or Divine Sentient Energy is the Supreme Conscious & Intellectual Energy which does all living work in the entire Cosmos. All the Incarnations, Messengers, Saints, Prophets and Divine Personalities were embodiments of the manifestation of this Divine Sentient Conscious Energy. In Mahabharata, the appearance of Virata, i.e., Disclosure of the Universal Cosmic Being was the highest Expression of Divine Sentient cosmic energy (Paramchaitanya, Divine Cool Breeze, Rooha, and Divine Vibrations).

Great Divine Personalities who are embodiments of this Divine Energy can perform supernatural and unexplainable feats every now and then. Auras are the expressions of Divine Energy Vibrations.

Everything is created, sustained, destroyed, and transformed by this Divine Sentient Cosmic Energy, which is the most powerful and subtle Supreme Conscious Energy in the Entire Cosmos, has the highest capacity to express, experience and enjoy. This energy flows through everything and everything exists in it. It is the Love, Desire, Will and Wish of The Lord.

All energies and consciousness are at the service of The God Almighty, the Supreme Spirit, which witnesses the Play of this Divine Spiritual Energy and Consciousness. Param Chaitanya -The Divine Sentient Cosmic Energy creates all beautiful aspects of existence like birth, life, sustenance, protection, prosperity, love, peace, bliss, happiness, joy and all that Governs the Life and Creation; and gives Energy and Power to all that is existing both Static and Dynamic.

Einstein's theory Energy E = MC2 Where E is Energy, M is the Mass of Atom and C is the speed of light. (186300 Miles/sec). The physical existence can be seen as Matter and Energy. Energies can be in bits, bytes, and packets and as Photon Energy, Electron Energy, Proton, Positron, Nuclear Energy, etc. Physical Energy forms are Light, Sound, Heat, Radio waves, Electromagnetic, Electrical, and Gravitational, etc. Conscious forms of Energies of

Mind, Intellect, Attention, Ego & Superego. The Primordial Divine Sentient Energy is the Basic Source of all Energies and Creation. It is the seed of creation. The process of cooling of the Universe (Nature) is continuing from the time of its Creation till today and which shall be continuing till eternity when everything may end causing another chain of action in Time.

Life of this Universe is approximately twenty-seven billion years as per scientific study.

E = MC2 either all mass is fully converted into energy, or all energy is fully converted into mass are two extreme States.

As per the latest scientific data, our Universe has completed 13.7 billion years; have passed half the way. Human body is Bio- Chemico - Electromagnetic in Nature. The fundamental unit of every living organism is a cell which consists of various Chemical Elements like Protoplasm, Chromatin etc. The Important Aspect of Chemical Structure is the Chemical reactions like oxidation, reduction, decarboxylation, deamination, hydrolysis, phosphorylation, etc. which all relate to either the removal or the addition of charged particles or ions which have an electrical charge associated with it.

Atomic structure of an atom consists of Positive (Nucleus having protons) and Negative charged particles called Electrons. The Chemical action allows formation of either positively charged or negatively charged or neutral particles depending upon the type of a chemical reaction. The Charged particles are formed by either the addition or removal of electron or many electrons from the Elements, Compounds and Ions.

Since these charged particles move in the system, this motion charged particles create an electromagnetic field, which can be sensed as radiation or vibration. Brain waves caused by electrical activity in Brain are radiated as alpha, beta, gamma, delta, and theta rays, which can be recorded. The nervous system which comprises of the brain, spinal cord and nerves in the body fully depends on the movement of electro chemical transmitters, the charged particles. Consequently, this movement creates associated electro-magnetic fields and radiations from the body.

Divine sentient energy- the will power of Lord, is the integrated force of your physical, mental, emotional, and causal bodies. The inner being which is our awareness is all energy. Energy contributes to physical manifestation of the object at gross and subtle levels whereas consciousness grants the capability to perceive and act. Both are integral part of the Divine Being. Divine sentient energy and consciousness are two fundamental attributes of every creation in existence.

While energy is defined with its frequency, Strength, direction, power, etc., consciousness is defined by level of awareness. Both exhibit themselves in action and behavior. The divine sentient energy is the ultimate in consciousness and energy source and manifests in all conceivable and unconceivable forms, and consciousness, the source of human awareness. Universal consciousness is the source of all creation. Consciousness is the capability of a being to perceive, feel, think, realize, understand and to know the reality, facts and truth of the object and subject in a particular situation. Consciousness is the source of all concepts, feelings, perception, understanding, etc.

This conscious awareness makes our intellect and mind work under the control of our Attention. Energy is the source and cover of all living and non-living entities in the Universe. Energy covers a spectrum of frequencies encompassing all seen and unseen material, subtle, and causal bodies, depicted as a spectrum covering frequency ranging from zero to infinity. Energy is the capacity and strength or the power to do work. Characteristics identifying energy are frequency, wavelength, strength, amplitude, direction, spin, speed, etc. Consciousness also exhibits as an activity which can be assigned a frequency and strength and hence a state of energy having certain capabilities and characteristics. It is for this nature of consciousness that it can perform tasks like telepathy telekinesis etc. Since energy can do work and performing tasks, various forms of consciousness and various levels of consciousness can perform certain tasks, which can be seen as the capability or characteristics of a level of person or object in existence.

A conversion / evolution in capability can take place. Consciousness can undergo transformation or conversion. Level of consciousness can be ranging from band Zero to infinity. Consciousness can also be destructive i.e... negative demonic & it can be constructive positive or Godly. It also has strength and amplitude.

- ❖ List your positive attitudes & values & ask yourself how fully & consistently you live them.
- ❖ Spiritual energy is the fuel, the gas, the fire for sustained behavioral change to have perseveration, to have the focus where you want to be.

- Value is an Aspiration, alignment occurs when the Value is matched by your behavior, that's the value in Action. It aligns fully with your Inner core values. Divine values are most important. Deeply built Values are the basis of spiritual fire. Values become Meaningful only when you live them fully & consistently.
- Deeply built values are the basis of spiritual fire.
- Live what you say. Behave Rightly & Correctly.
- Feel, behave & perform better with Excellence
- To Transmit the Effect of Peace, Love, Joy, Truth, Purity, Compassion...... to the Masses of People. The Formula is: The Meditative People Required = Square Root of 1% of Population to be benefited. (One Person can make change for 1000 people). Intense heartily intent is important.
- Thought, Emotion and Feeling is Vibration; When we think we are not only sending out waves which resonates the energy, we are sending out the frequency which is not heard by Human Ear which is outside the range of Human Hearing, we are sending out a sound, Everything, is sound. In the Beginning was word & the word was sound ("AUM", "Om"). It is sound that turns Matter & Energy into form. What you give out is what you create if the Sound Changes the Matter changes and the Energy Changes. When we think & feel, we create a Sound.
- Water is more than simply a physical substance. It's a certain concept & that Concept is connected in a special way, with the idea of Life. Human Vibrational energy, thoughts, words, ideas & music affect the molecular structure of water. The very same water that comprises over 70% (70% to 75%) of a mature Human body & covers the same amount of our planet. The molecular Structure of water is affected by our Consciousness, Intent & Sound.
- Earth is the living library of nature. Learn from each life on Earth. Earth is Cosmic Library with extraordinary Beauty. Information is stored in Frequencies & in a Genetic Process.
- Empty your mind, be formless & shapeless like water. If you put water into a cup it becomes the cup, you put in a body and it becomes the body. Water can flow, or it can crash. Be water my friend. – Bruce Lee

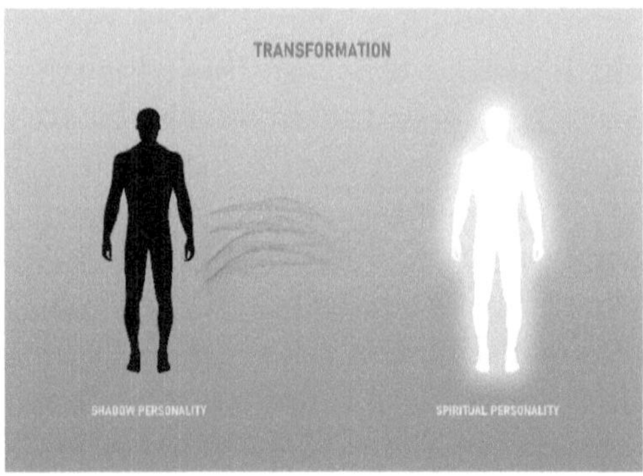

| | Parivartana - Spiritual Zero-Point Power Transformation | |

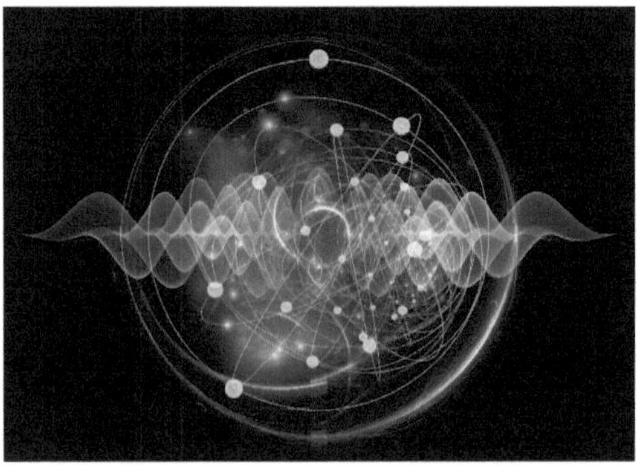

| | Zero-Point Energy Field Transformation | |

| | Spiral Galaxy Zero-Point Center | |

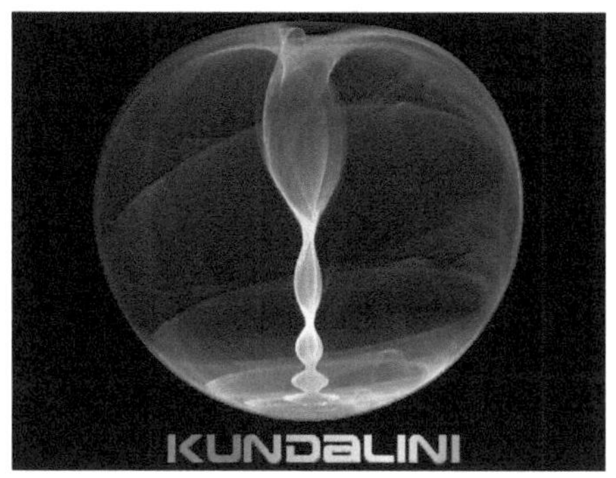

| | Meditation For Transformation | |

| | Spiritual Balance of Energies & Spirit | |

We are from the magnificent family of light. Our purpose on earth is to learn, elevate our consciousness, explore higher consciousness, and make difference with Infinite Possibilities. You are reminded what you already know. Go out & create & bring all things back to Me (The Supreme Creator). Earth is the living Library of Nature. What happens on Planet Earth affects the many Worlds and the entire Universe. At the Realization of the Self, you unfold the thousands of pages of divine ecstasy in a few seconds. There is a divine purpose and divine plan of which you are a part of. You hold the history and secrets of the universe within yourself; All physical, mental & Spiritual. You are evolving your DNA. You will become superbeings.

You must tune yourself to the higher frequencies of Heavens and the Spiritual Kingdom of God. You must be in complete receptive mode. Break the bars of confinement & fear & slavery. Liberate yourself from all bondages. Focus on the dance of your Inner Self. Get attuned with the dance of the Inner Real Self. Reach new heights of consciousness through creativity with infinite possibilities. Work with a team (Satsang). These higher frequencies are to be amplified. We are a Family of Light. And we have freedom of choice and freedom to Evolve. We are One, everything is interconnected, interdependent, interrelated, and integrated as a whole.

The field is the sole governing agency of the Particle. The field in the Universe & the field of each human being unteracts. You can heal yourself and heal others too; by harmonizing, by using positive vibration field, by positive thoughts, emotions, and feelings put into Synchronous Action with Intent and Intensity. The field of our Heart is part of the world around us. Be kind, cooperative, humble, loving, helping, compassionate, supportive, open hearted and joy giving. Exhilarating in full enjoyment of divinity in sublime synchronous harmony. The power of many Hearts in a state of Unity has the Awesome Potential to bring peace, happiness, joy and beauty to our planet.

- ❖ **The Law of Focus** ~ You can't think of two things at the same time. When our Focus is on Spiritual Values, it is impossible for us to have lower thoughts such as greed or anger.
- ❖ **The Law of Cause & Effect** ~ As you sow, so shall you reap. Whatever we put out in the Universe is what comes back to us.

- **The Law of Change** ~ History repeats itself until we learn the lessons that we need to change our path.
- There is no Time like The Present! Merge with NOW! Awaken & Live in this moment with Enjoyment.
- Enhance your Perception through 'Yoga'.
- **The law of Significance and Inspiration** ~ You get back from something whatever you've put into it, The Value of something is a direct result of the energy and intent that is put into it.

The Power of Intention:

- Connect to the power that created you to know the meaning of life.
- You are beyond the body & mind- the greatest truth is that you are the spirit.
- One must know the Spirit to know the Truth.
  Meditation is the only way to grow. The growth of awareness takes place in the silence of thoughtless doubtless awareness. Connect to the Power that created you, know that you are that Power, Commune with ... that power intimately, and meditate to allow that growth of Awareness to Take Place.
  - H.H. Shri. Mataji.
- Presence in Present, Pure Awareness, Be's in itself, Present in Now, this, isness, suchness, as it is, Stillness, Silence, in a Moment, Fullness, wholeness, Inclusiveness, Thoughtless, Doubtless, timeless, Spaceless, Transcending Consciousness, Eye of the I am. True Awakening in a moment, Accept as it is ... in bliss, peace, love, joy, beauty, and truth, whatever you accept you go beyond...... the perfect state is in Accepting 'Now' as it is, Moment by moment .... "You shall know the tree by its fruit".
- Be contentless consciousness, pure lightless light, beyond mind, beyond limited human intellect, perceptions, concepts, conditionings, etc.
- Transit from Relativity to Supreme Reality, the non-being essentiality,
- You are God to the Extent you know God.

The Subconscious Mind:

If you want to Change your life, you must change your Paradigm (your subconscious mind). When a Paradigm changes, your Life Changes. Paradigm is formed by Repetition of Information.

Your Thoughts, Emotions and Feelings with positive Greater Intensity with Intent will change the Programming of your Subconscious Mind very fast. As the Paradigm of subconscious Mind changes, your life will Change.

Replication of Idea → positive Affirmation e.g. I am so happy and grateful now that money comes to me in increasing quantities through multiple sources on a continuous basis.

Realization of the Self:

While meditating, always begin with understanding that I don't know! Now! With deep inquiry within your heart of hearts, ask yourself who am I? Known within yourself that you are not senses of this body, you are not this physical body, you are not this mental facility, you are not intellect, emotions, and the thinking mind; Not this... Not this...Not this.... then, who you really are? With your silent effulgent pure Awareness, you realize that you are part and parcel of this whole, which is Omniscient, Omnipresent, Omnipotent, Eternal, Blissful, Joyful and Beautiful. You are a glorious divine Soul, divine part of "The Almighty Lord" "MahaPrabhu".

When you realize this and see your Real Self by the Self, you immediately Act to change & transform which you are not- to be your real Self. Purity & cleanliness is Next to Godliness. Your consciousness changes and makes a shift to transform your physical gross body to make it dynamic and healthy, your mind pure and focused, your emotions gentle and effective, your intelligence sharp & discriminative with reality & truth, your brain intuitive, alert, and active, your heart full of love, joy, bliss, peace, compassion and with divine beauty. You remove all impurities, negativities, conditionings, ideations, all imbalances from within your body, mind, intellect, emotions, etc. This happens spontaneously & automatically because you now observe and notice clearly who you really are not.

By seeing non self or false self clearly, all your Actions under the control of Real Self become Real. Your actions are divinely spirited, pure, unconditional, powerful without any conceptualization, ideation, comparison, egoism, etc. You do Righteous actions as per Dharma because now you know complete Reality. You know what you really are and, what you are not. You totally surrender to the "Almighty Lord" and establish a harmonious connection of your Real Self with the Supreme Self. You are now fully aware of 'Maya' the illusionary play of the Divine.

At this moment of realization of your true Self, you start transforming, cultivating to attain your Selfhood, your Salvation, your Enlightenment, Mukti, Nirvana, Self- realization, Moksha (Liberation) and Freedom.

Antimatter is Spirit:

Matter & Spirit Co-exist. Spirit de-constructs everything. All transformation takes place because of Spirit. Matter & Energy follow the Spirit. Whole Cosmos is the Interplay of Spirit & Energy. Spirit is reflected in the energy and matter. They are interconnected by consciousness. Spirit Needs Energy. Spirit cannot do anything without Energy. Energy follows Spirit. Energy is useless without Spirit. Principle of Mutual co-existence of Spirit & Energy is everywhere, it is Universal. "The Soul" is the Witnessing, Enjoying Beauty.

❖ Beauty Awakens the Soul to Act.

- Dante Alighieri

❖ To Love Beauty is to See Light.

- Victor Hugo

❖ Of life's two chief Prizes, beauty & truth, I found the first in a loving heart & the second in a Laborer's hand.

- Khalil Gibran

❖ Beauty in things exists in the mind which contemplates them.

- David Hume

❖ Rare is the union of beauty & purity.

- Juvenal

❖ Vision is the Art of Seeing things invisible.

❖ Anyone who keeps the ability to see beauty never grows old.

- Franz Kafka.

❖ Everything has beauty, but not everyone sees it.

- Confucius

- Our mental conceptions cannot stand the potent light of truth.
- **It's all Beauty**, "God is Beauty", Beauty has truth, divinity, innate pure nature, dharma, divine wisdom, Param Chaitanya, Supreme Consciousness and Divine Pristine Awareness. It is Omniscient, Omnipresent, Omnipotent, Supreme Intelligence, Supreme Energy, Supreme Bliss, Serenity, Soundarya, Eternity and Divine Art. There is beauty everywhere. You just must find it, experience, and enjoy it. To be in Beauty is to be in Peace. Peace is when you are established in this Beauty. Love emerges when you are at peace with Beauty. Love is the fragrance of Beauty, it spreads spontaneously and automatically. Love for all Beautiful creation gives real divine Joy. Miracles happen from Beauty. Beauty is one unified and is everywhere. Life is Beauty of Enjoyment of Beauty.

Brahman Satyam Jagat Mithya:

Brahman (Ultimate Reality) is the only Truth, the World is illusory, and there is ultimately no difference between the individual Self and the Brahman.

Mithya means neither true nor false. The world cannot be false because we all clearly see and perceive it. Shankaracharya says that the world is not true either, because it is constantly changing and everything that the world has to offer is temporary, transient, and impermanent.

Realization of the individual Self, Atman in its purest state (without the ego) is nothing but realizing the Brahman. This point of realization of the Self, Atman as Brahman itself, is the Zero Point. Making the mind calm and quiet and directing the single-pointed concentration inwards, meditating on the Self with Shraddha (Faith) realize the true Self by the Self.

Om Asato Maa Sad-Gamaya |
Tamaso Maa Jyotir-Gamaya |
Mrtyor-Maa Amritam Gamaya |
Om Shaantih Shaantih Shaantih ||

"Om, lead us from Unreality (of transitory Existence) to the Reality (of the Eternal Self), lead us from the darkness (of Ignorance) to The Light (of Spiritual knowledge), Lead us from the fear of Death to the knowledge of Immortality. Om Peace, Peace, Peace."

Meditating on the inquiry of the Self, one Realizes one's Shadow Self and Real Self (Atman), which initiates the process of transformation from transitory illusory Self to Eternal Real Self, from darkness of ignorance to the light of knowledge of the Self (Atman), from mortal material world with fear of death to immortal Spiritual Eternal World, realizing the play of 'Maya' (divine illusory play) and Eternity.

Upon Self-realization and Enlightenment transformation is experienced From, Shava to Shiva, Shadow to Real, Darkness to Light, Ignorance to Knowledge of Atman, Illusion to Reality, Untruth to Truth, and from Mortal to Immortal.

E + Shava = Shiva (Shava = Dead, and E=Divine Energy)

It means when Divine Spiritual Energy flows into the dead body; it starts to live; hence called as Shiva.

Shiva is a mendicant. He remains in his bhadraasana and engrossed in his tapa. He does not move. He doesn't breathe as he's Yogeshwar and Yogis are said to have control over their breathing pattern. His eyes are shut and his gaze inwards.

Without Nature, mind ceases to exist. Without mind, the Nature remains unobserved and hence invisible. Thus, both mind and nature, Purusha and Prakriti complement and complete each other's purpose.

Being actively one with ParaBrahmn. Union of your divine Soul with 'The Supreme Soul' is the highest divine activity of Divine Friendship. Friendliness is a real essence of All Existences. Friendliness with love to yourself, with all beings, non-beings & with Nature is the life's purpose.

Practice spiritually to be surrendered to Supreme Paramatma. Be one with Nirakar Parabrahma. Be in pristine effulgent awareness of the Self in oneness with Sakaar and Nirakar Parabrahman. Be in a state of beauty, peace, bliss, love, and eternal joy. Be in a state of complete detachment with illusory world and steadfast with the reality and truth of the all-pervading Brahman "Mahaprabhu" ("The Almighty Lord").

Science of 'Zero–Point' Energy: It is the lowest possible energy of a quantum system or field. Quantum systems constantly fluctuate in their lowest energy state as described by the Heisenberg uncertainty principle. According to the quantum field theory, the Universe can be thought of not as isolated particles but continuous fluctuating fields: matter fields, whose quanta are fermions (i.e., leptons and quarks), and force fields, whose quanta are Bosons (e.g., Photons and gluons). All these fields have zero-point energy. These fluctuating zero-point fields lead to a kind of reintroduction of an aether in physics. Since some systems can detect the existence of this energy; however, this aether cannot be thought of as a physical medium if it is to be Lorentz invariant such that there is no contradiction with Einstein's theory of special relativity. Many physicists believe that the vacuum holds the key to a full understanding of Nature.

Zero-Point energy, vibrational energy that molecules retain even at the absolute zero of temperature. Zero-point energy, also known as ground state energy, could be the greatest gift the quantum world can ever give us. It's a byproduct of the fact that subatomic particles don't really behave like single particles, but like waves constantly flitting between different energy states. This means even the seemingly empty vacuum of Space is a roiling sea of virtual particles fluctuating in and out of existence, and all those fluctuations require energy. If there's as much energy in those fluctuations as some - though definitely not all - physicists believe, and if we could ever learn how to tap into this phenomenon, we would gain access to an unparalleled source of energy. Zero-Point energy could power the planet with the strength of multiple Suns, making it easy for us to solve Earth's energy problems forever or to travel beyond the solar system and take our place among the stars. However, we can only guess how much energy is contained in the vacuum.

Simply put, we don't know enough about the universe to figure out whether zero-point energy- vacuum energy - really is a bombastic fountain of staggering power.

Shunyata: In Buddhist philosophy, the voidness that constitutes ultimate reality; Shunyata is seen not as negation of existence but rather as undifferentiation out of which all apparent entities, distinctions and dualities arise. Madhyamika (middle way) is sometimes called the Shunyavaada or Doctrine that All is Void. (The Spirit and Energy in its purest essence form united and perfectly balanced as one) Shunyata means emptiness or voidness. It is the highest meditative state or experience. It is the primordial empty awareness, Eternal awareness. Shunyata in Sanskrit means devoid-ness, emptiness, hollow, hollowness, voidness. Shunya means zero, nothing, empty, void, hollow and 'ta' means "ness".

The term emptiness is used in three ways 1) as a meditative dwelling 2) as an attribute of objects, and 3) as a type of awareness - release.

Shunya - Emphasizes seeing phenomena as 'being empty'.

In the text, a series of contemplations is given for each aggregate: form is like 'a lump of foam'; sensation like 'a water bubble'; perception like "a mirage"; formations like "a plantain tree"; and cognition is like "a magical illusion" (maya).

"Monks, sensual pleasures are impermanent, hollow, false, deceptive; they are illusory (mayakatame), the prattle of fool." Emptiness as a mental state, means a mode of perception in which one neither adds anything to nor takes anything away from what is present, noting simply, 'There is this'.

Vedas Shunya (Zero-Point):

Everything is encoded in 'Vedic Mantras' .... even several births cannot derive all meanings of single 'Mantra'. The concept of 'Shunya', or Zero, Void, was originally conceived as the symbol of Brahman, expressing the sum of all distinct forms. Shunya in the decimal system of notation, it describes how the number increases by 10 by writing Zero in front of it. In fact, the concept of Shunya was not just mathematical or scientific but is deeply rooted in all branches of thought - especially metaphysics & cosmology. Shunya is the transition point between opposites, it symbolizes the real balance between divergent tendencies. Most ancient mathematicians defined zero as the sum to two equal and opposite quantities. Zero produces all figures but is itself not limited to certain value. Zero is the primary or final reservoir of all single numbers. Shoonya as Nothingness /Emptiness) void was originally conceived as the symbol of Brahman, expressing nothingness or void or mere emptiness. Void that exists in the space within and without. Zero /

Shunya is both negative and positive, and thus has a "presence" in both the realms.

The ancient Hindu symbol of a circle with a dot in the middle, known as 'Bindu', symbolizing the void and the negation of the Self, was probably instrumental in the use of a circle as a representation of the concept of Zero.

Indian Vedic philosophy has glorified concepts like the material world being an illusion (Maya), the act renouncing the material world (Tyaga) and the goal of merging into the Void of Eternity (Mukti, Liberation, Nirvana). In Vedas the terms used to describe Zero included Pujyam, Shunyam, Bindu the concept of Void or Blank was termed as Shukla and Shubra. In the Void there is Brahman in the form of Sat-Chit-Ananda (Truth-Consciousness-Bliss), which itself is complete. So, Voidness - and Completeness is Brahman itself. All is Brahman.

Vedic Mantra for Brahman (Completeness & Voidness):

> Om Purnamadah Purnamidam Purnat purnamudachyate |
> Purnasya Purnamadaya Purnamevavashishyate | |

> Meaning: That is full, this also is full. This Fullness came from that Fullness. Though this fullness came from that Fullness, That Fullness remains forever Full.

(That refers to Parabrahman; This refers to Brahman which is Nama Rupastha i.e., which is having name, form, i.e., entire Cosmos, Existence, infinite Brahman).

When we get the required knowledge (Divya Vidya), which removes the ignorance or veil that make us to differentiate between this two so called types of the same Brahman, then only the ParaBrahman which is the cause of everything, is that which remains. It is universally accepted that the concept of infinity, Zero and decimal system are the original contributions of ancient Vedic knowledge of India, which have played a very vital role for the progress of human civilization and culture on this planet. Several ideas like the origin and shape of the universe, meaning of time, the concepts of infinite God and infinitesimal Soul were the subject matter of academic discussions during the Vedic period.

According to the Vedas, "Mahaprabhu" ("The Great Lord", "God") is Ananta (Infinite): Let us have a clear understanding of the meaning of this word Infinite; and use it in its proper Sense. That which is not limited by Time and Space and not subject to the law of Causation, which is above time, space and beyond all laws, is infinite. God is not limited by time or space, neither has he any cause. He is Absolute. The infinite again must be one, otherwise it is finite. If there be any other thing beside that infinite, then it is no longer infinite; it is limited by that object, consequently it has become finite. Thus, if we admit that God is infinite, we deny the existence of any other thing besides God; otherwise, he would be limited by that thing, and be subject to time, space, and the law of causation. If we think of ourselves as separate from God, as independent of this Being, then in our thought we have denied His illimitable Nature. There is for the same reason, not a single particle of matter in the Universe that can exist independent of God's existence or outside God.

If He is infinite and one, our bodies and everything of the universe from the minutest atom to be largest planetary system, from the lowest animalcule to the highest Being, exists in and through that infinite Existence. If God is infinite and one, then mind and matter, subject and object, creator and creation, and all relative dual existences are within that Being, and not outside of it. The whole Universe is in God and God is in it; it is inseparable from God. I am in Him, and He is in me; each one of us in inseparable from His being; if one atom of my body exists, that existence cannot be separated from His existence. Now we know that Universal Soul is infinite. How can infinity have parts? How can it be broken up, divided?

Infinite can never be divided. If that were possible it would be no more infinite. Again, there can be no two infinities. If there be two infinities, how would you demarcate their respective spheres? The Infinite is spaceless and timeless; therefore, it is neither a cause nor an effect. Hence, when the full Universe comes from full (Purna) Almighty, nothing has happened. It may look as if God has not created the Universe at all if we go deep into it.

He is exactly in the same eternal glory that He was prior to that action that we are imputing to Him as creation. Having created, He is full (Purna). This universe also appears to be full for us in a relative sense. God is Absolute Fullness, and the Universe is relative fullness. Infinity makes a Divine being all-inclusive.

Infinity refers to something that has no end. In mathematical terms, we can express infinity as a numberless number. It does not increase by adding anything or decrease by subtracting anything from it.

In the Vedic Shloka "Infinity is born from Infinity and when we take infinity out of infinity, only infinity remains". It is very interesting to note the relationship between Zero and Infinity. Anything divided by Zero is Infinity. The first Purnam relates to the Infinity and the later one to Zero which is a root for Infinity.

In Taittariya Updanished, Brahman has been described as "Satyam Gynanam Anantam Brahman", which means Brahman is truth, knowledge, and infinity. In the Vedas, infinity Mantra reverberates through the Purnanic texts. This is the Shanti Mantra which unites us. The oneness Principle 'Akhandattva'.

'The Mahashoonya' (The Great Zero) means Nothingness, Void and Emptiness. To contemplate on infinity, you must first contemplate on 'The Mahashoonya' (The Great Zero). The Mahashoonya is symbolically, represented as Dot in a circle (Infinity). The idea of 'Poorna from Poorna' of Infinity Mantra (Shanti Mantra) represents a repeating motif. It is this repeating aspect that makes the mantra so significant. Bhartiya (Indian) tradition truly attempted to understand the Infinite. Sanskrit word 'Ananta' means infinite, infinity, endless, eternal, unlimited, boundless, limitless and unending. While describing the Veda, scholars begin with the description: "Ananta Vai Vedah", i.e. "The Vedas are verily endless".

Swami Vivekananda said, "It is an insult to a starving people to offer them religion; it is an insult to a starving man to teach him metaphysics".

Methematics: Zero:

The whole between –1 and 1, with the symbol '0' shows that there is no amount. Zero is not positive and is also not negative. When we add Zero to a number the result is just the number, unchanged. When we multiply a number by Zero, we get Zero,

$$A+0 = A,\ A-0 = A,\ A\times 0 = 0,\ A/0 = \text{undefined},$$
$$(\text{Infinity})?\ 0! = 1\ (0\ \text{factorial}=1)$$

Infinity: Infinity has no end. Infinity means "endless", "boundless" Infinity does not grow. Infinity is not "getting larger", it is already fully formed. Infinity does not do anything, it just is. Infinity is not a real number; it is an idea. An idea of something without an end. Infinity cannot be measured. Infinity is simple. Yes! It is simpler than things which do have an end. Because when something has end, we must define where that end is. A line goes in both directions without end.

Nasadiya Sukta (Hymn), (Hymn of Creation) (Rigveda):

It is concerned with cosmology and the origin of the universe.

"Then even non-existence was not there, nor existence, there was no air then, nor the space beyond it. What covered it? Where was it? In whose keeping? Was there then cosmic fluid, in depths unfathomed?

Nasadiya Sukta begins rather interestingly, with the statement. "Then, there was neither existence, nor non-existence." It ponders over the when, why, and by whom of creation in a very sincere contemplative tone and provides no definite answers. Rather, it Concludes that the Gods too may not know, as they came after creation. And maybe the supervisor of creation in the highest heaven knows, or maybe even he does not know.

Nasadiya Suktam:

> Nasadasinno Sadasittadanim Nasidrajo No Vyoma Paro Yat |
> Kimavarivah Kuha Kasya Sharmannambhah Kimasidgahanam Gabhiram | |

Synchronous:

Existing or occurring at the same time or speed. Simultaneously, happening, existing, or arising at precisely the same time. Occurring or recurring exactly together and at the same rate, instantaneous, synchronized, coordination in time, in unison.

Resonance: (used about sound) The quality of being resonant, 'Anunaad' ,'Gunj' Resonance the sound produced in an object by sound of a similar frequency from another object. The production of a sound because of, vibration of another object. (If a sound has resonance, it is deep, clear, and strong)' A resonance in the sound which is produced by an object when it vibrates at the same rate as the sound waves from another object.

Naad: Divine Sound, Divine music which is heard in higher state of meditation. It is the unstruck sound reverberating in the Cosmos.

Anahad Naad: Dhvani is the worldly sound which is produced. Naad is a fundamental sound of existence. When a mantra is chanted for a long time, Naad arises from within. It is a cosmic divine sound quite unlike the sounds of this world. Every sound of this world is produced through friction, contact, vibration, and obstruction, this is called Aahata. However, cosmic vibration, if one can hear it, is eternal and existent without any friction, this is called Anahata (Unstruck). All great Saints speak of this sound which can be heard in the spiritual center in one's heart region, the Anahata Chakra (Heart Chakra). It is not produced by us but only heard. A 'Yogi' can hear this. It is the subtlest sound.

'Chitta' or thought waves are difficult to control. So, one can get the mind (Chitta) to be entirely absorbed and concentrated by listening to the Naada, which arises from within, after mantra chanting. This sound, according to 'Naada Bindu Upanishad', acts like a sharp goad to control the maddened elephant of 'Chitta' or snare for binding the deer 'Chitta', or shore to the ocean waves of 'Chitta'.

NaadaBindu: Naadabindu refers to the union of Shiva and Shakti (Spirit and Energy), where Naada means Shiva and Bindu (Dot) (Energy) means Shakti.

Naada is like the sound made after closing both the lips, or like softly touching thumb and first finger. Naada is Consciousness about to manifest as the universe. It is the Subtlest Sound Vibration; this subtle sound vibration can best be explained by the Sanskrit letter म (ma). Humming sound after softly saying mantra "ॐ" (Om). There is no other way to explain this. Without Naada, Bindu Cannot be effective as 'Bindu' cannot be pronounced separately. Naad Bindu refers to the union of Shiva and Shakti, where Naada means Shiva and Bindu means Shakti (Power, Energy). Hence the universe is pervaded by Shiva and Shakti (Spirit and Energy). Bindu is the support of

Naada. The Universe has the support of Bindu. Both Bindu and Naada together support the entire Universe. Accordingly, "the entire universe consisting of the movable and the immovable is of the nature of Bindu (Dot) and Naada (Divine Sound Vibration). The unification of the Bindu and the Nanda is called Sakalikarana and the Universe takes its birth as a result of this Sakalikarana. The phallic emblem is the fusion of Bindu and Naada and is the cause of the Universe. "Goddess of the form Bindu (Shakti) is the mother and Shiva (Spirit) of the form of Naada is the father". The Supreme Brahman sounded his drum that gave out the Divine Naada. Its resonant, reverberating sound pervaded the three worlds heightening enthusiasm and called upon everyone in diverse ways.

Naada (नाद) - The evolution of the material world is complemented by that of the world of language encompassing transcendent, subtle, and gross sounds. The transcendent sound - principle is 'Naada' from which evolve articulate speech, letters, syllables, words, and sentences. Naada (The transcendent Spiritual Principle) Complements Bindu, the transcendent material principle. This is the fundamental principle of the science of mantras, and hence their relevance in building rites. The potency of the seed syllables (Bija / Beeja) owes to the conceived undifferentiated unity of naada and bindu in them.

In Sanskrit, Vyakarana (Grammar) meaning voice, resonance, tone, the sound caused by the vibration of the vocal cords, in the open glottis when the air passes through them. Sound, articulate sound generally without Sense, which is momentary. The highest Sound (Para Dhwani). Naada (voiced) refers to a type of abhyantara (internal effort) of articulation. Naada (voiced) occurs, for instance when pronouncing "Om", ga, ma, pa, dha. Naada is the universal pulse of life. It is the flowing stream of consciousness. In Yoga, Naada refers to the nasal sound often found in mystical words, mantras. The Naada or Shabda is the first expression of Creation. The Shabda Brahman is the cause of the manifest and differentiated word and meaning or the subtle and crude objects. Without understanding the meaning and significance of Sphota or the eternal word, one cannot become one with Brahman. The Supreme Bliss is accomplished only after the removal of Naada-Bindu ignorance. Tantra prescribes Naada-Bindu Yoga for the attainment of supreme oneness with

Param Shiva. Naada (reed) is mentioned in the Rigveda as growing in lakes, and in the Atharvaveda,it is described as Varshika (produced in the rains). Naada (roar), a prolonged or continuing sound, a reverberated sound (e.g. A lion's roar (Simha Naada) as it reverberates in The Jungle) (A Sound of a Cloud Thunder). To be or to keep under the hum and buzz of, i.e., to pursue intently and devotedly; to be engrossed by the desire of contemplation. To be lost or spoiled - the true sound of a vessel & as from a crack. To be no more-one's credit or great name. To destroy one's credit or great name. To draw after, to hold in expectation; make to dance. See quarrel from quarrel.

In Yoga Philosophy, the nasal sound (Naada) is represented by a semicircle. Naada is also a praise of "The Lord".

Naada in Vedic terminology refers to the unstruck sound or "Anahata Naada" (Hearts Throbbing); which is reported as a thin buzzing resonant sound being heard when the ears are closed with fingers; and upon whom meditating, a person attains the "Turya" state of meditation easily. This Anahata Nanda is heard in silence and deep meditative state.

A Yogin, at the start of his practice, concentrates in the inner side of right ear from inside and, hears many sounds proceeding from those like an ocean and clouds (It is said that this starts from sounds of flute, cymbals, and cloud thunder). These filter out, and over time, he can hear more subtle sounds such as single note of musical instruments at his will and get absorbed in whichever sound note he wants to, asserts the Vedic text. (The Yogin contemplates on Omkara ("OM"), as it leads one to the knowledge of Aatman or Self, helps him overcome his Karma's. Agyan (Ignorance) as the cause of bondage, to remove ignorance, yogin should listen to his inner voice in meditative state; the inner voice in the Heart of the Heart). This focus on sound notes helps the yogi destroy distractions from other senses and fluctuations of his mind, just like a bee focused on honey does not care about the odor that surrounds it. Such a Yogi does not care about fame or disgrace from others, he does not feel heat or cold, neither happiness nor sorrow, he is lost within, in his self, in Brahman-Pranava("OM"). The goal of Yoga, asserts the Vedic text, is to realize the transcendent Atman, its existence in everyone, and its oneness with Brahman through meditation and absorption into Naada Brahman, Divine Sound Vibration "OM".

AmrutaBindu Upanishad: Amruta Naada-Bindu is Zero-Point. The esoteric doctrine of Bindu (point) or Naada (Reverberation) of the word "OM" which signifies Brahman. Is a drop of Nectar which grants immortality (Divine Ambrosia). It is an Immortal Point. It differentiates between vocal recitation of the "OM" syllable and its non-vocal practice.

[NaadaBindu: Amruta Bindu, Tejo Bindu, Yogashikha, Dhyan Bindu, Brahman Bindu, Yogatattva.]

The text opens stating that it is wise, who after reading the textbooks repeatedly, throw away the books and proceed to the practice of Yoga with meditation on the silent, invisible "Om", in their pursuit of the Brahman–knowledge (Ultimate, Unchanging reality). The Upanishad differentiates the mind under impure and pure state and assigns its character as bondage and Liberation. Further enquiry into the crux of the matter reveals that Truth is realized within, which is our real Self.

The withdrawal of mind and sensory organs from external objects, and redirecting them to introspection, this is Pratyahara.

Pranayama breathing exercises consisting of Rechaka (exhaling completely), Puraka (inhaling Deeply) and Kumbhaka (retaining breath for various intervals). Dharana is concentrated introspection on Atman (Self, Soul) with one's mind. Taraka is reflecting and inner reasoning between one's Mind and Soul. Dhyanam is contemplation and meditation. Samadhi is communion with and in one's Soul.

A Yogin must drink enough water and breathe deeply to cleanse the body and senses. Yogin must practice various breathing exercises. Against fear, against anger, against sloth, against too much waking and sleeping. Against too much eating, against starvation. A yogin shall always be on his Guard.

Oneness of Atman in all beings: Cows are of various colors, milk is one –colored, the wise man looks upon Soul as milk, of bodies as cows of different garbs, knowledge is hidden, as butter in milk (Amrita Bindu Upanishad). The mind is the cause of bondage and liberation. A mind that craves for something else is in bondage, one that doesn't is liberated. Spirituality is geared to obtain inner purity, calmness of mind, and ultimately, liberation. In the state of liberation, the mental components like virtue and vice become irrelevant.

Amaita Bindu Vedanta theory of non-dualism (Advaita). It states that "there is only One-Self in all creatures, that one appears many just as the moon appears many when reflected in many water droplets", and the toughest connection yet most liberating connection one can make is with one's own Self (Soul), which is very difficult because it is concealed by Maya. When one successfully removes this veil, look within, one realizes the Self and its unity with the eternal, indestructible, unchanging truth that is one with the Universe. Asserting that one who has realized this True Divine Knowledge attains Liberation, Moksha, Nirvana.

Anahata Naada: The unstuck Sound vibration. The initial creative impulses arose as spandan or thought vibration of the Pure Being. The sound that emanated from the vibration was 'Om' AUM. In its transcendental aspect, it is difficult to establish contact with the Supreme Being. However, the nearest approach is Sound Vibration, also referred to as Aparam Brahman. Super-charged with transcendent Soul- force, sound is, in all Creation, reverberating, the one, powerful principle that widely influences and effectively brings under control all other manifestations. Self-realized beings, the Siddhas, Yogis, discovered that there exists a definite relationship between sound and mind. The mind, in the process of being attracted towards sound, loses awareness of the external world altogether. Through meditation, Seekers, Sadhakas, and Yogis endeavor to establish contact with the Divine Sound Vibration, which is all pervading, the Anahata Naada that helps in subduing the turbulent mind that keeps roving in the pleasure garden of sensual objects and giving it a new, inward direction. As the Sadhaka delves deeper within, he realizes that his physical and astral bodies, his senses, and the mind, all have sound as their basis. An analysis of one's individual existence takes one to sound before one reaches the Eternal Self. Anahata Naada also forms the basis in all the seven Chakras or Plexuses located within the Sushumna that extends from the base the spine to the crown of the head. The Brahmarandhra or the tenth door. Since the Lower three Chakras Muladhara, Swadhishthana and Manipura (Nabhi) are dominated by the tattvas Earth, water, and fire respectively, this Anahata Naada which is subtlest is not clearly heard in these. Anahata Chakra, which corresponds to the cardiac plexus in the physical body, is the center of Vayu Tattva. Anahata Naada, called the sound of the Shabda Brahman, emanates from this center.

Significantly, Anahata Naada is the unstruck, mystic sound that occurs spontaneously and is not the result of striking or beating certain things. Depending upon the intensity of a Saadhaka's concentration and the level of mental purity, Anahata Naada can be distinctly heard in deep meditation, paving the way for the seeker's evolution to the highest level of consciousness. Anahata Naada manifests itself in different ways ranging from the sound that is like the beating of the waves of the sea to the deafening peals of huge bells and the holy sound of the Conch (Shankh Naada). When the seeker hears the sound of flute, his entire being is permeated with Divine Bliss and he loses body-consciousness; the sound of the kettledrum bestows the seeker with powers of Clairvoyance and the ability to see distant objects. But the Naada that leads the Sadhaka to the goal of 'Yoga', Nirvikalpa Samadhi, is the Meghanaada, the Sound of thunder. Gurus say that constant hearing of Meghanaada for some days in deep meditation enables the seeker to enter the abode of Chiti, Pure Consciousness, where he experiences the tranquility of the supra-causal state of consciousness. The Saadhaka then begins to understand that there are two dimensions to Chiti: One is the supremely pure transcendent aspect which transcends the world, and the other is the immanent aspect, in which by free will, there is differentiation, attribution and the projection of the wondrous Universe on the canvas of the Supreme Being. Despite appearing as the Universe with myriad diversities and impurities, chiti retains her immaculate purity and remains absolutely untainted. Anahata Naada - Soundless sounds. These sounds are in all the parts of our body. Through Self-realization you become the Soul and get established in the Self (Brahmanishtha). Anahata Naada the Silent Sound. Nirvichaara (Thoughtlessness) is a state without thoughts, a state like a stone, Nirvikalpa is a state of no 'I' -ness. Except for a Gyani (Dnyani), Nirvikalpa state cannot be found anywhere. Knowing the Self, no worldly sadness, unhappiness will touch you.

Liberation (Mukti) - It is the Samadhi experience you get when you arrive at Zero-Point. There is nothing you have in your attention- No-Body, No-Mind, No-Thought, No-Emotions, No-Intellect, No-Ego, No-Relationships, Nothing of material Possessions, No-Desires,

No-Consciousness. Everything personal becomes absolutely Zero. Zero-Point is a gateway for Nowhere to Everywhere, Nothing to Everything, Merging to Expanding. Your real connection to the whole Universe takes place at this Zero-Point. You experience limitlessness, complete fullness, a State of Sat-Chit-Ananda, absolute peace, bliss, joy, and beauty. This is the point of Infinite possibilities, potencies, knowledge, creativity, transformation, experiencing reality, love, peace bliss, joy, and divine Beauty. It is a point of divine Revelation of "Mahaprabhu" ("The Great Lord").

Shunya shikhar par anahad baaje,
Nirbhay nirgun gun re gaunga. -- Sant Kabir

Introduction

Mool Kamal Dradh Aasan Bandhu-ji Ulti Pavan Chadaunga,
Man Mamta Ko Thir Kar Laun-ji Pancho Tat Milaunga,
Ingala Pingala Sukhman Nadi-ji Tirveni Pe Haun Nahaunga,
Panch Pachhison Pakad Mangaun-ji Ek Hi Dor Lagaunga,
Shunya Shikhar Par Anhad Baje-ji Raag Chattis Sunaunga,
Kahat Kabir Suno Bhai Sadho-ji Jeet Nishan Ghuraunga,

Translation

Fearlessly I Will Sing the Attributes of the One without Attributes.
Using the Base Lotus as the Steady Seat. I Will Make the Wind Rise in Reverse. Steadying the Mind's Attachments. I Will Unify the Five Elements.
Ingila, *Pingala* and *Sukhman* are the Channels. I Will Bathe at the Confluence of the Three Rivers.
The Five and Twenty-Five I Will Master by my Wish, And String them Together by One Common Thread.
At the Summit of Aloneness, the Un-struck *Anahad* Sound Reverberates, I Will Play the Thirty-Six Different Symphonies.
Says Kabir Listen Oh Practicing Aspirant I Will Wave the Flag of Victory.

Explanation

In this song, Kabir clearly shows the "real" meaning of certain phrases used in ancient texts. Often these are mistaken to be reference to physical places while in reality an internal experience is actually being told.

Fear is the first and the biggest obstacle to spiritual realization. And a state of fearlessness shows that a person has actually-accepted the environment or physical reality for what it is. In that state of accepting oneness, Kabir says that he is going to expound on the attributes of the ultimate.

Mapping out the procedure for this spiritual journey, Kabir says that we must start by rooting ourselves (as the tree or plant roots itself) at the base or seat of the energy. The lotus is a reference to a spiritual experience of energy that "flowers" much like a lotus rising above the negativ ity and fear. Note that the source for nourishment of this lotus is indeed coming from the same swampy muck of negativity. In other words, the negativity or fear is not intrinsically "bad" but really needs to be channeled into more creative expressions. In such a re-channeling of energy, the subtle life force (much like a wind or molecular energy current) starts defying gravity (of our limitations) and moves in a reverse elevating fashion. The further it moves up the less constrained it becomes, - in effect integrating all of reality into a universal oneness.

What pulls the energy down is the gravitational force of our attachments. Therefore, the mind needs to be steadied to a state of equilibrium where these attachments are no longer forcing us downward to the realm of fear. In such a state of upward transition, the earthy reality of fear gets transformed to the watery reality of creativity, then the fiery reality of power onto the airy reality of love and finally the ethereal realm of freedom and total spatial detachment. In effect, the five elements of Earth, Water, Fire, Air and Ether are merged in a transcendental fashion.

At this stage of the journey, the pair of opposites are balanced. That is, the cold dispassionate channel and the hot passionate channel are balanced in the center channel through a dynamic equilibrium. However, reality is still flowing, and time is not transcended. Only when the triad of flows (cold, hot, and lukewarm, or past, future, and present, or left, right and center) merge that one is able to overcome the grip of Kala or time. It is then that the three rivers or channels merge at the confluence of Triveni and one takes a Holy dip of immortality. Why immortality? Because, at this point, the constraints of both space (through the unifying of the five elements) and time (through the merging of the three channels) have been removed. In fact, the holy dip in the immortality of Triveni is an internal experience and the physical location of Prayag (Allahabad, India) is only a reminder of this inner truth. In other words, Kabir is indicating that only when one experiences such holy bathing within, does one become immortal and not by a mere dip in the waters of the three rivers at Allahabad.

When such a confluence is achieved, one has the ability of controlling the five senses and twenty-five ways of experiencing world and stringing them with the oneness of your inner self much like a garland. Since there is nothing but yourself, Kabir calls it the summit of nothingness. The feat of reaching the summit of creation is celebrated by the waving of a flag of victory and sounds of a myriad of rhythmic symphonies coming from the eternal un-struck sound that brings forth the entire creation itself.

MahaSadhaka – MahaSatsangSeva – MahaGurukripa – MahaAvahana

The Great Spiritual Seeker - Serving Divine Collective - Blessings of MahaGuru – Great Appeal

MahaSaadhaka - The Great Spiritual Seeker.

'Maha' means Great and 'Saadhaka' means the Seeker of Truth. 'Sadhya' means Goal and 'dhyas' means driven by intense aspiration. 'Saadhaka' means the Seeker who is driven by intense aspiration on the path of seeking; or driven towards Goal. Faithful yearning towards spiritual Goal. The word Sadhaka is a combination of three virtues of God. 'Saa' means 'manifestation in the form of Principles, 'dha' means retention in the form of activities and 'ka' means proficiency in the form of capability. He who is adorned with these three virtues, is a Saadhaka. Manifestation in the form of Principle generates dhyas for Chaitanya (Divine Consciousness), retention in the form of activities puts the dhyas in activity form and proficiency in the form of capability culminates the dhyas in gains in the form of Anand (Bliss). Without Saadhana, there is no certain goal in life; without a goal, there is no stability; without Stability, there is no Brahman; without realizing Brahman, there is no liberation; without liberation, there is no merging with God; without merging, there is no Moksha (Final Liberation); without Moksha, there is no knowledge about Ultimate Truth. One who, without wasting any time, runs through this sequential process, gaining momentum during the course by way of yearning, conquering the pinnacle of Saadhana in the form of Moksha and thereby reaching the Ultimate Anand (Divine Peace, Bliss, and Joy) is a Saadhaka. While progressing through these stages, a Saadhaka must conquer many a peak of spiritual difficulties. Only the Grace of Sadguru (Divine Spiritual Master) can facilitate overcoming the peaks of spiritual difficulties. Whoever crosses the Spiritual barrier successfully becomes a Saadhaka. Saadhaka is the one who follows Sadhana to realize the spiritual Goal. In Sanskrit, Saadhu, 'Saadh' means 'to accomplish'. As long the one has yet to reach the goal, they are a Saadhaka, while one who has reached the goal is called a Siddha. Saadhaka removes dark thought and desires, increases intelligence, memory, wisdom, and self-Esteem. Saadhaka must get initiated by a Guru (spiritual master) into the path of spiritual realization. Saadhaka is the instrument of a spiritual Divine Activity. Saadhaka is the practioner to attain certain Siddhis. Saadhaka becomes "Yogi" or "Yogini". Saadhaka is Accomplishing, fulfilling effecting, completing, Efficient, Skilful, Adept, Magical, helping, Assisting, one who develops supernatural powers. Saadhaka is instrumental, conducive and promotive. The Saadhaka who performs Sadhana is engaged in Parmartha Chinthana ceaselessly, is in Equanimity and is content in the thought that Al l's 'Lord's' and nothing is his; he is never in grief or loss, anger or hatred, selfishness, hunger, thirst, or fickleness. He journeys through life with fortitude, courage, joy, peace, and humility. Sadhana is necessary to realize God. Saadhaka is engaged uninterruptedly in the contemplation of the Lord. Instead of quarrelling for every tiny little thing, losing one's temper, becoming sad at the slightest provocation, getting angry at the smallest insult, worried at thirst, hunger and loss of sleep, these can never be the characteristics of a Saadhaka. Those who are immersed in External Illusions and Avidyamaya are "Men"; those who are immersed in internal illusions or Vidya Maya is "Sadhakas". He who has no external illusions, becomes a Sadhaka and when such Saadhaka has no internal illusions gets Self Realized. Marga (Path) and Sadhana (Method Process) is necessary to become devoid of Gunas its effects. In this world, there is no tapas higher than fortitude, no happiness greater than contentment, no Punya a holier than mercy, no weapon more effective than Patience. Bhaktas should consider the body as the field, good deeds as seeds and cultivate the name of the "Lord", with the help of the heart as the 'ryot' to get the harvest, The Lord Himself. As the Milk, so the cream; as the fuel, so the fire, so also, as the Sadhana, so the Saakshaathkaara. Even if the attainment of Mukti is not directly realized as the consequence of taking up the Lord's name, the four fruits are certainly evident to those, who have had the experience. They are: 1) The company of the great, 2) Truth, 3) Contentment, 4) The control of the senses. Through whichever of these gates one may enter, whether he be a householder or recluse, or a member of any other class, he can reach the "Lord" without fail. This is certain. In the midst of the worldly pleasures, one rarest of the rare entertains the deep desire for attaining "The Lord". Of various types of bhakti,Namasmarana bhakti (Remembering Name of 'Lord') is the Best. In the kaliyuga, the name is the Path for saving oneself. Jayadeva, Gouranga, Chaitanya, Tukaram, Kabir, Ramdas, all these great Bhaktas attained "The Lord " through just this one Nama. Even Prahlada and Dhruva were able to enjoy the Darshan, Sparshan and Sambhashana of the "Lord" through Nama only. Minimise the Evil deeds and Maximise the Good Deeds. You must be, as you want others to be. Miserliness must be transformed to Generosity. Anger and Hatred must be transformed into compassion and love. One single name must be used for Japam and Dhyanam. One has also to get the strong conviction that all the Lord's Names and all the Lord's forms are but the name and the form which one is repeating in Japam and meditating on, during Dhyanam. That Name and that form must not give any slightest feeling of dislike or disaffection. Saadhaka should immerse his soul in Love, Truthfulness. He must always be on the path of Righteousness, he must be compassionate. Sadhaka the one who does sadhana to Sadhu (master) / perfect own self and be buddha (self-realized). Saadhaka does sadhana to contain, retain and be centered in true being, to be medium to spread the essence, fragrance of truth, beauty, joy, and grace for perpetual eternal bliss all around, as trees and plants give fruits and flowers. One needs to work on the self to uncover and realize that inner truth to be That...The only journey that is worth undertaking is within. Awaken people, enlighten masses, do something rather than cribbing and complaining. Manifestation of consciousness is for the welfare and wellbeing of humanity.

Maha Satsang Seva (Serving Divine Collective)

All Saadhakas must do SadGuru Seva and Satsang Seva. Seva is selfless Service. Service is Paramount. "The best way to find yourself is to lose yourself in the service of others", said Mahatma Gandhi. Through service, one loses one's sense of self-importance and becomes humble. But we can share only what we have within ourselves. You cannot share / pour from empty Cup. Self-care and Self-Development is very important. Practice replenishing ourselves. Be full and overflowing with Divine essence and qualities. Everything we get is from satsang, meditation, Seva, and by Sadguru kripa, blessings, and God's Grace, without which our spiritual development and upliftment is not possible. Doing seva is of utmost importance. Meditation is seva. The purpose of meditation is to prepare us to accept what the Lord gives, to prepare us not to expect. In prayer, we always expect, but in meditation, we always accept. We pray because we're expecting something; we do meditation because we are preparing to accept what He wants to give us. In prayer we speak to the Lord; in meditation we hear Him. So, meditation itself is a seva. First, clean the utensil, then, fill it with Amrita (divine nectar). This is also known by mystics as seva. "If you learn to love repeating the name of "The Lord", the web of illusion will be torn away, the ocean of the world will evaporate. In this age of darkness, tell me, has anyone ever made the crossing by another practice, however great? Reading or teaching scriptures can't do it - just repeat the Name. Rituals can't achieve it with yoga or austerity. You earn the fortune of devotion only in the company of mystics. God has given me his promise, says Namdev, no other method is needed. (-Namdev in many voices, One Song) Meditation builds the relationship with the Master. Meditation helps lighten our karmic load. It helps us control and still the mind; it helps us to let go of the worries of the world. Eventually we learn that meditation is the solution to everything that comes our way. Meditation is the most important tool the masters give to their disciples (Saadhakas). Meditation gives us the strength to gracefully fulfil our destiny. Meditation helps us break down the barriers that hold us (Greed, lust, anger, attachment, ego, hatred, etc.) Medita tion helps us to Realize the true Self.

| | Vandana - Prayer - Namaste | |

| | Guru - Shishya (Master - Disciple) Acquiring Knowledge | |

| | Sadhaka Dhyana Sadhana (Seeker in Meditation) | |

| | Buddha in Samadhi – Meditative Enlightened Consciousness | |

| | Drop in Ocean - Ocean in Drop | |

**| | MahaSatsang AnandaUtsav
(The Great Spiritual Collective Joy Celebration) | |**

MahaGuru kripa (Blessings of MahaGuru):

Saadhaka can cross the Bhavasagar (ocean of Earthly concern, ocean of worldly life) by the Grace of a SadGuru (True spiritual Master). Saadhaka must acknowledge the path of the master as true. Follow the teachings prescribed by the Master. The Master protects the Saadhaka from all negative powers; and blesses the saadhaka with Divine Powers. The Saints teach us that true happiness can only be found if we search within, for the Kingdom of heaven lies within us. 'The Lord's' name is the creative power or spirit out of which all the creation is aroused and which sustains all life. The Sadguru is a realized being, who bears witness to the Word and who can awaken others to its presence within. Salvation of Saadhaka is possible by Sadguru kripa in this lifetime. Saadhaka must do his sadhana under the complete guidance from a living spiritual master (SadGuru). The spiritual Master suggest that the truly brave are those who make meditation the center of their lives. The Stillness and happiness can be experienced in this lifetime. Meditation is simple but not easy. Its importance can never be ignored. Meditation, the masters tell us, will eventually answer all our questions, and give us everything we need.

By Gurukripa and divine grace saadhaka experiences intense personal transformation leading to finally Self-Realization. Gurukripa is the only way by which the Saadhaka may transcend the bondage of lifetimes of Karma, go beyond the effects of Prarabdha karma, Sanchita Karma. Gurukripa is not a gift from God, but rather must be earned through Heartily Seva of Sadguru and Satsang by complete Surrendering and offering of body, heart, and wealth (Tan-Man-Dhan). As per Vedas everything belongs to "The Almighty Lord" "MahaPrabhu". In Lord's Aarti "Om Jai Jagadish Hare" the last stanza states: 'Tan Man Dhan Sab Hai Tera, Tera Tujiko Arpan, Kya Lage Mera' (The body, mind-Heart-Soul, and wealth-all belongings are all Yours. What is Yours I offer to You, nothing is mine). By such offerings of selfless service, volunteer service, Seva, Donations, Charity, Contributions to spread the Glory of "MahaPrabhu", Saadhaka develops non-attachment for Illusiory worldly affairs, and gains Good Merits for his spiritual upliftment.

As Krishna says to Arjuna in the final chapter of the Bhagavad Gita, "Setting aside all meritorious deeds (Dharma), just surrender completely to my will (with firm faith and loving contemplation). I shall liberate you from all sins. Do not fear."

The Skanda Purana mentions the grace of a Guru, in Guru Stotram (known as Guru Gita), in the form of dialogue between Shiva and Uma (Shakti).

"Gurur Brahma Gurur Vishnu Gurur Devo Maheshwara Guru Sakshat Param Brahma Tasmai Shri Gurave Namah", "Dhyana Moolam Guru Murti, Puja Moolam Gurur Padam, Mantra Moolam Gurur Vakyam, Moksha Moolam Guru Kripa". By GuruKripa Saadhaka earns and experiences Grace of the Self (Aatma Utthan), Grace of Spiritual Divine Scriptures, and Grace of "MahaPrabhu" ("The Almighty Lord"). The spiritual path of GuruKripa is a faster path to moksha, or liberation. The Saadhaka receives spiritual energy directly from Guru. To obtain Guru Kripa, the Yogi must follow the path of the Guru, work in service of the Guru and Satsang to spread Divinity and be dedicated and devoted on spiritual Journey, The Guru bestows his grace by resolving to do so simply by the power of his presence. "Guru Kripa Hi Kevalam" is a Sanskrit expression, mantra and song that means "The Guru's Grace is absolute and the only reality." Vedas and other spiritual scriptures state that Guru Kripa is a wonderful, mysterious factor that will enable the aspirants to seek and to attain the summum bonum of life, Self-realization, Darshan of God, or Moksha. On the spiritual Plane, Guru Kripa takes one to transcendental Bliss. There is nothing except Guru Kripa needed for to attain perfection in Life. Guru Kripa has not only to be bestowed, not only to be given, but it has also to be received. In receiving it, we immortalize ourselves, divinize ourselves. Unlimited charity may be bestowed by a generous-hearted donor who calls upon all who are in need to come and take. But not all the wealth of the world will be of any avail to an indigent one if he will not avail of this great opportunity and become a receiver of Guru Kripa, Guru's Grace and Blessings. And therefore, it is that the great Lord Jesus said: "Seek and it shall be found; knock and it shall open unto you; ask and it shall be given," It is not as though there is any dearth of divine munificence, divine grace of Guru Kripa. Light is not lacking, but then there is a law, that is we must ask, we have to seek, and we have to knock, and having done it, we must be ready to receive. If this is present, then Guru Kripa works all wonders; it will flow into us and raise us to the highest realm of immortality, eternal light, and infinite Bliss. By acceptance of Discipleship of a Guru and by faithful conduct and practice of spirituality, one becomes ready to receive his Grace. For, the question of Guru and Guru Kripa arises only for the disciple. For those who are not of the category named disciple, it is said that mercy, compassion, grace, and ashirwad will be given, but not GuruKripa. GuruKripa is something special, something mysterious, and something that bestows not anything merely of this Earth but gives the highest thing which human life is here for. For the attainment of the Gift of Gurukripa, one should be a fully surrendered, dedicated, and devoted Disciple of a Guru. In as much as GuruKripa takes us to the highest state, true discipleship is qualifying ourselves to attain that highest state, or the realization of ourselves as Satchidananda. Service is that mysterious something which pulls down the barrier that stands between us and the influence of Guru Kripa. Ego is the greatest barrier. Our old self-conceit and preconceived notions form formidable second barrier. For all of this, Seva Service is the effective barrier-breaker. True service of the Guru is to try our level best to carry out his upadesha, his teachings, upon his sublime instructions we should mold our life. The secret of carrying out the instructions of the Guru to our humble best is a willing obedience in spirit -That is the most important thing, Readiness to bow completely down to the earth. Accept him as the Leader, Master and obey him. There must be Joy in obedience to the Guru; and there should be a real craving in the Spirit that "I should Obey". For a true disciple, the nature of the Guru is not human. we should be completely blind to the human side of the Guru, and we should be conscious of the Divinity that he is. Then alone will we be able to partake of this Guru Kripa which will transform us from the lower human into the transcendental divine. Our relationship with the Guru is purely divine, purely spiritual. By the Guru's Grace and Blessings, problems of this worldly life (Prapanch) will also be solved. Our Sadhana should be to generate divine consciousness and shed our human consciousness. By Guru Kripa, we generate Divine consciousness and realize our reality that we are not just human beings, but we are Divine Souls in bondage. We are divine beings, we are immortal beings, we are in essence Satchidananda. Patience and humility in the spiritual realm, is to be extended for a period for Guru Kripa. Humbly leave everything to the Guru. Pray to the Guru, 'O Ocean of Mercy and compassion make me a proper disciple and give me the spirit of willing obedience. Help me in trying to follow thy instructions. Help me in trying to mold myself upon the pattern set up by thee'. This must be our constant prayer to make our life fruitful. The perfect way of praying is trying and practicing our best to be a real disciple.

For the sake of the Goal, a disciple must be willing to give up everything petty, and most important of all, be willing to give oneself up, to renounce one's little self, to renounce the very reality of one's temporary, earthly being: "Whoever Clings to his life shall lose it, and whoever loses his life shall save it". Kill this little 'I'. Die to live. Lead the Divine Life. The Guru imparts knowledge to remove ignorance that is the cause of bondage, sorrow, and suffering. The Guru takes away one's illusion and shows Reality. The essence of the disciple is a keen eagerness, a great desire to be free from ignorance - the essential nature of which is ego-and attain illumination. Hundreds of Gurus cannot help unless the disciple has a great desire, willingness for Enlightenment, liberation. Guru bhakti and Guru seva are important factors in spiritual life. Real Guru Seva is to live your life and conduct yourself in such a manner that your behavior and character bring good name to the Guru. A tree is known by its fruits.

A Guru helps us navigate through life, teaches us the ways and means of living, shows ways to face current problems and difficulties, answer out questions, removes doubt's, leads us on the spiritual path. Having a living Guru is as important as having a Guru in spirit form. A living Guru is of this world and can explain things to you through the ways of this world in its current form. Everything in this world must be done through instruments. The divine must be transmitted through a Living Divine Instrument. So, Guru is the Living Divine Instrument through whom the Divine Energies, Powers, Principles, Essence, Param Chaitanya, and Divine knowledge is transmitted. Similarly, the elevated Disciples of the Guru transmit the Divine Powers. Disciples who follow the Guru continue to bring these teachings to others in a living way. As the Guru initiates his disciples, the elevated disciples can also initiate new disciples. In the Bible, we see that Jesus Christ initiated others through his disciples. It's still his power, but it's living; it's like a baton that's been passed on but energized by the Guru's touch. Only reading spiritual books and scriptures won't help that much as to gain faster from a living Guru. The divine knowledge is perpetuated through living Guru, which is vibrant, vital, alive. The living Guru is Pratyaksha, the Divine Presence. Complete surrendering to the living Guru is the key for all attainment. The presence of a live Guru is a big blessing. Guru guides you but it is you who need to walk. No one else can walk for you. It is by your Sanchita Punya Karmas, (past virtuous Deeds) that you get a genuine SadGuru. Guru gives you a push which is necessary for right development and spiritual upliftment.

MahaAvahana (Great Appeal for Donation) Daana, Samarpan:

Saadhaka must have devotion, dedication, and heartily contribution by all ways and means to MahaPrabhuyoga MahaSatsang. All Saadhakas should give a heartily Donation, Daana, Samarpan for a great cause to spread Divinity, Divine knowledge, Love, Bliss, Peace, Joy, Beauty and MahaPrabhuyoga which is the innermost and innate requirement for the growth and spreading of MahaPrabhuyoga MahaSatsang. Cultivate giving without thinking and expecting about what you might get in return. Everything you have is a gift from God to be freely shared. Contribute with generous heart as much as you can. Get others to join you in giving. It is in giving that we receive everything. Giving is a sacred art. Giving is a blessing which creates divine connections. "A bit of fragrance always clings to the hand that gives roses." Generosity gives you Joy and Blessings. You get the power to transform yourself and contribute to Change the world a little. Donate Heartily and Joyously with a smile. 'Even a Smile is Charity'. Giving charity does not deplete wealth. Giving and sharing creates a great flow of Abundance. We channelize the flow of Divinity. "Abundance is not measured by what flows in, but by what flows over." It's not how much we are each able to give that matters as much as that we give regularly. Generosity is a spiritual practice that reflects an attitude of heart and mind. Giving is an act of Love, is honoring our True self. Spiritual science places more importance on the inner intent (cause) than on the action (Effect) of giving to Charity. Charity done with the unity of the mind, speech and conduct receives tremendous benefits. This world is in the form of an echo. Charity means to give and then receive in multiplicity. There will be echoes of whatever good you do it returns to you with addition, you gain merit of good karmas. Your inner intent and hearts feeling (Bhaava) is important. Consecration is the act of dedicating one's life, time, talent, and resources to building the Heavenly kingdom of "Mahaprabhu" "The Almighty lord." Being Charitable is an imperative for the wellbeing and betterment of humanity. Saadhaka must be kind, compassionate and generous. If you believe God is Love, then Charity, faith, and spirituality are central to everything you do. The most rewarding purpose is to serve others with body, mind, spirit, and possessions. The wisdom of an age-old proverb: "When the right hand washes the left, the right gets cleansed too." Healing ourselves, making ourselves whole by helping others. The greatest help can be extended by spreading the Divine knowledge, Light, Love, Life, Bliss, Peace, Joy, and Beauty through "MahaPrabhuYoga". Contribute by donating as much as you can to 'MahaPrabhuYoga MahaSatsang'. Volunteer Seva, service to MahaSatsang. "The friendship of man for God", which "Unites us to God". "The habit of charity extends not only to the love of God, but also to the love of our neighbor". Charity is Love. It is spiritual love that is extended from God to man and then reflected by man, who is made in the image of God, back to God. God gives man the power to act as God (God is Love), the man then reflects God's power in his own human actions towards others. One example of this movement is "Charity Shall cover the multitude of sins". "The practice of charity brings us to act toward ourselves and others out of love alone, precisely because each person has the dignity of a beloved child of God. Charity is held to be the ultimate perfection of the human spirit because it is said to glorify and reflect the nature of God. Charity is divinely infused into the Soul; it resides in the will. Charity is an absolute requirement for happiness, which he holds as man's last goal. Charity is one's love for Self, neighbors (All Humanity and Nature), and Love for God. "So, faith, hope, love and Charity remain." Charity is a Great Virtue. The fruits of Charity are Happiness, Peace, Bliss, mercy, compassion, Love and Joy of Divinity. "The Love which God lavishes upon us and which we in turn must share with others." Charity is loving Kindness and friendliness. In Sanskrit "Daana" connotes the virtue of generosity, charity, giving of alms, sharing with fellow human beings and other living plant and animal Kingdom of Mother Nature, which is considered in the Vedas as the highest of spiritual divine Merits that one can earn. Daana is a Practice of Cultivating generosity. Daana means Giving. It is the act of giving something. Daana is giving volunteer service, Donation, Charity, Helping, giving gifts. Daana is a benevolent Deed. The Upanishad states that three characteristics of a good divinely elevated person are self-restraint (Damah), compassion, and love for all sentient life (Daya), and Charity (Danna). Daana (Donation, Charity) must be Sattvikam (Good, enlightened, pure); given for Great Noble Cause. Charity is also by Deeds (body), words (speech) and thoughts (mind). It states that a brightly beaming smile, the kindly light of loving eye, and saying pleasant words with sincere heart is a form of charity that every human being should strive to give. The highest of all Daana's is Vidyadaana, Dynanadaana, and Abhayadaana. The spiritual knowledge which is given by the Guru to his disciples. Daana is best done with shraddha (faith), goodwill, cheerfulness and delight. Daana is characterized and unattached and unconditional generosity, giving and letting go. The left hand should not know what is given by the right hand. Daana leads one to "perfections". Which leads to greater spiritual wealth. One gains positive Karma by Daana. Wisdom of Daana is of not giving oneself credit for giving Daana (Charity, Donation), just give heartily and forget about it, rest is taken care of by Nature.

Volunteering is an incredible way to share your talents, meet new friends, enrich lives, and be of Service to create a world that works for all. Volunteering is one of the best qualities of a spiritual Saadhaka to promote spirituality so that everyone lives an awakened harmonious life in happiness, peace, bliss, love, and Joy. "The best way to find yourself is to lose yourself in the service of others." The happiest people are not those getting more, but those who are giving and serving more. Research has shown that people who volunteer often live a peaceful, happy, and joyous life and live longer. No act of kindness, no matter how small, is ever wasted. Three keys to more abundant living are caring about others, daring for others, sharing with others. Volunteers are the jewels of the society. When you give yourself, you receive more than you give. Volunteering is at the very core of being a human. No one has made it through life without someone else's help. We make life by contribution. "Alone we can do so little; together we can do so much." Volunteering is the real selfless service (seva) for the betterment of the world.

Saadhaka must have a higher purpose in life, must have clear understanding and responsibility. Purpose must be worthy and significant. To attain the highest form of knowledge; for the highest Good; for happiness, wellbeing, flourishing, achieving excellence, good merits through good karmas, peace, bliss and joy; Freedom from all suffering, Living virtuous life in harmony with universal divine order, with wisdom and self-control. Living with devotion, dedication, and subservience to God. Living virtuous life with Love, compassion, harmony, generosity, and selfless service.

Life's purpose is to seek divine salvation through the grace of God, to attain union (Yoga) with God and to be a Great Glorious Divine Personality to do greater good for humanity and all living on Earth. For this great glorious noble cause and purpose 'MahaPrabhuyoga MahaSatsang' is committed to working and serving for spreading Divine Love, Peace, Bliss, Happiness, Joy, and Beauty all around the World. Aims that every person orients himself to give great meaning to his life by fulfilling the life's higher purpose. To get one's Self-Realization and to promote Enlightenment to the masses to experience Divine Life on Earth and Enjoy its Magnificent Beauty. Your individual contribution is collective growth of 'MahaPrabhuYoga MahaSatsang'. For this great collective divine work, we make an Aavahana, a heartily invoking to join and contribute for this great noble cause. It's a timely call and we invite you to give your Heartily Monetary contribution as donation, daana, samarpan with joyous loving kind Heart as per your wish and pure desire as much as you can to 'Mahaprabhuyoga MahaSatsang'. We have complete faith that this great Monetary Contribution and sacrifice shall bring all of us good health, lots of blessings, well wishes, prosperity, happiness, love, peace, bliss, joy, glory, and Beauty. 'May God bless us.'

www.ingramcontent.com/pod-product-compliance
Ingram Content Group UK Ltd.
Pitfield, Milton Keynes, MK11 3LW, UK
UKHW041856190726
13854UKWH00002B/942

9 789390 640232